Ports of Call 1998

Reprinted from *Fodor's Worldwide Cruises and Ports of Call 1998*

Fodor's Travel Publications, Inc.
New York • Toronto • London • Sydney • Auckland
www.fodors.com/

Copyright

First Edition

ISBN 0-679-03553-2

Fodor's Europe Ports of Call

Editor: M. T. Schwartzman
Contributors: Robert Blake, Janet Foley, Jennifer Paull, Heidi Sarna, Dinah A. Spritzer
Creative Director: Fabrizio La Rocca
Cartographer: David Lindroth
Cover Photograph: Princess Cruises/Island Princess/Santorini, Greece (top photo), Michele & Tom Grimm/Tony Stone Images (bottom photo)
Cover Design: Allison Saltzman
Text Design: Vignelli Associates

Special Sales

Fodor's Travel Publications are available at special discounts for bulk purchases for sales promotions or premiums. Special editions can be created in large quantities for special needs. For more information, contact your local bookseller or write to Special Markets, Fodor's Travel Publications, 201 E. 50th St., New York, NY 10022; Random House of Canada, Ltd., Marketing Dept., 1265 Aerowood Dr., Mississauga, Ontario L4W 1B9; or Fodor's Travel Publications, 20 Vauxhall Bridge Rd., London SW1V 2SA, England.

PRINTED IN THE UNITED STATES OF AMERICA
10 9 8 7 6 5 4 3 2 1

Contents

Maps

Please Write to Us

Everyone who has worked on *Europe Ports of Call 1998* has taken enormous care to ensure the accuracy of the text. All prices and opening times we quote are based on information supplied to us at press time. However, the passage of time will always bring changes, so it's always a good idea to call ahead to confirm information in this guide when it matters—particularly if you have to travel far from your ship. Fodor's cannot accept responsibility for any errors that may have occurred.

Was your ship as we described it? Was the food better? The service worse? The cabins smaller? Did our restaurant picks exceed your expectations? Positive and negative, we love your feedback. So please send us a letter or postcard (we're at 201 East 50th Street, New York, NY 10022). If you have complaints, we'll look into them and revise our entries when the facts warrant it. We'll look forward to hearing from you. And in the meantime, have a wonderful cruise!

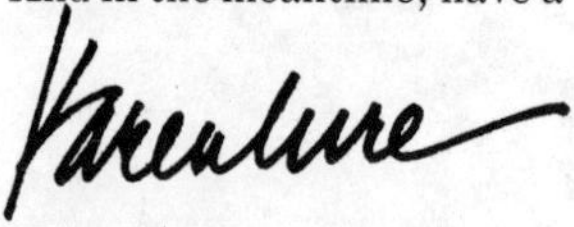

Karen Cure
Editorial Director

1 Cruise Primer

Choosing Your Cruise

The right ship is one that makes you comfortable. Every ship has its own personality, depending upon its size, when it was built, and its purpose. Big ships are more stable and offer a huge variety of activities and facilities. Smaller ships feel intimate, like private clubs. Each type of ship satisfies a certain type of passenger, and for every big-ship fan there is somebody who would never set foot aboard one of these "floating resorts."

Comparing Ships

In order to compare cruise ships, you need to speak "ship talk." Vessels are generally described according to their passenger capacity, gross registered tonnage, passenger-to-crew ratio, and space ratio. A ship's passenger capacity is usually based on double occupancy, meaning the normal cruise complement of the vessel with two passengers in each cabin. This does not include third or fourth passengers in a cabin, which on some ships can greatly increase the total passenger count. Gross registered tonnage is commonly used to measure a vessel's size. Technically, it is a measurement of the ship's volume, with 1 cubic foot equal to 1 gross registered ton. Passenger-to-crew ratio indicates the number of passengers served by each crew member—the lower the ratio, the better the level of service. Space ratio, the ship's tonnage divided by its passenger capacity, allows you to compare a ship's roominess. The higher the ratio, the more spacious a vessel will feel. The roomiest ships have ratios of 40:1 or better; ships with ratios of less than 28:1 may feel cramped.

But when choosing your cruise, the size of the ship isn't the only factor to consider. You also need to find out about the nature of the experience you will have—the lifestyle and activities available by day and after dark, the mealtime hours and dining-room dress codes, how roomy the ship is, and how good the service is apt to be. Equally important are your itinerary, the accommodations, and the cost of the cruise.

Types of Ships

Although all ocean liners are equipped with swimming pools, spas, nightclubs, theaters, and casinos, there are three distinct types: classic liners, cruise liners, and megaships. Many **classic liners,** ships constructed between 1950 and 1969 for transatlantic or other ocean crossings, are still sailing in the fleets of many cruise lines. Beginning in the 1960s, ship lines began to create vessels specifically for cruising. Some of these **cruise liners** were brand new; others were converted ferries or freighters. Vessels known as **megaships,** the biggest cruise ships ever built, first appeared in the late 1980s and, with their immense proportions and passenger capacities, immediately established a new standard of cruise-ship design.

Cruises are also available aboard a number of specialty ships: cruise yachts, expedition ships, and motor-sailing ships.

Classic Liners

With their long, sweeping hulls and stepped-back passenger decks, these vessels defined passenger-ship design for decades. Now serving cruise duty, they were originally configured to keep passengers happy during long ocean crossings. Typically, their cabins and closets are larger than those on vessels built for cruising. Deck space is sheltered, with fully or partially enclosed promenades that allow you to relax on deck even during foul weather. A few are still steam powered, without the vibrations sometimes associated with diesel power. Rich wood panels the walls, and fixtures may be the original brass. Smaller ships may feel cramped because of low ceilings in the lobby and corridors. But on the most opulent vessels, public spaces designed to inspire still do. There are balconies above the dining room, where musicians can serenade diners; stained glass graces the cinemas and other public spaces; and grand staircases lead from one deck to another. Such traditional features have proved so enduring they have been incorporated in the plans for some of today's newest vessels.

Although classic ships typically carry between 600 and 1,000 passengers and register between

20,000 and 30,000 tons, a couple of them are among the largest passenger ships afloat.

Cruise Liners When shipbuilders stopped constructing vessels for transportation and started designing them for vacationing, the cruise liner entered the scene. On these ships, outdoor deck space is plentiful; stateroom space is not. Many have a wraparound outdoor promenade deck that allows you to stroll or jog the perimeter of the ship. Older cruise liners resemble the transatlantic ships from which they are descended: Decks are stacked one atop the other in steps, and the hull amidships may appear to droop, so the bow and stern seem to curve upward. In the newest cruise liners, traditional meets trendy. You find atrium lobbies and expansive sun and sports decks, picture windows instead of portholes, and cabins that open onto private verandas. The smallest cruise liners carry 500 passengers and are no bigger than 10,000 tons, while the largest accommodate 1,500 passengers, exceed 50,000 tons, and are stuffed with diversions—almost like megaships.

Megaships The centerpiece of most megaships is a three-, five-, or seven-story central atrium. However, these giant vessels are most easily recognized by their boxy profile: The hull and superstructure rise straight out of the water, as many as 14 stories tall, topped out by a huge sun or sports deck with a jogging track and swimming pool, which may be Olympic size. Some megaships, but not all, also have a wraparound promenade deck. As on the latest cruise liners, picture windows are standard equipment, and cabins in the top categories have private verandas. From their casinos and discos to their fitness centers, everything is proportionally bigger and more extravagant than on other ships. Between 1,500 and 2,500 passengers can be accommodated, and tonnage ranges from 60,000 to 70,000 or more.

Cruise Yachts At the opposite end of the spectrum from the megaship is the tiny cruise yacht. These intimate vessels carry from 100 to 300 passengers, register between 4,000 and 15,000 tons, and are like miniature ocean liners, with big-ship amenities such as fitness centers, casinos, lounges, and swimming pools. What sets these yachts apart from typical ocean liners is that passengers are treated like royalty. Cabins are all outside suites equipped with every creature comfort on the high seas—from VCRs and stocked minibars to marble baths. Built into the stern of some of these vessels are retractable platforms, which are lowered for water sports when the ship is at anchor in calm waters.

Expedition Ships Vessels of this type are designed to reach into the most remote corners of the world. Shallow drafts allow them to navigate up rivers, close to coastlines, and into shallow coves. Hulls may be hardened for sailing in Antarctic ice. Motorized rubber landing craft known as Zodiacs, kept on board, make it possible for passengers to put ashore almost anywhere. However, because the emphasis during cruises aboard expedition ships tends to be on learning and exploring, the ships don't have casinos, showrooms, multiple bars and lounges, and other typical ocean-liner diversions. Instead, they have theaters for lectures, well-stocked libraries, and enrichment programs, led by experts, as entertainment. The smallest expedition ships carry fewer than 100 passengers and register just over 2,000 tons. The largest carries nearly 200 people and registers 9,000 tons.

Motor-Sail Vessels A number of cruise vessels were designed as sailing ships. With their sails unfurled, they are an impressive sight. But since they must keep to a schedule, they cannot rely solely on wind power. So all are equipped with engines as well. Usually they employ both means of propulsion, a technique known as motor sailing, to put on a good show and make the next port on time. These vessels range from small windjammers carrying a handful of passengers to rather large clipper-style ships that approach the size of a small ocean liner and accommodate almost 400 passengers.

The Cruise Experience

Your cruise experience will be shaped by several factors, and to determine whether a particular ship's style will suit you, you need to do a bit of research. Is a full program of organized activities scheduled by day? What happens in the evening? Are there one or two seatings in the dining room? If there is more than one, you will not be allowed to arrive and exit as the spirit moves you but instead must show up promptly when service begins—and clear out within a specified time. What kind of entertainment is offered after dark? And how often do passengers dress up for dinner? Some cruises are fancier than others.

Although no two cruises are quite the same, even aboard the same ship, the cruise experience tends to fall into three categories.

Formal Formal cruises embody the ceremony of cruising. Generally available on ocean liners and cruise yachts sailing for seven days or longer, formal cruises recall the days when traveling by ship was an event in itself. By day, shipboard lifestyle is generally unstructured, with few organized activities. Tea and bouillon may be served to the accompaniment of music from a classical trio in the afternoon. Ashore, passengers may be treated to a champagne beach party. Meals in the dining room are served in a single seating, and passengers are treated to the finest cuisine afloat. Jackets and ties for men are the rule for dinner, tuxedos are not uncommon, and the dress code is observed faithfully throughout the evening. Pianists, cabaret acts, and local entertainers provide nighttime diversion. Service is extremely attentive and personalized. Passenger-to-crew and space ratios are best. Because these cruises tend to attract destination-oriented passengers, shore excursions—such as private museum tours—sometimes are included in the fare, as are pre- or post-cruise land packages and sometimes even tips.

Semiformal Semiformal cruises are a bit more relaxed than their formal counterparts. Meals are served in two seatings on ocean liners or one seating on specialty ships, menu choices are plentiful, and the cuisine is on a par with that available in better restaurants. Men tend to wear a jacket and tie to dinner most nights. Adding a distinct flair to the dining room is the common practice of staffing the restaurant with waiters of one nationality. Featured dishes may be prepared table-side, and you often are able, with advance notice, to order a special diet, such as kosher, low-salt, low-cholesterol, sugar free, or vegetarian. There is a daily program of scheduled events, but there's time for more independent pursuits; passengers with similar interests are often encouraged to meet at appointed times for chess or checkers, deck games, and other friendly contests. Production-style shows are staged each evening, but the disco scene may not be too lively. Passenger-to-crew and space ratios assure good service and plenty of room for each passenger. Look for semiformal cruises aboard classic liners, cruise liners, megaships, and a few expedition ships on voyages of seven days or longer.

Casual Casual cruises are the most popular. Shipboard dress and lifestyle are informal. Meals in the dining room are served in two seatings on ocean liners and one seating on specialty ships; menus are usually not extensive, and the food is good but not extraordinary; your options may be limited if you have special dietetic requirements. Men dress in sport shirts and slacks for dinner most nights, in jackets and ties only two or three evenings of a typical seven-day sailing. Aboard casual ocean liners, activities are more diverse than on formal and semiformal ships, and there is almost always something going on, from bingo to beer-chugging contests. Las Vegas–style variety shows or Broadway revues headline the evening entertainment. Discos bop into the wee hours. Passenger-to-crew and space ratios are generally good, but service tends to be less personal. On the smallest ships, activities on board will be limited as indicated in Types of Ships, *above*.

Look for casual cruises aboard classic liners, cruise liners, and megaships; expedition ships; and motor-sailing ships.

How Long to Sail

After you choose the type of ship and cruise experience you prefer, you must decide how long to sail. Two key factors to keep in mind are how much money you want to spend and how experienced are you at cruising.

You may want to try a week long cruise. For some people, seven days is still too short—just when you learn your way around the ship, it's time to go home. On **10- or 11-day sailings,** you get more ports as well as more time at sea, but you won't pay as much as on **two-week sailings.** Many experienced cruisers feel it's just not worth the effort to board a ship for anything less than 14 days, so they opt for either a single 14-day itinerary or two seven-day trips back-to-back, combining sailings to eastern and western Mediterranean ports of call, for example—and taking advantage of the discounts offered by some lines for consecutive sailings. Cruises that last longer than two weeks—**very long cruises**—require a lot of time and money and a love of cruising. If you have all these, then cruising can become more than a vacation—it can be a way of life.

Ship Itineraries

In choosing the best cruise for you, a ship's itinerary is another important factor. The length of the cruise will determine the variety and number of ports you visit, but so will the type of itinerary and the point of departure. Some cruises, known as **loop cruises,** start and end at the same point and usually explore ports close to one another; **one-way cruises** start at one port and end at another and range farther afield.

Note: Cruise itineraries listed in Chapter 3 are for the 1998 Europe season but are subject to change. Contact your travel agent or the cruise line directly for up-to-the-minute itineraries.

Cost

For one price, a cruise gives you all your meals, accommodations, and onboard entertainment. The only extras are tips, shore excursions, shopping, bar bills, and other incidentals. The axiom "the more you pay, the more you get" doesn't always hold true: While higher fares do prevail for better ships, which have more comfortable cabins, more attractive decor, and better service, the passenger in the least-expensive inside cabin eats the same food, sees the same shows, and shares the same amenities as one paying more than $1,000 per day for the top suite on any given ship. (A notable exception is aboard the *Queen Elizabeth 2*, where your dining-room assignment is based on your cabin category.)

A handy way to compare costs of different ships is to look at the per diem—the price of a cruise on a daily basis per passenger, based on double occupancy. (For instance, the per diem is $100 for a seven-day cruise that costs $700 per person when two people share the same cabin.)

Booking Your Cruise

Using a Travel Agent

Since nearly all cruises are sold through travel agents, the agent you choose to work with can be just as important as the ship you sail on. So how do you know if an agent or agency is right for you? Talk to friends, family, and colleagues who have used an agency to book a cruise. The most qualified agents are members of CLIA (Cruise Lines International Association). Agents who are CLIA Accredited Cruise Counsellors or Master Cruise Counsellors have had extensive cruise and ship inspection experience. If you opt for a cruise-only agency (*see below*), they should also be a member of NACOA (National Association of Cruise-Only Agencies). These agents are also experienced cruisers. Finally, the most reputable agencies, both full-service and cruise-only, are members of ASTA (American Society of Travel Agents).

If you're undecided about a ship or line, an agent's personal account of his or her own cruise can be invaluable. However, keep in mind that agencies often have "partnerships" with certain cruise lines. In some cases, the agency may actually block space on a ship; in other cases, the agency agrees to sell a certain amount of space. Either way, the agency gets a favorable rate from the cruise line; the agency can then afford to offer a "discounted" price to the public. But since agents often receive higher commissions on these cruises, they might steer you toward a cruise that might not be for you. *A good travel agent puts your needs first.*

Larger agencies often have more experienced cruisers on their staff and can provide the biggest discounts. Smaller agencies may compete with their personalized service. Whether you choose a large or small agency, a good agent takes the time to learn as much as possible about you and your cruise companion(s). An agent who asks a few cursory questions before handing you a brochure is a mere order taker; an agent who asks you to fill out a questionnaire about your personal interests is a professional. A travel agent might not know what ship is right for you; a good agent *will* know which ones are wrong.

Of course, you want the best price. When it comes down to it, the top agencies can more or less get you the same price on most cruises, because they'll guarantee that if the cruise line lowers the price in a promotion, you'll get the better deal. So look for an agency that offers this guarantee. But the overall value of your cruise depends on an agency's service, and agencies that are willing to go the extra mile for their clients by providing free cruise-discount newsletters, cabin upgrades, dollar-stretching advice, and 24-hour service in case of a problem are your best bet.

Cruise-Only Travel Agents As the name implies, "cruise-only" travel agencies specialize in selling cruises. However, these agencies can sell you air tickets and other travel arrangements, too, as part of your cruise package. Sometimes, your choice may be limited to a package put together by the cruise line. Increasingly, though, cruise-only agencies are putting together their own custom-designed cruise vacations.

Full-Service Travel Agents Full-service agents have broad travel experience but may be less knowledgeable about cruise lines than their cruise-only counterparts. If you know exactly what line and ship you want to sail on and are more concerned about your pre- or post-cruise land arrangements, a full-service agent may be more helpful. (But keep in mind that full-service agencies may not have the same discounts as cruise-only agencies.) If you choose to use a full-service agency, look for one that has a "cruise" desk with agents who sell only cruises. Then, you get the best of both worlds.

Spotting Swindlers Always be on the lookout for a scam. Although reputable agencies far outnumber crooks, a handful of marketeers use deceptive and unethical tactics. The best way to avoid being fleeced is to pay for your cruise with a credit card, from deposit to full payment. That way, if an agency goes out of business before your cruise departs, you can cancel payment on services not rendered. Two tip-offs that an agency may be a bad apple: It doesn't accept credit cards and it asks for a deposit that is more than what the cruise line has requested (check the brochure). To avoid a disreputable agency, make sure the one you choose has been in business for at least five years. Check its reputation with the local Better Business Bureau or consumer protection agency *before* you pay any deposits. If a cruise price seems too good to be true, it could mean the agency is desperate to bring in money and may close its doors tomorrow, so don't be tempted by agencies that claim they can beat any price. Be wary of bait-and-switch tactics: If you're told that an advertised bargain cruise is sold out, don't be persuaded to book a more expensive substitute. Also, if you're told that your cruise reservation was canceled because of overbooking and that you must pay extra for a confirmed rescheduled sailing, demand a full refund. Finally, if ever you fail to receive a voucher or ticket on the promised date, place an inquiry immediately.

Getting the Best Cruise for Your Dollar

By selecting the right agent, you have the greatest chance of getting the best deal. But having a basic knowledge of how and why cruises are discounted can only benefit you in the end. Since your vacation experience can vary greatly depending on the ship and its ports of call, it's best to pick your vessel and itinerary first, and then try to get the best price. Remember, it's only a deal if the cruise you book, no matter what the price, meets your expectations.

Like everything in retail, each cruise has a brochure list price. But like the sticker price on a new car, nobody actually pays this amount. These days, if you asked any 10 cruise passengers on any given ship what they paid, they would give you 10 different answers. Discounts from cruise lines and agencies can range from 5% on a single fare to 50% on the second fare in a cabin.

Approach deep discounts with skepticism. Fewer than a dozen cabins may be offered at the discounted price, they may be inside cabins, and the fare may not include air transportation or transfers between the airport and the ship. Finally, do the math. A promotion might sound catchy, but if you divide the price by the number of days you'll be cruising and include the cost of air and accommodations, you might find that the deal of the century is really a dud.

Deals and Discounts

Seasonal Discounts

Cruise-brochure prices are typically divided into three categories based on the popularity of sailing dates and weather: high season, shoulder season, and low season. Before you take advantage of a low-season rate, have your agent check on the specific weather conditions and on other factors (such as mosquitoes) in your cruise destination.

Early-Bird Specials

Almost all cruise lines provide a discount for passengers who book and put down a deposit far in advance; an additional discount may be provided if payment is made in full at the time of booking. These discounts, given to passengers who book at least six months before departure, range from 10% to 50% off the brochure rate. (Brochures are usually issued a year or more in advance of sailing dates.) Booking a popular cruise early is the best way to get the best price; there will likely be no last-minute deals on these sailings. The other advantage of booking far in advance is that you're more likely to get the cabin and meal seating you want. On most cruises, the cheapest and most expensive cabins sell out first.

Last-Minute Savings

In recent years, cruise lines have provided fewer and fewer last-minute deals. However, if a particular cruise is not selling well, a cruise line may pick certain large cruise-only travel agencies to unload unsold cabins. These deals, sometimes referred to by agents as "distressed merchandise," are typically available three weeks to three months before the cruise departs. These specials are unadvertised but may be listed in the agencies' newsletters and on their cruise telephone hot lines (*see* Agencies to Contact, *below*). Keep in mind that your choice of cabin and meal seating is limited for such last-minute deals. Distressed merchandise on older ships, those built before the 1980s, may be limited to smaller cabins in undesirable areas of the ship. Last-minute deals may only be available in certain regions.

Mixed Bag Besides the major discounts mentioned above, agencies and cruise lines might attract passengers with price promotions such as "Sail for 12 Days and Pay for Only 10," "Free Hotel Stay with Your Cruise," and "Two Sail for the Price of One." Read the fine print before you book. The offer may be a bargain—or just slick advertising. How can you tell? Compare the advertised price to the standard early-booking discount, and check if the promotion includes airfare. Also check on senior-citizen discounts and "cruise dollars" accrued on participating credit cards. Cruise lines that target families sometimes take on a third or fourth cabin passenger for free. Some of the best cruise prices are available on repositioning cruises at the beginning or end of the summer season.

Upgrades There are two types of cabin upgrades: One is guaranteed; the other is not. The first kind of upgrade is a promotional offer by the cruise line. For example, you may be offered a two-category upgrade if you book by a certain date. In this case, the cabin assignment that you receive with your documents prior to sailing should reflect your better accommodations. The second kind of upgrade is dispensed on board at the discretion of the cruise line. Like airlines, cruise lines overbook at their cheapest price in order to attract as many passengers as possible. When the number of bookings at these low rates exceeds the number of cabins available, some people are given better accommodations. How does the cruise line decide? Sometimes, those passengers who booked early get priority for upgrades. Other times, passengers who booked through top-selling travel agencies are at the top of the upgrade list—just two more reasons to book early and book with a cruise-only agency that does a lot of business with your line.

Payment

Once you have made a reservation for a cabin, you will be asked to put down a deposit. Handing money over to your travel agent constitutes a contract, so before you pay, review the cruise brochure to find out the provisions of the cruise contract. What is the payment schedule and cancellation policy? Will there be any additional charges before you can board your ship, such as transfers, port fees, or local taxes? If your air connection requires you to spend an evening in a hotel near the port before or after the cruise, is there an extra cost?

If possible, pay your deposit and balance with a credit card. This gives you some recourse if you need to cancel, and you can ask the credit-card company to intercede on your behalf in case of problems.

Deposit Most cruises must be reserved with a refundable deposit of $200–$500 per person, depending upon how expensive the cruise is; the balance is due 45–75 days before you sail. If the cruise is less than 60 days away, however, you may have to pay the entire amount immediately.

Cancellation Your entire deposit or payment may be refunded if you cancel your reservation between 45 and 75 days before departure; the grace period varies from line to line. If you cancel later than that, you will forfeit some or all of your deposit (*see* Protection, *below*). An average cancellation charge is $100 one month before sailing, $100 plus 50% of the ticket price between 15 and 30 days prior to departure, and $100 plus 75% of the ticket price between 14 days and 24 hours ahead of time. If you simply fail to show up when the ship sails, you will lose the entire amount. Many travel agents also assess a small cancellation fee. Check their policy.

Protection Cruise lines sell two types of policies that protect you in the event of cancellation or trip interruption. **Waivers** provide a full refund if you cancel your trip for any reason, usually up to 72 hours before sailing; the cost to cover a seven-day cruise is about $75. **Insurance,** sold by an insurance broker and through travel agencies, protects against cancellation for specified reasons plus trip delay, interruption, medical expenses, emergency evacuation, and lost, stolen, or damaged luggage; the cost to cover a seven-day cruise is about $99. The insurance does not cover cancellations, interruptions, or delays caused by a preexisting medical condition. Keep in mind that a waiver is only available at the time of booking; insurance policies are best purchased after you have paid a significant portion of your cruise, which you will lose in the case of cancellation. Neither insurance nor waivers protect you against cruise-line default. For that, you'll need special default insurance, sold only by a select number of companies, such as Travel Guard (tel. 800/826–1300).

Agencies to Contact

The agencies listed below specialize in booking cruises, have been in business at least five years, and emphasize customer service as well as price.

Cruise Only

Cruise Fairs of America (2029 Century Park E, Suite 950, Los Angeles, CA 90067, tel. 310/556–2925 or 800/456–4386, fax 310/556–2254), established in 1987, has a fax-back service for information on the latest deals. The agency also publishes a free twice-yearly newsletter with tips on cruising. Cruise Fairs can make independent hotel and air arrangements for a complete cruise vacation.

Cruise Holidays of Kansas City (7000 N.W. Prairie View Rd., Kansas City, MO 64151, tel. 816/741–7417 or 800/869–6806, fax 816/741–7123), a franchisee of Cruise Holidays, a cruise-only agency with outlets throughout the United States, has been in business since 1988. The agency mails out a free newsletter to clients every other month with listings of cruise bargains.

Cruise Line, Inc. (150 N.W. 168th St., N. Miami Beach, FL 33169, tel. 305/653–6111 or 800/777–0707, fax 305/653–6228), established in 1983, publishes *World of Cruising* magazine three times a year and a number of free brochures, including "Guide to First Time Cruising," "Guide to Family Cruises," and "Guide to Cruise Ship Weddings and Honeymoons." The agency has a 24-hour hot line with prerecorded cruise deals that are updated weekly.

Cruise Pro (2527 E. Thousand Oaks Blvd., Thousand Oaks, CA 91362, tel. 805/371–9884 or 800/222–7447; 800/258–7447 in CA; fax 805/371–9084), established in 1983, has special discounts listed in its two-times-per-month mailings to members of its Voyager's Club ($15 to join).

CruiseMasters (300 Corporate Pointe, Suite 100, Culver City, CA 90230, tel. 310/568–2040 or 800/242–9000, fax 310/568–2044), established in 1987, gives each passenger a personalized, bound guide to their ship's ports of call. The guides provide money-saving tips and advice on whether to opt for a prepackaged port excursion or strike out on your own. The agency's Family Cruise Club serves parents cruising with their children. A World Cruise Desk is dedicated to booking very long cruises. CruiseMasters also specializes in theme cruises.

Cruises, Inc. (5000 Campuswood Dr., E. Syracuse, NY 10357, tel. 315/463–9695 or 800/854–0500, fax 315/434–9175) opened its doors in 1981 and now has nearly 200 cruise consultants, including many CLIA Master Cruise Counsellors and Accredited Cruise Counsellors. Services provided by the agency include complimentary accident insurance for up to $250,000 per cruise, a monthly bargain bulletin ($19 a yr), and a free twice-a-year cruise directory with cruise reviews, tips, and discounts.

Cruises of Distinction (2750 S. Woodward Ave., Bloomfield Hills, MI 48304, tel. 810/332–2020 or 800/634–3445, fax 810/333–9743), established in 1984, publishes a free 80-page cruise catalog four times a year. For a fee of $39, which is credited to your first cruise booking, you can receive notification of unadvertised specials by mail or fax.

Don Ton Cruise Tours (3151 Airway Ave., E–1, Costa Mesa, CA 92626, tel. 714/545–3737 or 800/318–1818, fax 714/545–5275), established in 1972, features a variety of special-interest clubs, including a short-notice club, singles club, family cruise club, and adventure cruise club. The agency is also experienced in personalized pre- and post-cruise land arrangements.

Golden Bear Travel (16 Digital Dr., Novato, CA 94949, tel. 415/382–8900; 800/551–1000 outside CA; fax 415/382–9086) acts as general sales agent for a number of foreign cruise ships and specializes in longer, luxury cruises. Its Cruise Value club sends members free twice-a-month mailings with special prices on "distressed merchandise" cruises that are not selling well. The agency's Mariner Club runs escorted cruises for passengers who would like to travel as part of a group.

Kelly Cruises (1315 W. 22nd St., Suite 105, Oak Brook, IL 60521, tel. 630/990–1111 or 800/837–7447, fax 630/990–1147), established in 1986, publishes a quarterly newsletter highlighting new ships and special rates. Passengers can put their name on a free mailing list for last-minute deals.

National Discount Cruise Co. (1409 N. Cedar Crest Blvd., Allentown, PA 18104, tel. 610/439–4883 or 800/788–8108, fax 610/439–8086) is a five-year-old cruise division launched by GTA Travel, an American Express representative that has served travelers since 1967. The cruise division specializes in high-end cruises and includes shipboard credits, exclusive to American Express, on most of the sailings it books. A three-times-a-year newsletter highlights the agency's latest discounts.

Vacations at Sea (4919 Canal St., New Orleans, LA 70119, tel. 504/482–1572 or 800/749–4950, fax 504/486–8360), established in 1983, puts together its own pre- and post-cruise land packages and escorted land tours. The agency also publishes a free six-times-a-year newsletter with cruise reviews and discounts.

Full Service

Ambassador Tours (120 Montgomery St., Suite 400, San Francisco, CA 94104, tel. 415/981–5678 or 800/989–9000, fax 415/982–3490), established in 1955, does 80% of its business in cruises. Three times a year, the agency distributes a free 32-page catalog, which lists discounts on cruises and land packages, plus free monthly discount alerts.

Time to Travel (582 Market St., San Francisco, CA 94104, tel. 415/421–3333 or 800/524–3300, fax 415/421–4857), established in 1935, does 90% of its business in cruises. It mails a free listing of cruise discounts to its clients three to five times a month. Time to Travel specializes in pre- and post-cruise land arrangements and claims its staff of 19 has been nearly everywhere in the world.

White Travel Service (127 Park Rd., West Hartford, CT 06119, tel. 860/233–2648 or 800/547–4790; 860/236–6176 prerecorded cruise hot line with discount listings; fax 860/236–6177), founded in 1972, does most of its business in cruises and publishes a free 40-page brochure listing the latest cruise discounts.

Before You Go

Tickets, Vouchers, and Other Travel Documents

After you make the final payment to your travel agent, the cruise line will issue your cruise tickets and vouchers for airport-ship transfers. Depending on the airline and whether you have purchased an air-sea package, you may receive your plane tickets or charter-flight vouchers at the same time; you may also receive vouchers for any shore excursions, although most cruise lines issue these aboard ship. Should your travel documents not arrive when promised, contact your travel agent or call the cruise line directly. If you book late, tickets may be delivered directly to the ship.

Once aboard, you may be asked to turn over your passport for group immigration clearance (*see* Passports and Visas, *below*; Embarkation *in* Arriving and Departing, *below*) or to turn over your return plane ticket so the ship's staff may reconfirm your flight home. Otherwise, keep travel documents in a safe place, such as the safe in your cabin or at the purser's office.

Passports and Visas

Carrying a passport is always a good idea, and entry requirements do change, so read your cruise documents carefully to see what you'll need for embarkation. (You don't want to be turned away at the pier!)

If you are boarding a ship outside the United States, you'll need the appropriate entry requirements for that country. On cruises to or from some countries, you may be required to obtain a visa in advance. Check with your travel agent or cruise line about specific requirements. If you do need a visa for your cruise, your travel agent should help you obtain it, through a visa service by mail or directly from the consulate or embassy. (There may be a charge of up to $25 for this service, added to the visa charge.)

Passport Applications For information on obtaining or renewing a passport, contact the Office of Passport Services (tel. 202/647–0518).

Non-U.S. Citizens Depending on your country of origin, you may need a passport, visa, or both. Contact your cruise line or travel agent about entry requirements and any visas you may have to obtain in advance.

Passport Applications Canadian citizens should contact the Passport Office (tel. 819/994–3500 or 800/567–6868). Citizens of the United Kingdom interested in obtaining or renewing a passport should contact the London Passport Office (tel. 0990/21010).

What to Pack

For European ports of call, pack as you would for any American city: casual clothes by day, dressier fashions for going out on the town at night. For visits to churches, cathedrals, and mosques, avoid shorts and other outfits that could be considered immodest. In Italy, women should cover their shoulders and arms (a shawl will do). In Turkey, women must have a head covering; a long-sleeve blouse and long skirt or slacks are also required.

Generally speaking, plan on one outfit for every two days of cruising, especially if your wardrobe contains many interchangeable pieces. Ships often have convenient laundry facilities as well. And don't overload your luggage with extra toiletries and sundry items; they are easily available in port and in the ship's gift shop (though usually at a premium price). Soaps, and sometimes shampoos and body lotion, are often placed in your cabin compliments of the cruise line.

Take an extra pair of eyeglasses or contact lenses in your carry-on luggage. If you have a health problem that requires a prescription drug, pack enough to last the duration of the trip or have your doctor write a prescription using the drug's generic name, because brand names vary from country to country. Always carry prescription drugs in their original packaging to avoid problems with customs officials. Don't pack them in luggage that you plan to check in case your bags go astray. Pack a list of the offices that supply refunds for lost or stolen traveler's checks.

Arriving and Departing

If you have purchased an air-sea package, you will be met by a cruise-company representative when your plane lands at the port city and then shuttled directly to the ship in buses or minivans. Some cruise lines arrange to transport your luggage between airport and ship—you don't have to hassle with baggage claim at the start of your cruise or with baggage check-in at the end. If you decide not to buy the air-sea package but still plan to fly, ask your travel agent if you can use the ship's transfer bus anyway; if you do, you may be required to purchase a round-trip transfer voucher ($5–$20). Otherwise, you will have to take a taxi to the ship.

If you live close to the port of embarkation, bus transportation may be available. If you are part of a group that has booked a cruise together, this transportation may be part of your package. Another option for those who live close to their point of departure is to drive to the ship. The major U.S. cruise ports all have parking facilities.

Embarkation

Check-In On arrival at the dock, you must check in before boarding your ship. (A handful of smaller cruise ships handle check-in at the airport.) An officer will collect or stamp your ticket, inspect or even retain your passport or other official identification, ask you to fill out a tourist card, check that you have the correct visas, and collect any unpaid port or departure tax. Seating assignments for the dining room are often handed out at this time, too. You may also register your credit card to open a shipboard account, although that may be done later at the purser's office.

After this you may be required to go through a security check and to pass your hand baggage through an X-ray inspection. These are the same machines in use at airports, so ask to have your photographic film inspected visually.

Although it takes only five or 10 minutes per family to check in, lines are often long, so aim for off-peak hours. The worst time tends to be immediately after the ship begins boarding; the later it is, the less crowded. For example, if boarding begins at 2 PM and continues until 4:30, try to arrive after 3:30.

Boarding the Ship Before you walk up the gangway, the ship's photographer will probably take your picture; there's no charge unless you buy the picture (usually $6). On board, stewards may serve welcome drinks in souvenir glasses—for which you're usually charged between $3 and $5 cash.

You will either be escorted to your cabin by a steward or, on a smaller ship, given your key by a ship's officer and directed to your cabin. Some elevators are unavailable to passengers during boarding, since they are used to transport luggage. You may arrive to find your luggage outside your stateroom or just inside the door; if it doesn't arrive within a half hour before sailing, contact the purser. If you are among the unlucky few whose luggage doesn't make it to the ship in time, the purser will trace it and arrange to have it flown to the next port.

Visitors' Passes Some cruise ships permit passengers to invite guests on board prior to sailing, although most cruise lines prohibit all but paying passengers for reasons of security and insurance liability. Cruise companies that allow visitors usually require that you obtain passes several weeks in advance; call the lines for policies and procedures.

Most ships do not allow visitors while the ship is docked in a port of call. If you meet a friend on shore, you won't be able to invite him or her back to your stateroom.

Disembarkation

The last night of your cruise is full of business. On most ships you must place everything except your hand luggage outside your cabin door, ready to be picked up by midnight. Color-coded tags, distributed to your cabin in a debarkation packet, should be placed on your luggage before the crew collects it. Your designated color will later determine when you leave the ship and help you retrieve your luggage on the pier.

Your shipboard bill is left in your room during the last day; to pay the bill (if you haven't already put it on your credit card) or to settle any questions, you must stand in line at the purser's office. Tips to the cabin steward and dining staff are distributed on the last night.

The next morning, in-room breakfast service is usually not available because stewards are too busy. Most passengers clear out of their cabins as soon as possible, gather their hand luggage, and stake out a chair in one of the public lounges to await the ship's clearance through customs. Be patient—it takes a long time to unload and sort thousands of pieces of luggage. Passengers are disembarked by groups according to the color-coded tags placed on luggage the night before; those with the earliest flights get off first. If you have a tight connection, notify the purser before the last day, and he or she may be able to arrange faster preclearing and debarkation for you.

Customs and Duties

U.S. Customs Before your ship lands, each individual or family must fill out a customs declaration, regardless of whether anything was purchased abroad. If you have less than $1,400 worth of goods, you will not need to itemize purchases. Be prepared to pay whatever duties are owed directly to the customs inspector, with cash or check.

Allowances. You may bring home $400 worth of foreign goods duty-free if you've been out of the country for at least 48 hours and haven't already used the $400 exemption, or any part of it, in the past 30 days. Note that these are the *general* rules, applicable to most countries; if you're returning from a cruise that called in the U.S. Virgin Islands, the duty-free allowance is higher—$1,200.

Alcohol and Tobacco. Travelers 21 or older may bring back 1 liter of alcohol duty-free, provided the beverage laws of the state through which they reenter the United States allow it. In the case of the U.S. Virgin Islands, 5 liters are allowed. In addition, 100 non-Cuban cigars and 200 cigarettes are allowed, regardless of your age. From the U.S. Virgin Islands, 1,000 cigarettes are allowed, but only 200 of them may have been acquired elsewhere. Antiques and works of art more than 100 years old are duty-free.

Canadian Customs

Allowances. If you've been out of Canada for at least seven days, you may bring in C$500 worth of goods duty-free. If you've been away less than seven days but more than 48 hours, the duty-free exemption drops to C$200. You cannot pool exemptions with family members. Goods claimed under the C$500 exemption may follow you by mail; those claimed under the lesser exemption must accompany you.

Alcohol and Tobacco. Alcohol and tobacco products may be included in the seven-day and 48-hour exemption. If you meet the age requirements of the province or territory through which you reenter Canada, you may bring in, duty-free, 1.14 liters (40 imperial ounces) of wine or liquor *or* two dozen 12-ounce cans or bottles of beer or ale. If you are 16 or older, you may bring in, duty-free, 200 cigarettes, 50 cigars or cigarillos, and 400 tobacco sticks or 400 grams of manufactured tobacco. Alcohol and tobacco must accompany you on your return.

U.K. Customs

Allowances. If your cruise was wholly within European Union (EU) countries, you no longer need to pass through customs when you return to the United Kingdom. If you plan to bring back large quantities of alcohol or tobacco, check in advance on EU limits. When returning from cruises that called at countries outside the European Union, you may import duty-free 200 cigarettes, 100 cigarillos, 50 cigars or 250 grams of tobacco; 1 liter of spirits or 2 liters of fortified or sparkling wine or liqueur; 2 liters of still table wine; 60 milliliters of perfume; 250 milliliters of toilet water; plus £136 worth of other goods, including gifts and souvenirs.

2 Ports of Call

Going Ashore

Traveling by cruise ship presents an opportunity to visit many different places in a short time. The flip side is that your stay will be limited in each port of call. For that reason, cruise lines invented shore excursions, which maximize passengers' time by organizing their touring for them. There are a number of advantages to shore excursions: In some destinations, transportation may be unreliable, and a ship-packaged tour is the best way to see distant sights. Also, you don't have to worry about being stranded or missing the ship. The disadvantage is that you will pay more for the convenience of having the ship do the legwork for you. Of course, you can always book a tour independently, hire a taxi, or use foot power to explore on your own.

Disembarking

When your ship arrives in a port, it either ties up alongside a dock or anchors out in a harbor. If the ship is docked, passengers just walk down the gangway to go ashore. Docking makes it easy to go back and forth between the shore and the ship.

Tendering If your ship anchors in the harbor, however, you will have to take a small boat—called a launch or tender—to get ashore. Tendering is a nuisance. When your ship first arrives in port, everyone wants to go ashore. Often, in order to avoid a stampede at the tenders, you must gather in a public room, get a boarding pass, and wait until your number is called. This continues until everybody has disembarked. Even then, it may take 15–20 minutes to get ashore if your ship is anchored far offshore. Because tenders can be difficult to board, passengers with mobility problems may not be able to visit certain ports. The larger the ship, the more likely it will use tenders. It is usually possible to learn before booking a cruise whether the ship will dock or anchor at its ports of call. (For more information about where and whether ships dock, tender, or both, *see* Coming Ashore for each port, *below*.)

Before anyone is allowed to walk down the gangway or board a tender, the ship must first be cleared for landing. Immigration and customs officials board the vessel to examine passports and sort through red tape. It may be more than an hour before you're actually allowed ashore. You will be issued a boarding pass, which you must have with you to get back on board.

Returning to the Ship

Cruise lines are strict about sailing times, which are posted at the gangway and elsewhere as well as announced in the daily schedule of activities. Be certain to be back on board at least a half hour before the announced sailing time or you may be stranded. If you are on a shore excursion that was sold by the cruise line, however, the captain will wait for your group before casting off. That is one reason many passengers prefer ship-packaged tours.

If you are not on one of the ship's tours and the ship does sail without you, immediately contact the cruise line's port representative, whose name and phone number are often listed on the daily schedule of activities. You may be able to hitch a ride on a pilot boat, though that is unlikely. Passengers who miss the boat must pay their own way to the next port of call.

Europe and the Mediterranean

For sheer diversity, there is no cruise destination quite like Europe. From the majesty of Norway's fjords to the ruins of ancient Greece, the Old World has more than one could possibly hope to see in a single cruise vacation.

The hardest part of cruising in Europe is deciding what to see. Do you want to sail the Mediterranean, with ports of call in Greece, Turkey, Israel, Egypt, and Spain? Or would you prefer Northern Europe, perhaps including a few cities in the former Soviet Union? Or maybe Western Europe, with the glamorous beaches and resort cities of the French Riviera? You will have to choose.

Select your ship as carefully as you choose your itinerary. Look especially at the mix of passengers: Are they all North Americans or a mix of Americans and Europeans?

When to Go Cruise lines sail in Europe from April to November. Peak season runs from May through August; the weather is usually at its best during this time, which means you will be joining the crowds. Early spring and late fall are a good time to visit if you want to avoid the fray—and get lower prices. Temperatures can be very comfortable, and it is possible to swim in the Mediterranean through early October. Some lines operate European itineraries year-round featuring the Canary Islands, a popular spot among Europeans for winter getaways.

Currency Currencies vary by country, and U.S. dollars are accepted at some ports. It is advisable to change only a small amount on your ship or ashore for purchasing trinkets or snacks. When making major purchases and eating at better restaurants, use credit cards, which offer the best exchange rate.

Passports and Visas All U.S. citizens will need a passport to travel to Europe. Several countries, including Israel, Egypt, and Russia, require visas. Your cruise documents will specify whether visas are needed, and, generally, the line or your travel agent can obtain the visa for you for a fee.

Europe

Reykjavík
ICELAND
NORWAY
Bergen
SCOTLAND
NORTHERN IRELAND
Edinburgh
North Sea
Skagerrak
Belfast
IRELAND
Irish Sea
DENMARK
Dublin
UNITED KINGDOM
Cork
WALES
Hamburg
ENGLAND
NETHERLANDS
Cardiff
Amsterdam
The Hague
London
Rotterdam
ATLANTIC OCEAN
English Channel
GERM
Brussels
Bonn
BELGIUM
Frankfurt
Paris
LUXEMBOURG
FRANCE
Zürich
Munic
Bern
SWITZERLAND
Lyon
LIECHTENSTEI
Milan
Veni
Monte Carlo
Nice
MONACO
Marseille
ANDORRA
PORTUGAL
Madrid
Florence
Lisbon
Corsica
Barcelona
SPAIN
Sardinia
Seville
Granada
Balearic Islands
Tyrrheni
Gibraltar
Mediterranean Sea
MOROCCO
ALGERIA
0
400 miles
TUNISIA
0
600 km

FINLAND
Gulf of Bothnia
SWEDEN
Helsinki
Gulf of Finland
St. Petersburg
Tallinn
Stockholm
ESTONIA
Göteborg
Riga
LATVIA
Moscow
Copenhagen
LITHUANIA
Baltic Sea
Kaunas
RUSSIA
Vilnius
RUSSIA
Kaliningrad
Minsk
POLAND
BELARUS
Warsaw
Kraków
Kiev
Prague
CZECH REPUBLIC
UKRAINE
SLOVAKIA
Vienna
Bratislava
Salzburg
AUSTRIA
Budapest
MOLDOVA
Chişinău
HUNGARY
SLOVENIA
Zagreb
ROMANIA
CROATIA
Novi Sad
BOSNIA AND HERZEGOVINA
Belgrade
Bucharest
SERBIA
Black Sea
Adriatic Sea
Sarajevo
BULGARIA
MONTENEGRO
Priština
Sofia
Skopje
Podgorica
F.Y.R. of MACEDONIA
Istanbul
Tiranë
Naples
ALBANIA
Ankara
TURKEY
GREECE
Aegean Sea
Ionian Sea
Athens
CYPRUS
Crete
Mediterranean Sea

What to Pack A priority item for cruising Europe is a comfortable pair of shoes—walking is the best and sometimes only way to really explore in port. Wardrobes will be determined by your cruise itinerary. In the Mediterranean, casual summer wear will do. In countries such as Egypt, Turkey, and Morocco, women will want to dress conservatively, covering their arms and legs. Pack clothing that can be layered and that is suitable for hot days and cooler evenings.

Telephones and Mail Unless money is no object, don't use the satellite phones aboard ship. At major ports where ships dock, there typically will be telephones at or near the pier. If your ship is tendering into port, ask at the shore-excursion office for the nearest calling center.

As a rule, cruise ships sell local stamps at the front desk, and you can send postcards from an onboard mailbox as well, eliminating the need to find a post office.

Shore Excursions Due to its diversity and wealth of attractions, Europe is well suited to shore excursions, which are usually bus tours. However, depending on the port, you may want to explore on your own. Often, this is possible on foot. In larger ports, you can hire a local guide at the pier. A group of four to six will find this more economical and practical than will a couple or a single person. Renting a car is often more of a pain than a pleasure, given the limited time you have ashore. On some islands, motor scooters are an option—but they are notoriously dangerous. It's better to hire a car and driver. Ask your shore-excursions office for recommended companies in each port.

Amsterdam, The Netherlands

If you've come to Holland expecting to find its residents shod in wooden shoes, you're years too late; if you're looking for windmills at every turn, you're looking in the wrong place. The bucolic images that brought tourism here in the decades after World War II have little to do with the Netherlands of the '90s. Modern Holland is a marriage of economic power and cultural wealth, a mix not new to the Dutch: In the 17th century, for example, money raised through colonial outposts was used to buy or commission portraits and paintings by young artists such as Rembrandt, Hals, Vermeer, and van Ruisdael.

Amsterdam is the cultural focal point of the nation. Small and densely packed with fine buildings, many dating from the 17th century or earlier, it is easily explored on foot. The heart of the city consists of canals, with narrow streets radiating out like spokes of a wheel.

Currency The unit of currency in Holland is the guilder, written as NLG (for Netherlands guilder), Fl., or simply F. Each guilder is divided into 100 cents. At press time, the exchange rate for the guilder was 1.7 Fl. to the U.S. dollar.

Telephones All towns and cities have area codes that are used only when you are calling from outside the area. Coin-operated public phone booths are being replaced with equipment that requires phone cards. Pay phones in bars and restaurants take 25¢ or Fl. 1 coins. Phone cards may be purchased from post offices, railway stations, and newsagents for Fl. 10 or Fl. 25. Dial 0800/0410 for an English-speaking operator. Direct-dial international calls can be made from any phone booth. To reach an **AT&T** long-distance operator, dial 0800/022–9111; for **MCI**, dial 0800/022–9122; for **Sprint**, dial 0800/022–9119.

Shore Excursions The following is a good choice in Amsterdam. It may not be offered by all cruise lines. Time and price are approximate.

City Tour & Cruise. By motor coach and canal boat, you'll see Amsterdam's major sights, including the Royal Palace, New Church, and Rijksmuseum. The route also passes some of Amsterdam's architectural highlights, such as Mint Tower and Weeping Tower. *3 hrs. Cost: $36.*

Coming Ashore Ships dock at the cruise terminal; it's about a 10-minute drive to the main square. Central Station, the hub of the city, is the most convenient point to begin sightseeing. Across the street, in the same building as the Old Dutch Coffee House, is a tourist information center that offers helpful advice.

Getting Around Amsterdam is a small, congested city of narrow streets, which makes it ideal for exploring on foot. The most enjoyable way to get to know Amsterdam is by taking a boat trip along the canals. There are frequent departures from points opposite Central Station. Taxis are expensive: A 5-km (3-mi) ride costs around Fl. 15. Rental bikes are readily available for around Fl. 10 per day with a Fl. 50–Fl. 200 deposit. Several rental companies are close to the central train station.

Exploring Amsterdam

Numbers in the margin correspond to points of interest on the Amsterdam map.

1 The **Centraal Station** (Central Station), designed by P. J. H. Cuijpers, was built in 1884–89 and is a good example of Dutch architecture at its most flamboyant. It provides an excellent viewpoint for both the Beurs van Berlage and the Scheepvaartshuis, two of the city's best examples of early-20th-century architecture. The street directly in front of the station square is Prins Hendrikkade.

The most important of Amsterdam's museums
2 is the **Rijksmuseum** (State Museum), easily recognized by its towers. It was founded in 1808, but the current, rather lavish, building dates from 1885. The museum's fame rests on its unrivaled collection of 16th- and 17th-century Dutch masters. Of Rembrandt's masterpieces, make a point of seeing *The Nightwatch*, concealed during World War II in caves in Maastricht. The painting was misnamed because of its dull layers of varnish; in reality it depicts the Civil Guard in daylight. Also worth searching out are Frans Hals's family portraits, Jan Steen's drunken scenes, van Ruisdael's romantic but menacing landscapes, and Vermeer's glimpses of everyday life bathed in his usual pale light. *Stadhouderskade 42, tel. 020/6732121. Admission: Fl. 12.50. Open daily 10–5.*

3 The not-to-be-missed **Rijksmuseum Vincent van Gogh** (Vincent van Gogh Museum) contains the world's largest collection of the artist's works—200 paintings and nearly 500 drawings—as well as works by some 50 of his contemporaries. *Paulus Potterstraat 7, tel. 020/5705200. Admission: Fl. 10. Open daily 10–5.*

4 The **Stedelijk Museum** (Municipal Museum) has a stimulating collection of modern art and ever-

changing displays of contemporary art. Before viewing the works of Cézanne, Chagall, Kandinsky, and Mondrian, check the list of temporary exhibitions in Room 1. *Paulus Potterstraat 13, tel. 020/5732911. Admission: Fl. 7.50. Open daily 11–5.*

Arguably the most famous house in Amsterdam
5 is **Anne Frankhuis** (Anne Frank House), which was immortalized by the poignant diary kept by the young Jewish girl from 1942 to 1944, when she and her family hid here from the German occupying forces. A small exhibition on the Holocaust can also be seen in the house. *Prinsengracht 263, tel. 020/5567100. Admission: Fl. 8. Open June–Aug., Mon.–Sat. 9–7, Sun. 10–7; Sept.–May, Mon.–Sat. 9–5, Sun. 10–5.*

The infamous *rosse buurt* (red-light district) is bordered by Amsterdam's two oldest canals (Oudezijds Voorburgwal and Oudezijds Achterburgwal). In the windows at canal level, women in sheer lingerie slouch, stare, or do their nails. Although the area can be shocking, with its sex shops and porn shows, it is generally safe. If you do decide to explore the area, take care; purse-snatchers and pickpockets are a problem.

6 Dominating Dam Square is the **Het Koninklijk Paleis te Amsterdam** (Royal Palace at Amsterdam), a vast, well-proportioned structure that was completed in 1655. It is built on 13,659 pilings sunk into the marshy soil. The great pedimental sculptures are an allegorical representation of Amsterdam surrounded by Neptune and mythological sea creatures. *Dam, tel. 020/6248698. Admission: Fl. 5. Open Tues.–Thurs. 1–4; daily 12:30–5 in summer. Sometimes closed for state events.*

From 1639 to 1658, Rembrandt lived at Joden-
7 breestraat 4, now the **Museum Het Rembrandthuis** (Rembrandt's House). For more than 20 years, the ground floor was used by the artist as living quarters; the sunny upper floor was his studio. It contains a superb collection of his etchings. From St. Antonies Sluis Bridge, just by the house, there is a canal view that has barely changed since Rembrandt's time. *Jodenbreestraat 4–6, tel. 020/6249486. Admission: Fl. 7.50. Open Mon.–Sat. 10–5, Sun. 1–5.*

Anne Frankhuis, **5**
Centraal Station, **1**
Het Koninklijk Paleis te Amsterdam, **6**
Museum Het Rembrandthuis, **7**
Rijksmuseum, **2**
Rijksmuseum Vincent van Gogh, **3**
Stedelijk Museum, **4**

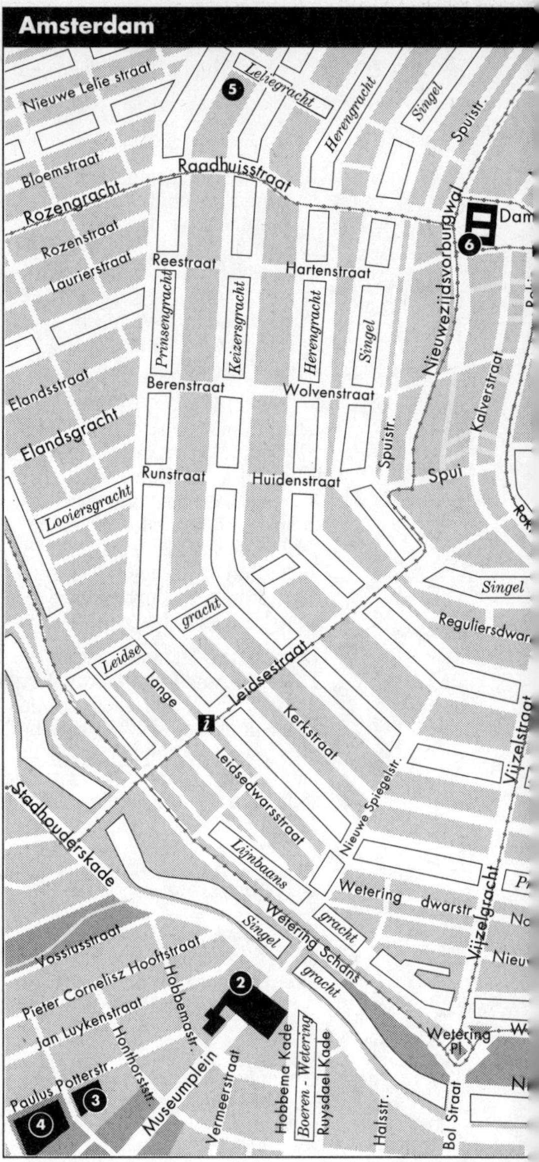

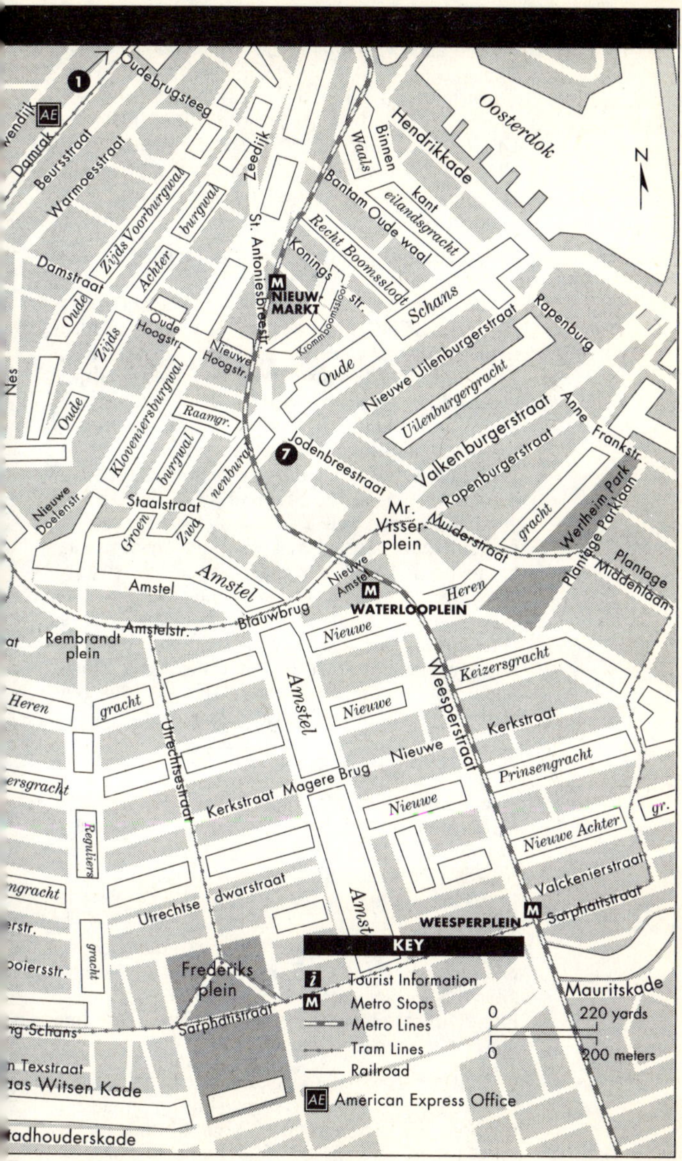

Oudebrugsteeg
Damrak
Beursstraat
Warmoesstraat
Zeedijk
Zijds Voorburgwal
Achter
burgwal
Damstraat
Oude
Zijds
Oude Hoogstr.
Nieuwe Hoogstr.
Nes
Oude
Kloveniersburgwal
Raamgr.
burgwal
nenburg
Nieuwe Doelenstr.
Staalstraat
Groen
Zwa
Amstel
Amstel
Amstelstr.
Blauwbrug
Rembrandt plein
St. Antoniesbreestr.
NIEUWMARKT
Konings str.
Krommeboomssloot
Recht Boomssloot
Bantam Oude waal
Waals
Binnen kant
eilandsgracht
Hendrikkade
Oosterdok
N
Schans
Oude
Nieuwe Uilenburgerstraat
Uilenburgergracht
Rapenburg
Anne Frankstr.
Valkenburgerstraat
Rapenburgerstraat
gracht
Jodenbreestraat
Mr. Visser plein
Muiderstraat
Wertheim Park
Plantage Parklaan
Plantage Middenlaan
Nieuwe Amstel
WATERLOOPLEIN
Heren
Nieuwe
Keizersgracht
Amstel
Nieuwe
Weesperstraat
Kerkstraat
Nieuwe
Prinsengracht
Heren
gracht
Utrechtsestraat
Kerkstraat
Magere Brug
Nieuwe
Nieuwe Achter
gr.
Valckenierstraat
Sarphatistraat
WEESPERPLEIN
Reguliers
gracht
Utrechtse
dwarstraat
Amst
Frederiks plein
Sarphatistraat
Mauritskade
n Texstraat
Witsen Kade
Stadhouderskade
Schans
KEY
Tourist Information
Metro Stops
Metro Lines
Tram Lines
Railroad
American Express Office
0
220 yards
0
200 meters

Beer lovers will want to visit the **Heinekenontvangstgebouw,** formerly the Heineken Brewery. The guided weekday tours take in a slide presentation, the old brewery stables, and, of course, include free beer at the end of the tour. *Van der Helstraat, tel. 020/5239436. Admission: Fl. 2. Tours year-round 9:30 and 11, additional summer tours at 1 and 2:30. Children under 18 not admitted.*

Shopping Amsterdam is a cornucopia of interesting markets and quirky specialty shops selling antiques, art, and diamonds. The chief shopping districts, which have largely been turned into pedestrian-only areas, are the **Leidsestraat, Kalverstraat, Utrechtsestraat,** and **Nieuwendijk.** The **Rokin,** hectic with traffic, houses a cluster of boutiques and renowned antiques shops selling 18th- and 19th-century furniture, antique jewelry, Art Deco lamps, and statuettes. By contrast, some of the **Nieuwe Spiegelstraat's** old curiosity shops sell a less expensive range of goods. Haute couture and other fine goods are at home on **P.C. Hooftstraat, Van Baerlestraat,** and **Beethovenstraat.** For trendy small boutiques and unusual crafts shops, locals browse through the **Jordaan.** For A-to-Z shopping in a huge variety of stores, visit the **Magna Plaza** shopping center, built inside the glorious old post office behind the Royal Palace.

Athens/Piraeus, Greece

Athens is essentially a village that outgrew itself, spreading out from the original settlement at the foot of the Acropolis. Back in 1834, when it became the capital of modern Greece, the city had a population of fewer than 10,000. Now it houses more than a third of the Greek population—around 4.3 million. A modern concrete city has engulfed the old village and now sprawls for 388 square km (244 square mi), covering almost all the surrounding plain from the sea to the encircling mountains.

The city is crowded, dusty, and overwhelmingly hot during the summer. It also has an appalling air-pollution problem. Still, Athens is an experience not to be missed. Its tangible vibrancy makes it one of the most exciting cities in Europe, and the sprawling cement has failed to overwhelm the few astonishing reminders of ancient Athens.

Currency The Greek monetary unit is the drachma (dr.). At press time, there were approximately 241 dr. to the U.S. dollar.

Telephones The country code for Greece is 30. Telephone kiosks are easy to find, although some can only be used for local calls. The easiest way to make a local or an international call is with a phone card, available at kiosks, convenience stores, or Hellenic Telecommunications Organization (OTE) offices. Go to an OTE office for convenience and privacy if you plan to make several international calls; there are several branches in Athens. For an **AT&T** long-distance operator, dial 00/800–1311; **MCI,** 00/800–1211; **Sprint,** 00/800–1411.

Shore Excursions The following are good choices in Athens. They may not be offered by all cruise lines. Times and prices are approximate.

Athens and the Acropolis. A must for the first-time visitor. Drive by motor coach to Athens, passing the Olympic Stadium, the former Royal Palace, and the Tomb of the Unknown Warrior on the way to the Acropolis, where a guide will lead an extensive walking tour. *4 hrs. Cost: $40.*

Agora and Plaka. The Acropolis, where Sophocles once taught, and Athens's old shopping district are the centerpieces of this half-day tour into historic Greece. *4 hrs. Cost: $38.*

Coming Ashore Cruise ships dock at Piraeus, 10 km (6 mi) from Athens's center. From Piraeus, you can take the nearby metro right into Omonia Square. The trip takes 20 minutes and costs 100 dr. Alternatively, you can take a taxi, which may well take longer due to traffic and will cost around 1,100 dr. Cruise lines nearly always offer bus transfers for a fee.

The central area of modern Athens is small, stretching from the Acropolis to Mt. Lycabettus, with its little white church on top. The layout is simple: Three parallel streets—Stadiou, Venizelou (a.k.a. Panepistimiou), and Akademias—link two main squares—Syntagma and Omonia.

Getting Around Many of the sights you'll want to see, and most of the hotels, cafés, and restaurants, are within the central area of Athens, and it's easy to walk everywhere. Taxis are plentiful and heavily used. Although you'll eventually find an empty one, it's often faster to call out your destination to one carrying passengers; if the taxi is going in that direction, the driver will pick you up. Most drivers speak basic English and are familiar with the city center. The meter starts at 200 dr., and there is a basic charge of 58 dr. per kilometer, which increases to 113 dr. between midnight and 5 AM. There is an additional 160 dr. charge for trips from the port.

Exploring Athens *Numbers in the margin correspond to points of interest on the Athens map.*

1 A steep, zigzag path leads to the **Akropolis** (Acropolis). After a 30-year building moratorium at the time of the Persian wars, the Athenians built this complex during the 5th century BC to honor the goddess Athena, patron of the city. It is now undergoing conservation as part of an ambitious 20-year rescue plan launched with international support in 1983 by Greek architects.

The first ruins you'll see are the Propylaea, the monumental gateway that led worshipers from the temporal world into the spiritual world of the sanctuary; now only the columns of Pentelic marble and a fragment of stone ceiling remain. Above, to the right, stands the graceful Naos Athenas Nikis or Apterou Nikis (Wingless Victory). The temple was mistakenly called the latter because common tradition often confused Athena with the winged goddess Nike. Athenians claimed the sculptor had purposely omitted the wings on the temple's statue to ensure Victory would never fly away from the city. The elegant and architecturally complex Erechtheion temple, most sacred of the shrines of the Acropolis and later turned into a harem by the Turks, has emerged from extensive repair work. Dull, heavy copies of the Caryatids (draped maidens) now support the roof. The Acropolis Museum houses five of the six originals, their faces much damaged by acid rain; only four are on display, since one is being restored. The sixth is in the British Museum in London.

2 The **Parthenonas** (Parthenon) dominates the Acropolis and indeed the Athens skyline. It was completed in 438 BC and is the most architecturally sophisticated temple of that period. Even with hordes of tourists wandering around the ruins, you can still feel a sense of wonder. The architectural decorations were originally painted in vivid red and blue, and the roof was of marble tiles, but time and neglect have given the marble pillars their golden-white shine, and the beauty of the building is all the more stark and striking. The British Museum houses the largest remaining part of the original 532-ft frieze (the Elgin Marbles). The building has 17 fluted columns along each side and eight at the ends, and these lean slightly inward and bulge to cleverly counterbalance the natural optical distortion. The Parthenon has had a checkered history: It was made into a brothel by the Romans, a church by the Christians, and a mosque by the Turks. The Turks also stored gunpowder in the Propylaea, and when this was hit by a Venetian bombardment in 1687, a fire raged for two days and 28 columns of the Parthenon were blown out, leaving the temple in its present condition. *Top of Dionyssiou Areopagitou, tel. 01/321–0219. Admission: 2,000 dr., joint ticket to Acropolis and museum. Open weekdays 8:30–6:30 (winter 8–4), weekends 8–3.*

3 The **Museo Akropoleos** (Acropolis Museum), tucked into one corner of the Acropolis, contains some superb sculptures from the Acropolis, including the Caryatids and a large collection of colored *korai* (statues of women dedicated by worshipers to the goddess Athena, patron of the ancient city). *Tel. 01/323–6665. Admission: 2,000 dr., joint ticket to the Acropolis. Open Mon. 11–6:30, Tues.–Fri. 8:30–6:30, weekends 8:30–2:30.*

On Areopagus, the rocky outcrop facing the Acropolis, St. Paul delivered his Sermon to the Unknown God. Legend also claims that Orestes was tried here for the murder of his mother. To
4 the right stands the **Archaia Agora** (Ancient Agora), which means "marketplace," the civic center and focal point of community life in ancient Athens.

Akropolis, **1**
Archaia Agora, **4**
Ethniko Archaiologiko Museo, **8**
Goulandri Museo Kikladikis ke Archais Technis, **9**
Hephaisteion, **5**
Museo Akropoleos, **3**
Museo tis Agoras, **6**
Parthenonas, **2**
Plaka, **7**
Vizantino Museo, **10**

Athens

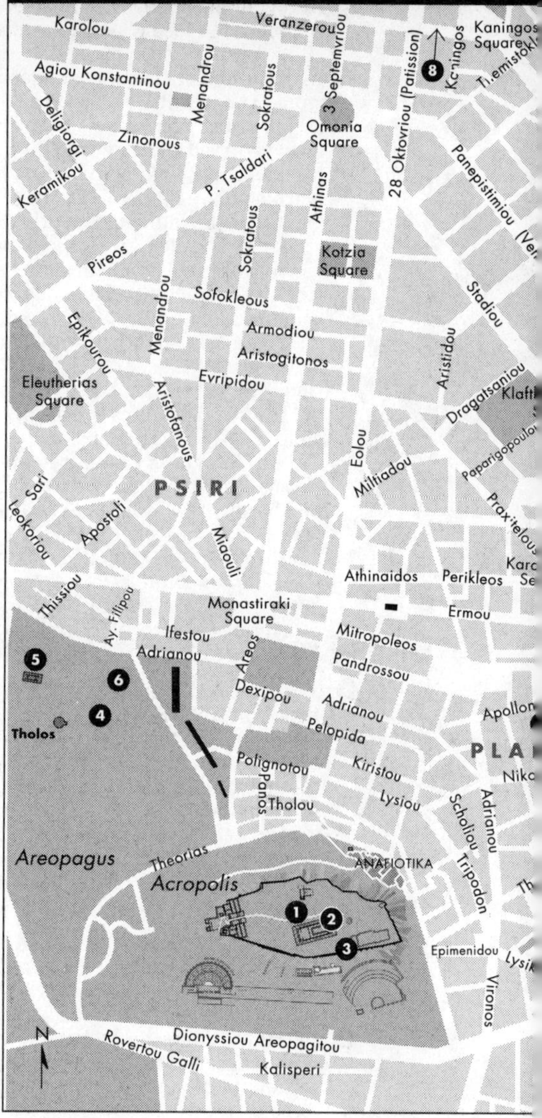

LIKAVITOS
Ayios Giorgios
KOLONAKI
Municipal Cultural Center
Schliemann's Mansion
Kolonaki Square
Syntagma Square
National Gardens
Zappion
Ardittos Hill
Em. Benaki
Zoodohou Pigis
Harilaou Trikoupi
N. Mavromichali
Navarinou
Ippokratous
Dervenion
Arachovis
Didotou
N. Ouranou
Dafnomili
Sarantapichou
Marasli
Akademias
Asklepiou
Skoufa
Chersonos
Massalias
Solonos
Sina
Korai
Omirou
Lykavitou
Anagnostopoulou
Aristipou
Kleomenous
Loukianou
Spefsipou
Dimokritou
Voukourestiou
Amerikis
Ch. Lada
Pindarou
Patriarhou Ioakim
Alopekis
Karneadou
Ypsilantou
Irodotou
Kolokotroni
Kanari
Merlin
Koumbari
Georgiou I
Vasilissis Sofias
Mitropoleos
Pendeli
Voulis
Nikis
Filellinon
Amalias
Herod Atticus
Rigilis
Vasileos Georgiou B'
Souri
Kidathineon
Amalias Ave.
Vasileos Konstantinou
Pafsaniou
Eratosthenous
Arianou
Agras
Goura
Pitakou
Vasilissis Olgas
KEY
American Express Office
0
220 yards
0
200 meters

The sprawling confusion of stones, slabs, and foundations at the Agora is dominated by the best-preserved temple in Greece, the **Hephaisteion** (often wrongly referred to as the Theseion), built during the 5th century BC. Like the other monuments, it is roped off, but you can walk around it to admire its 34 columns.

The impressive **Stoa Attalou** (Stoa of Attalos II), reconstructed by the American School of Classical Studies in Athens with the help of the Rockefeller Foundation, houses the **Museo tis Agoras** (Museum of the Agora Excavations). *Three entrances: from Monastiraki, on Adrianou street; from Thission, on Apostolos Pavlou street; from Acropolis, on descent along Ag. Apostoli. Tel. 01/321–0185. Admission: 1,200 dr. Open Tues.–Sun. 8:30–2:45.*

The **Plaka** is almost all that's left of 19th-century Athens. During the 1950s and '60s, the area became garish with neon as nightclubs moved in and residents moved out. Renovation in recent years has restored the Plaka, with its winding lanes, neoclassical houses, and sights such as the Museo Laikis Technis (Greek Folk Art Museum; Kidathineon 17); the Aerides (Tower of the Winds), a 1st-century BC water clock near the Roman Agora; and the Mnimeio Lysikratous (Monument of Lysikrates; Herefondos and Lysikratous Sts.). Above the Plaka, at the base of the Acropolis, is Anafiotika, the closest thing you'll find to a village in Athens. To escape the city bustle, take some time to wander among its whitewashed, bougainvillea-framed houses and its tiny churches. *Stretching east from the Agora.*

Make time to see the **Ethniko Archaiologiko Museo** (National Archaeological Museum). Despite being somewhat off the tourist route, a good 10-minute walk north of Omonia Square, it is well worth the detour. It houses one of the most exciting collections of antiquities in the world, including sensational archaeological finds made by Heinrich Schliemann at Mycenae; 16th-century BC frescoes from the Akrotiri ruins on Santorini; and the 6½-ft-tall bronze sculpture *Poseidon*, an original work of circa 470 BC, possibly by the sculptor Kalamis, which was found in the sea off Cape Artemision in 1928. *28 Oktovriou (Patission) 44, tel. 01/821–7717. Ad-*

mission: 2,000 dr. Open Mon. 12:30–7, Tues.–Fri. 8–7, weekends and holidays 8:30–3.

9 The **Goulandri Museo Kikladikis ke Archaias Technis** (Goulandris Museum of Cycladic and Ancient Art) collection spans 5,000 years, with nearly 100 exhibits of the Cycladic civilization (3000–2000 BC), including many of the slim marble figurines that so fascinated artists such as Picasso and Modigliani. *Neofitou Douka 4 or Irodotou 1, tel. 01/722–8321. Admission: 400 dr. Open Mon. and Wed.–Fri. 10–4, Sat. 10–3.*

10 Housed in an 1848 mansion built by an eccentric French aristocrat is the **Vizantino Museo** (Byzantine Museum). Since the museum is undergoing renovation, not all its pieces are on display, but it has a unique collection of icons, recreations of Greek churches throughout the centuries, and the very beautiful 14th-century Byzantine embroidery of the body of Christ, in gold, silver, yellow, and green. Sculptural fragments provide an excellent introduction to Byzantine architecture. *Vasilissis Sofias 22, tel. 01/721–1027 and 01/723–1570. Admission: 500 dr. Open Tues.–Sun. 8:30–2:50.*

Shopping Better tourist shops sell copies of traditional Greek jewelry, silver filigree, Skyrian pottery, onyx ashtrays and dishes, woven bags, attractive rugs (including *flokatis*—shaggy wool rugs, often brightly colored), worry beads called *koboloi* in amber or silver, and blue-and-white amulets to ward off the *mati* (evil eye). Some museums sell replicas of small items that are in their collections. The best handicrafts are sold in the **National Welfare Organization shop** (Vas. Sofias 135, Platia Mavili; Ipatias 6 and Apollonos, Plaka) and the **Center of Hellenic Tradition** (Mitropoleos 59 or Pandrossou 36, Monastiraki). Other shops sell dried fruit, packaged pistachios, and canned olives. Natural sponges also make good gifts.

Barcelona, Spain

Barcelona thrives on its business acumen and industrial muscle. Its hardworking citizens are proud to have and use their own language (Catalan)—with street names, museum exhibits, newspapers, radio programs, and movies all in this native tongue. In 1992, the city realized a long-cherished goal—the hosting of the Olympic Games. The Olympics were of singular importance to the city's modernization, spurring significant improvements in roads and community buildings. This thriving metropolis has a rich history and an abundance of sights. For medieval atmosphere, few places can rival the narrow alleys of its Gothic Quarter. Barcelona has a sophistication built on its obsession with design, from Antonio Gaudí at the turn of the century right up to the present day. Make time to see the elegance and distinction of its **Moderniste Eixample** area and the fantasies of Gaudí's whimsical imagination.

Currency The unit of currency in Spain is the peseta (pta.). There are bills of 1,000, 2,000, 5,000, and 10,000 ptas. Coins are 1, 5, 25, 50, 100, 200, and 500 ptas. Note that the 2- and 10-pta. coins and the old 100-pta. bills are no longer legal tender. At press time, the exchange rate was about 145 ptas. to the U.S. dollar.

Telephones The country code for Spain is 34. Pay phones generally take the new, smaller 5- and 25-pta. coins; the minimum charge for short local calls is 25 ptas. Area codes always begin with a 9 and are different for each province. In Madrid province, the code is 91; in Cantabria, it's 942. If you're dialing from outside the country, drop the 9. International calls can be done from any pay phone marked TELÉFONO INTERNACIONAL. Use 50-pta. (or 100-pta. if the phone takes them) coins initially, then coins of any denomination to prolong your call. Dial 07 for international calls, wait for the tone to change, then 1 for the United States or 0101 for Canada. For lengthy international calls, go to the *telefónica*, a telephone office, where an operator assigns you a private booth and collects payment at the end of the call; this is the least expensive and by far the easiest way of phoning abroad. **AT&T** (tel. 900/99–00–11); **MCI** (tel. 900/99–00–14); **Sprint** (tel. 900/99–00–13).

Shore Excursions The following is a good choice in Barcelona. It may not be offered by all cruise lines. Time and price are approximate.

Barcelona Highlights. This comprehensive excursion winds its way from the pier to the Gothic

Quarter. Along the way you'll see the unfinished Sagrada Familia cathedral and visit Montjuïc, one of the city's highest points, before reaching Plaza Catalunya for a walking tour of the Gothic Quarter. *3½ hrs. Cost: $30–$50.*

Coming Ashore Ships visiting Barcelona dock near Portal de la Pau and the Columbus Monument.

Getting Around Modern Barcelona above the Plaça de Catalunya is mostly built on a grid system, though there's no helpful numbering system as in the United States. The Gothic Quarter from the Plaça de Catalunya to the port is a warren of narrow streets, however, and you'll need a good map to get around. Most sightseeing can be done on foot—you won't have any other choice in the Gothic Quarter—but you'll need to use the metro or buses to link sightseeing areas. The subway is the fastest way of getting around, as well as the easiest to use. For both subways and city buses, you pay a flat fare of 150 ptas. or purchase a *tarjeta multiviatge*, good for 10 rides (800 ptas.). Taxis are black and yellow and when available for hire show a LIBRE sign in the daytime and a green light at night. The meter starts at 325 ptas., and there are small supplements for rides to the port. There are cab stands all over town; cabs may also be flagged down on the street.

Exploring Barcelona *Numbers in the margin correspond to points of interest on the Barcelona map.*

At the Plaça de la Seu, step inside the magnifi-
1 cent Gothic **Catedral de la Seu** (cathedral) built between 1298 and 1450, though the spire and Gothic facade were not added until 1892. Highlights are the beautifully carved choir stalls, Santa Eulàlia's tomb in the crypt, the battle-scarred crucifix from Don Juan's galley in the Lepanto Chapel, and the cloisters. *Plaça de la Seu, tel. 93/315–1554. Admission free. Open daily 7:45–1:30 and 4–7:45.*

Barcelona's most eccentric landmark is Gaudí's
2 **Temple Expiatori de la Sagrada Família** (Expiatory Church of the Holy Family). Far from finished at his death in 1926—Gaudí was run over by a tram and died in a pauper's hospital—this striking creation will cause consternation or

Casa Milà, **10**
Catedral de la Seu, **1**
Mançana de la Discòrdia, **9**
Monument a Colom, **6**
Museu Nacional d'Art de Catalunya, **11**
Museu Marítim, **7**
Museu Picasso, **3**
Palau Güell, **8**
Plaça Sant Jaume, **5**
Santa Maria del Mar, **4**
Temple Expiatori de la Sagrada Família, **2**

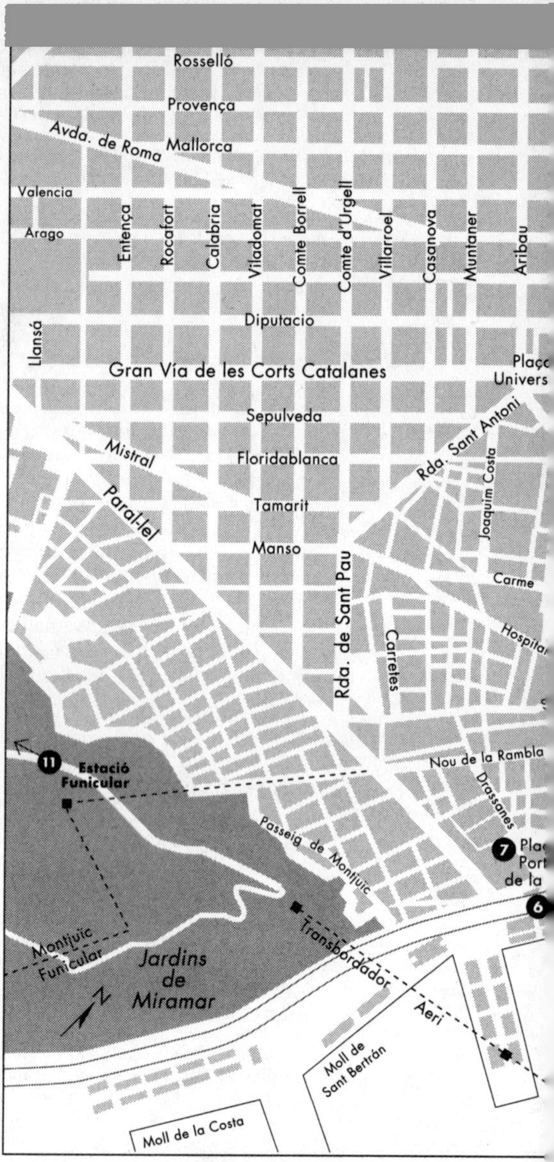

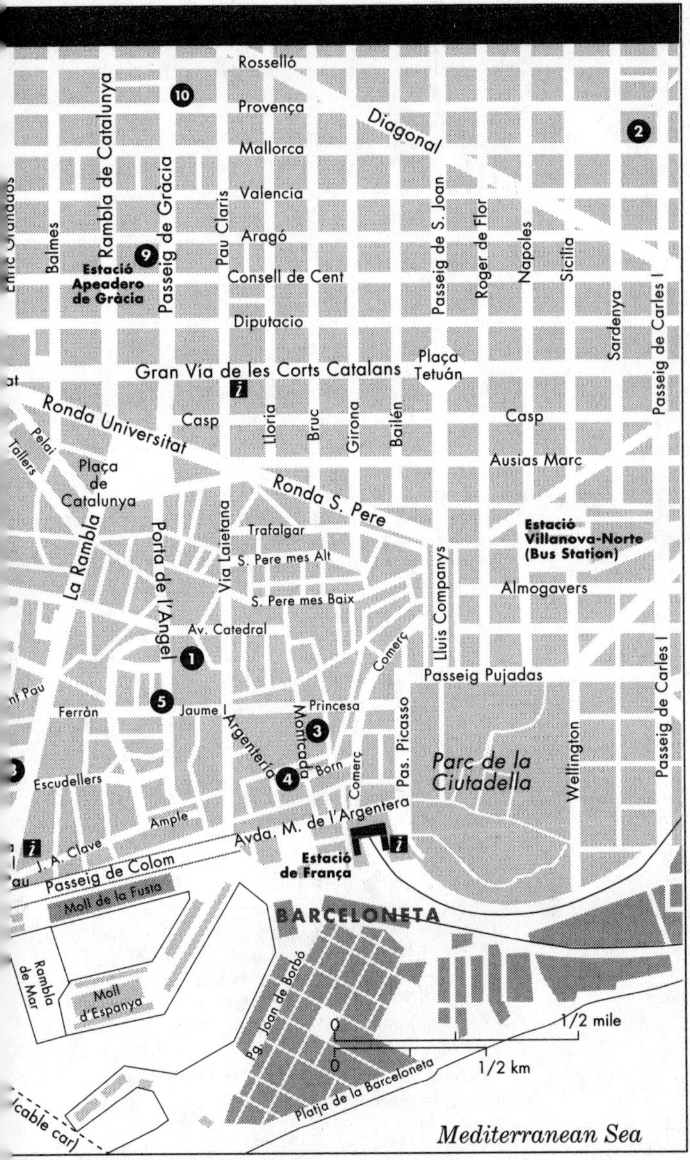
Rosselló
Provença
Mallorca
Valencia
Aragó
Consell de Cent
Diputacio
Gran Vía de les Corts Catalans
Diagonal
Rambla de Catalunya
Passeig de Gràcia
Pau Claris
Balmes
Estació Apeadero de Gràcia
Passeig de S. Joan
Roger de Flor
Napoles
Sicilia
Sardenya
Passeig de Carles I
Plaça Tetuán
Casp
Lloria
Bruc
Girona
Bailén
Casp
Ausias Marc
Ronda Universitat
Pelai
Tallers
Plaça de Catalunya
Ronda S. Pere
La Rambla
Porta de l'Angel
Via Laietana
Trafalgar
S. Pere mes Alt
S. Pere mes Baix
Estació Villanova-Norte (Bus Station)
Almogavers
Lluis Companys
Av. Catedral
Comerç
Passeig Pujadas
Ferràn
Jaume I
Princesa
Argentería
Montcada
Born
Comerç
Pas. Picasso
Parc de la Ciutadella
Wellington
Passeig de Carles I
Escudellers
Ample
Avda. M. de l'Argentera
J. A. Clave
Passeig de Colom
Estació de França
Moll de la Fusta
BARCELONETA
Rambla de Mar
Moll d'Espanya
Pg. Joan de Borbó
Platja de la Barceloneta
0
1/2 mile
0
1/2 km
(cable car)
Mediterranean Sea

wonder, shrieks of protest or cries of rapture. In 1936, during the Spanish Civil War, the citizens of Barcelona loved their crazy temple enough to spare it from the flames that engulfed all their other churches except the cathedral. An elevator takes visitors to the top of one of the towers for a magnificent view of the city. Gaudí is buried in the crypt. *C. de Sardenya between C. de Mallorca and C. de Provença, tel. 93/455–0247. Admission: 700 ptas. Open Sept.–May, daily 9–7; June–Aug., daily 9–9.*

One of Barcelona's most popular attractions, the
3 **Museu Picasso** (Picasso Museum) is actually two 15th-century palaces that provide a striking setting for the collections donated in 1963 and 1970, first by Picasso's secretary, then by the artist himself. The collection ranges from early childhood sketches to exhibition posters done in Paris shortly before his death. Of particular interest are his Blue Period pictures and his variations on Velázquez's *Las Meninas. Carrer Montcada 1519, tel. 93/319–6310. Admission: 650 ptas; Wed. ½ price, free 1st Sun. of month. Open Tues.–Sat. 10–8, Sun. 10–3.*

4 **Santa Maria del Mar** (Saint Mary of the Sea) is Barcelona's best example of a Mediterranean Gothic church and is widely considered the city's loveliest. It was built between 1329 and 1383 in fulfillment of a vow made a century earlier by Jaume I to build a church for the Virgin of the Sailors. Its simple beauty is enhanced by a stunning rose window and magnificent soaring columns. *Plaça Santa Maria. Open weekends 9–12:30 and 5–8.*

An impressive square built in the 1840s in the
5 heart of the Gothic Quarter, the **Plaça Sant Jaume** features two imposing buildings facing each other. The 15th-century Ajuntament, or City Hall, has an impressive black and gold mural (1928) by Josep María Sert (who also painted the murals for New York's Waldorf Astoria) and the famous Saló de Cent, from which the Council of One Hundred ruled the city from 1372 to 1714. You can wander into the courtyard, but to visit the interior, you will have to arrange an entrance with the protocol office. The Palau de la Generalitat, seat of the Catalan Regional Gov-

ernment, is a 15th-century palace open to the public on special days or by appointment. *Meeting of C. de Ferràn and C. Jaume I.*

6 Head to the bottom of Rambla and take an elevator to the top of the **Monument a Colom** (Columbus Monument) for a breathtaking view over the city. Columbus faces out to sea, pointing, ironically, east. (Nearby you can board the cable car that crosses the harbor to Barceloneta or goes up to Montjuïc.) *Admission: 300 ptas. Open Tues.–Sat. 10–2 and 3:30–6:30, Sun. 10–7.*

7 The **Museu Marítim** (Maritime Museum) is housed in the 13th-century Drassanes Reiales, the old Royal Shipyards. The museum is packed with ships, figureheads, nautical paraphernalia, and several early navigation charts, including a map by Amerigo Vespucci and the oldest chart in Europe, the 1439 chart of Gabriel de Valseca from Mallorca. *Plaça Portal de la Pau 1, tel. 93/318–3245. Admission: 350 ptas., Wed. 175 ptas., free 1st Sun. of month. Open Tues.–Sat. 10–2 and 4–7, Sun. 10–2.*

8 Gaudí's **Palau Güell** mansion was built between 1885 and 1890 for his patron, Count Eusebi de Güell, and is the only one of Gaudí's houses that is open to the public. *Nou de la Rambla, 3. Admission: 350 ptas. Open Tues.–Sat. 10–1:30 and 4–7:30.*

Above the Plaça de Catalunya you come into modern Barcelona and an elegant area known as the **Eixample,** which was laid out in the late 19th century as part of the city's expansion scheme. Much of the building here was done at the height of the Moderniste movement, a Spanish and mainly Catalan offshoot of art nouveau, whose leading exponents were the architects Gaudí, Domènech i Montaner, and Puig i Cadafalch. The principal thoroughfares of the Eixample are the Rambla de Catalunya and the Passeig de Gràcia, where some of the city's most elegant shops and cafés are found.

9 Moderniste houses are one of Barcelona's special drawing cards, so walk up Passeig de Gràcia until you come to the **Mançana de la Discòrdia** (Block of Discord), between Consell de Cent and Aragó. Its name is a pun on the word *mançana,*

which means both "block" and "apple." The houses here are quite fantastic. At No. 43 is Gaudí's Casa Batlló. Farther along the street on the right, on the corner of Provença, is Gaudí's

10 **Casa Milà** (Passeig de Gràcia 92), more often known as La Pedrera (Stone Quarry). Its remarkable curving stone facade with ornamental balconies actually ripples around the corner of the block.

11 One of the leading attractions here is the **Museu Nacional d'Art de Catalunya** (National Museum of Catalan Art) in the Palau Nacional atop a long flight of steps. The collection of Romanesque and Gothic art treasures—medieval frescoes and altarpieces, mostly from small churches and chapels in the Pyrénées—is simply staggering. *Montjuïc, tel. 93/423–7199. Admission: 650 ptas. Open Tues.–Sun. 9–2.*

Shopping There are no special handicrafts associated with Barcelona, but you'll have no trouble finding typical Spanish goods anywhere in town. If you're into fashion and jewelry, then you've come to the right place, as Barcelona makes all the headlines on Spain's booming fashion front. **Xavier Roca i Coll** (Sant Pere mes Baix 24, just off Laietana) specializes in silver models of Barcelona's buildings. Barcelona and Catalonia have passed along a playful sense of design ever since Antonio Gaudí began creating shock waves more than a century ago. Stores and boutiques specializing in design items (jewelry, furnishings, knickknacks) include **Vinçon** (Passeig de Gràcia 96), **Bd** (Barcelona Design, at Mallorca 291–293), and **Dos i Una** (Rosselló 275).

Bergen, Norway

Norway has some of the most remote and dramatic scenery in Europe. Along the west coast, deep fjords knife into steep mountain ranges. In older villages, wooden houses spill down toward docks where Viking ships—and later, whaling vessels—once were moored. Norway is most famous for its fjords, which were formed during an ice age a million years ago. The entrances to most fjords are shallow, about 500 ft, while inland depths reach 4,000 ft.

Bergen is the gateway to the fjord region. The town was founded in 1070 and is now Norway's second-largest city, with a population of 219,000. Bergen was a member of the medieval Hanseatic League and offered an ice-free harbor and convenient trading location on the west coast. Despite numerous fires in its past, much of medieval Bergen has remained.

Currency The unit of currency in Norway is the krone, written as Kr. on price tags but officially written as NOK (bank designation), NKr, or kr. The exchange rate at press time was NKr 6.42 to the U.S. dollar.

Telephones The country code for Norway is 47. Norway's phone system is not as expensive as one might fear. International calls can be made from any pay phone. For calls to North America, dial 00–1, then the area code and number. You will need to dial 00 for an international connection. To reach an **AT&T** long-distance operator, dial 80019011; **MCI,** 180019912; **Sprint,** 1800 19877.

Shore Excursions The following are good choices in Bergen. They may not be offered by all cruise lines. Times and prices are approximate.

City Tour. Head past the central harbor area to Bryggen, where rows of gabled merchants' houses line the streets. Stop at Troldhaugen, once the estate of composer Edvard Grieg, for a tour and concert. *3 hrs. Cost: $40.*

Viking History. Viking relics are the highlight of this short tour, which visits the Museum of Cultural History and the Maritime Museum. *3 hrs. Cost: $35.*

Coming Ashore Ships calling at Bergen dock at the harbor area at Bryggen. Seven surrounding mountains set off the weathered wooden houses, cobbled streets, and Hanseatic-era warehouses along the waterfront. Bergen is small and easily toured by foot.

Exploring Bergen The best way to get a feel for Bergen's medieval trading heyday is to visit the **Hanseatisk Museum** on the Bryggen. One of the oldest and best-preserved of Bergen's wooden buildings, it is furnished in 16th-century style. The guided tour is excellent. *Bryggen, tel. 55316710. Admission: NKr 35. Open June–Aug., daily 9–5; May and Sept., daily 11–2; Oct.–Apr., Mon., Wed., Fri., Sun. 11–2.*

On the western end of the Vågen is the **Rosenkrantz tårnet** (tower), part of the Bergenhus, the 13th-century fortress guarding the harbor entrance. The tower and fortress were destroyed during World War II but were meticulously restored during the 1960s and are now rich with furnishings and household items from the 16th century. *Bergenhus, tel. 55314380. Admission: NKr 15. Open mid-May–mid-Sept., daily 10–4; mid-Sept.–mid-May, Sun. noon–3, or upon request.*

From Ævregaten, the back boundary of Bryggen, you can walk through the meandering back streets to the popular **Fløybanen,** the funicular (a cable railway in which ascending cars counterbalance descending cars). It climbs a steep 1,070 ft to the top of Fløyen, one of the seven mountains guarding the city.

Shopping

Galleriet, on Torgalmenningen, is one of the best downtown shopping malls. Here you will find the more exclusive small shops along with all the chains, like Hennes & Mauritz and Lindex. **Prydkunst-Hjertholm** (Olav Kyrresgt. 7) is full of excellent locally made glassware and pottery. **Husfliden** (Vågsalmenning 3) includes a department of traditional Norwegian costumes; also, don't miss the troll cave.

Canary Islands, Spain

Traditionally a popular spot for winter holidays, Spain's Canary Islands are becoming a year-round destination favored by sunseekers and nature lovers alike. The Canaries lie 112 km (70 mi) off the coast of southern Morocco in the Atlantic Ocean and enjoy mild, sunny weather throughout the year, except for the north coast of Tenerife, which has above-average rainfall for the Canaries and below-average temperatures year-round. Each of the seven volcanic islands in the archipelago is distinct. Some have lush tropical vegetation, poinsettias as tall as trees, and banana plantations, while others are arid and resemble an exotic moonscape of lava rock and sand dunes. Mt. Teide (12,198 ft), Spain's highest peak, snowcapped for much of the year, is here. The islands are also home to national parks and dozens of other protected ecological zones in which visitors can hike through mist-shrouded forests of virgin laurel trees, climb mountains, eat food cooked by nature over volcanic craters, or scuba dive off long stretches of unspoiled coastline.

Currency The unit of currency in the Canary Islands is the peseta (pta.). At press time, the exchange rate was about 145 ptas. to the U.S. dollar.

Telephones The country code for Spain is 34. Pay phones generally take the new, smaller 5- and 25-pta. coins; the minimum charge for short local calls is 25 ptas. Area codes always begin with a 9 and are different for each province. In Madrid province, the code is 91; in Cantabria, it's 942. If you're dialing from outside the country, drop the 9. Calling abroad can be done from any pay phone marked TELÉFONO INTERNACIONAL. Use 50-pta. (or 100-pta. if the phone takes them) coins initially, then coins of any denomination to prolong your call. Dial 07 for international calls, wait for the tone to change, then dial 1 for the United States or 0101 for Canada. **AT&T** (tel. 900/99–00–11); **MCI** (tel. 900/99–00–14); **Sprint** (tel. 900/99–00–13).

Shore Excursions The following are good choices in the Canary Islands. They may not be offered by all cruise lines. Times and prices are approximate.

In Tenerife **Mt. Teide and Countryside.** A motor coach takes you through the Esperanza mountain range to Mount Teide National Park with picturesque scenery along the way. *4½ hrs. Cost: $40.*

Botanical Gardens. This motor-coach excursion takes you to the Orotava Valley, with its banana plantations and views of Mount Teide, before reaching the Botanical Gardens. *4½ hrs. Cost: $33.*

In Lanzarote **Timanfaya National Park and Winery Tour.** By motor coach, this tour visits the park of Timanfaya (fire mountains), before heading off to El Golfo, Los Hervideros, and Janubio, which feature a variety of different forms of volcanic activity. A visit to the La Geria vineyards includes a tasting. *4 hrs. Cost: $40.*

Coming Ashore Ships dock in Tenerife at the Santa Cruz pier in the island's provincial capital.

Getting Around Most visitors rent a car or Jeep—it is by far the best way to explore the countryside. **Hertz** and **Avis** have locations in both Tenerife and Lanzarote, though better rates can be obtained from the Spanish company **Cicar** (tel. 928/802790), located at airports.

Exploring the Canary Islands

Tenerife The **Museo Arqueológico Provincial** (Provincial Archaeology Museum) contains ceramics and mummies from the stone-age culture of the Guanches, the native people who inhabited the islands before they were conquered and colonized by the Spanish in the 15th century. *Bravo Murillo 5, tel. 922/24–20–90. Open Tues.–Sun. 10–8.*

The best thing to visit in Santa Cruz is the colorful morning market, **Mercado de Nuestra Señora de Africa** (Market of Our Lady of Africa), which sells everything from tropical fruits and flowers to canaries and parrots. *Av. de San Sebastín. Open Mon.–Sat. 5 AM–noon.*

Inland, past banana plantations, almond groves, and pine forests, is the entrance to **Parque Nacional del Tiede** (Mt. Teide National Park). Before arriving at the foot of the mountain, you pass through a stark landscape called Las Cañadas del Teide, a violent jumble of rocks and minerals created by millions of years of volcanic activity. A cable car will take you within 534 ft of the top of Mt. Teide, where there are good views of the southern part of the island and neighboring Gran Canaria. *Cable car: 1,000 ptas. Open daily 9–5, last trip up at 4. Visitor center open daily 9–4.*

Also worth a visit are the north-coast towns of **Icod de los Vinos,** which boasts a 3,000-year-old, 57-ft-tall dragon tree once worshiped by the ancient Guanches and a plaza surrounded by typical wood-balconied Canarian houses; and, farther west, **Garachico,** the most peaceful and best-preserved village on this touristy isle.

Lanzarote The **Parque National Timanfaya,** popularly known as the fire mountains, takes up much of the southern part of the island. Here you can have a camel ride, take a guided coach tour of the volcanic zone, and eat lunch at one of the world's most unusual restaurants, El Diablo, where meat is cooked over the crater of a volcano using the earth's natural heat. *4 km/2½ mi north of Yaiza, tel. 928/84–00–57. Admission: 850 ptas. Open daily 9–5.*

The **Jameos del Agua** (Water Cavern) is a natural wonder, created when molten lava streamed through an underground tunnel and hissed into the sea. Ponds in the caverns are home to a unique species of albino crab. The site also features an auditorium with fantastic acoustics for concerts and a restaurant-bar. *Rte. GC710, 21 km/13 mi north of Arrecife. Admission: 1,100 ptas at night. Open daily 11–6:45, Tues. and Sat. also 7 PM–3 AM.*

Shopping
In Tenerife

Tenerife is a free port, meaning no value-added tax is charged on luxury items such as jewelry and electronics. The streets are packed with shops selling these items, but the prices do not represent a significant savings for Americans. The Canary Islands are famous for lacy, hand-embroidered tablecloths and place mats. The largest selection is available in Puerto de la Cruz at **Casa Iriarte** (San Juan 17). Contemporary crafts and traditional musical instruments can be found at the government-sponsored shop **Casa Torrehermosa** (Tomas Zerolo 27) in Orotava.

Beaches
In Tenerife

Las Teresitas beach, 7 km (4 mi) east of Santa Cruz, was constructed using white sand imported from the Sahara Desert and is popular with local families. **Playa del Medano,** on the southern coast, a large bay surrounded by yellow sand, is considered the best beach on Tenerife.

In Lanzarote

Playa de la Garita is a wide bay with crystal-clear water that's great for snorkeling. The **Playa Blanca** resort area, reached by traveling down hard-packed dirt roads on Punta de Papagayo, features white-sand beaches.

Copenhagen, Denmark

When Denmark ruled Norway and Sweden in the 15th century, Copenhagen was the capital of all three countries. Today it is still a lively northern capital, with about 1 million inhabitants. It's a city meant for walking, the first in

Europe to recognize the value of pedestrian streets in fostering community spirit. As you stroll through the cobbled streets and squares, you'll find that Copenhagen combines the excitement and variety of big-city life with a small-town atmosphere. If there's such a thing as a cozy metropolis, you'll find it here.

You're never far from water, be it sea or canal. The city itself is built upon two main islands, Slotsholmen and Christianshavn, connected by drawbridges. The ancient heart of the city is intersected by two heavily peopled walking streets—part of the five such streets known collectively as Strøget—and around them curls a maze of cobbled streets packed with tiny boutiques, cafés, and restaurants—all best explored on foot. In summer Copenhagen moves outside, and the best views of city life are from the sidewalk cafés in the sunny squares. The Danes are famous for their friendliness and have a word—*hyggelig*—for the feeling of well-being that comes from their own brand of cozy hospitality.

Currency The monetary unit in Denmark is the krone (kr., DKr, or DKK), which is divided into 100 øre. At press time, the krone stood at about 6.5 kr. to the U.S. dollar.

Telephones The country code for Denmark is 45. Pay phones take 1-, 2-, 5-, and 10-kr. coins. You must use area codes even when dialing a local number. Calling cards, which are sold at DSB stations, post offices, and some kiosks, cost DKr25, DKr50, or DKr100 and may be used at certain phones. For international calls dial 00, then the country code, the area code, and the number. To reach an **AT&T** long-distance operator, dial 8001–0010; **MCI,** 8001–0022; **Sprint,** 8001–0877.

Shore Excursions The following are good choices in Copenhagen. They may not be offered by all cruise lines. Times and prices are approximate.

City Tour. This quick overview of the sights takes you to the Little Mermaid statue, Renaissance castle, City Hall Square, Tivoli Gardens, Christiansborg Palace, the Borsen Stock Exchange, the Canal District, and the courtyard of Amalienborg Palace. *3 hrs. Cost: $41.*

Royal Castle Tour. Castle aficionados can see two on this tour: Christiansborg Palace and Rosenborg Castle, as well as other sites. *3 hrs. Cost: $50.*

Coming Ashore Ships visiting Copenhagen dock at Langelinie Pier, a short distance from the central part of the city.

Getting Around Copenhagen is a city for walkers, not drivers. Attractions are relatively close together, and public transportation is excellent. Buses and suburban trains operate on a ticket system and divide Copenhagen and its environs into three zones. Tickets are validated on the time system: On the basic ticket, which costs 10 kr. for an hour, you can travel anywhere in the zone in which you started. The computer-metered taxis are not cheap. The base charge is DKr15, plus DKr8–DKr10 per km.

Exploring Copenhagen *Numbers in the margin correspond to points of interest on the Copenhagen map.*

1 Copenhagen's best-known attraction is **Tivoli.** In the 1840s, the Danish architect Georg Carstensen persuaded King Christian VIII that an amusement park was the perfect opiate for the masses, preaching that "when people amuse themselves, they forget politics." In the season from May to September, about 4 million people come through the gates. Tivoli is more sophisticated than a mere amusement park: It offers a pantomime theater and an open-air stage; elegant restaurants; and numerous classical, jazz, and rock concerts. On weekends there are elaborate fireworks displays. Try to see Tivoli at least once by night, when the trees are illuminated along with the Chinese Pagoda and the main fountain. *Vesterbrogade 3, tel. 33/15–10–01. Open May–mid-Sept., daily 11 AM–midnight.*

The hub of Copenhagen's commercial district is Rådhus Pladsen, which is dominated by the
2 mock-Renaissance building **Københavns Rådhus** (city hall), completed in 1905. A statue of Copenhagen's 12th-century founder, Bishop Absalon, sits atop the main entrance. Inside, you can see the first World Clock, an astrological timepiece invented and built by Jens Olsen and put in motion in 1955. If you're feeling energetic, take a

Amalienborg, **7**
Børsen, **6**
Christiansborg Slot, **4**
Den Lille Havfrue, **9**
Frihedsmuseet, **8**
Københavns Rådhus, **2**
Nationalmuseet, **3**
Rosenborg Slot, **10**
Thorvaldsens Museum, **5**
Tivoli, **1**

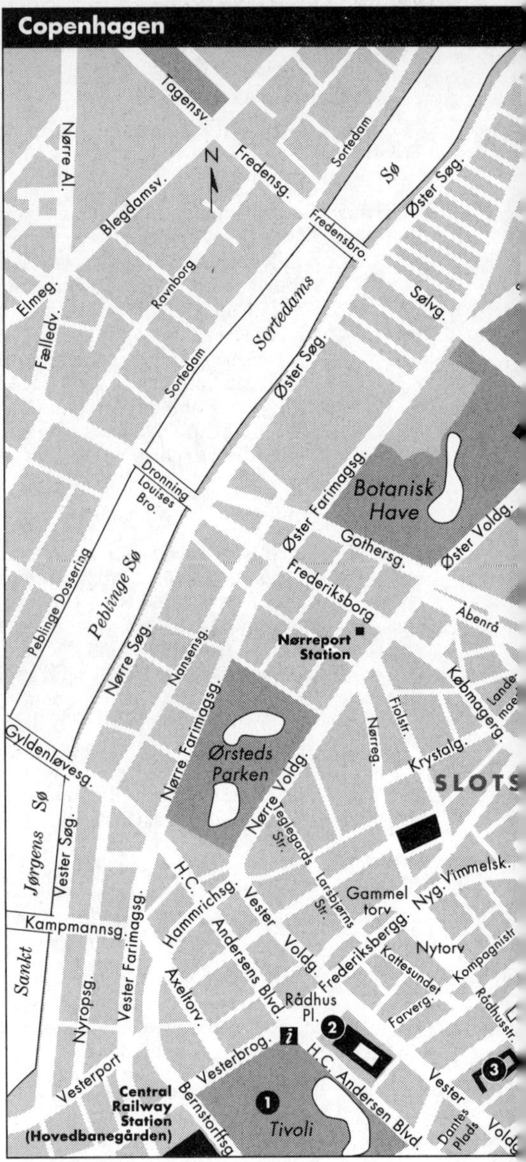

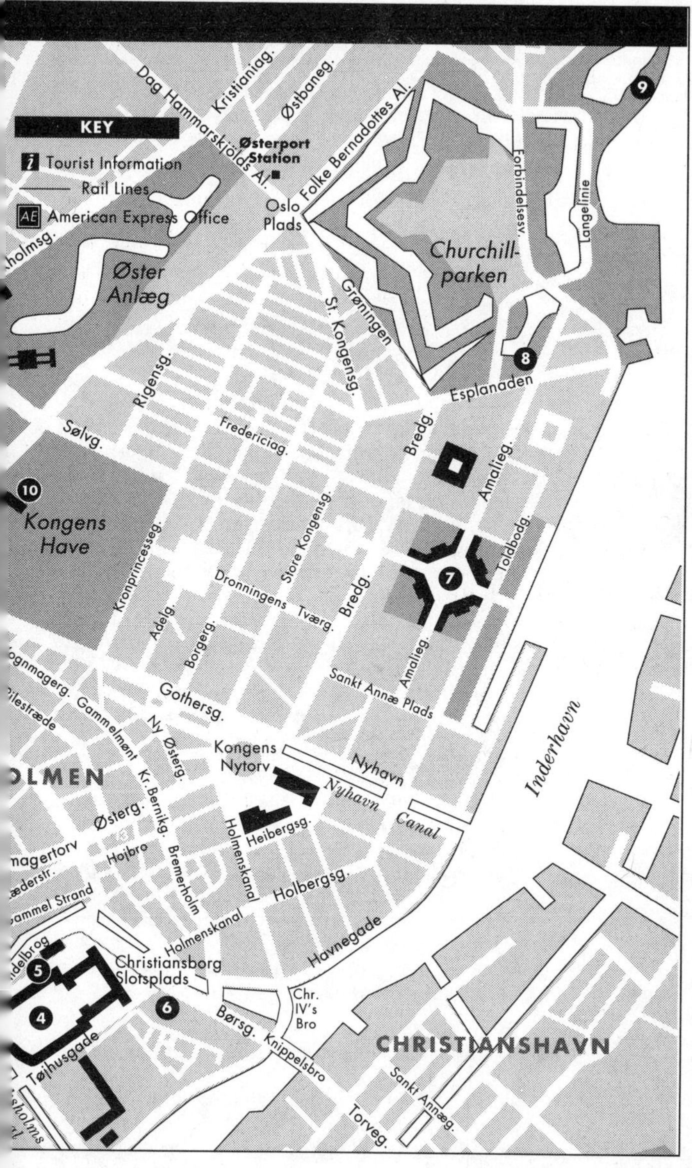
KEY
Tourist Information
Rail Lines
American Express Office
Dag Hammarskjölds Al.
Kristianiag.
Østbaneg.
Østerport Station
Folke Bernadottes Al.
Oslo Plads
Forbindelsesv.
Langelinie
Churchill-parken
Øster Anlæg
Grøningen
St. Kongensg.
Rigensg.
Esplanaden
Sølvg.
Fredericiag.
Bredg.
Amalieg.
Kongens Have
Kronprincesseg.
Store Kongensg.
Toldbodg.
Dronningens Tværg.
Adelg.
Borgerg.
Sankt Annæ Plads
Gothersg.
Gammelmønt
Ny Østerg.
Kongens Nytorv
Nyhavn
Nyhavn Canal
Inderhavn
Kr. Bernikg.
Østerg.
Højbro
Holmenskanal
Heibergsg.
Bremerholm
Holbergsg.
Gammel Strand
Havnegade
Christiansborg Slotsplads
Chr. IV's Bro
Børsg.
Knippelsbro
Tøjhusgade
CHRISTIANSHAVN
Sankt Annæg.
Torveg.

guided tour partway up the 350-ft tower for a panoramic view. *Rådhus Pladsen, tel. 33/66–25–82. Admission: tour 20 kr., tower 10 kr. Open Mon.–Wed. and Fri. 9:30–3, Thurs. 9:30–4, Sat. 9:30–1. Tours in English weekdays at 3, Sat. at 10. Tower tours Mon.–Sat. at noon; additional tours June–Sept. at 10 and 2.*

3 The city's **Nationalmuseet** (National Museum) houses extensive collections that chronicle Danish cultural history to modern times and displays Egyptian, Greek, and Roman antiquities. Viking enthusiasts may want to see the Runic stones in the Danish cultural-history section. *Ny Vestergade 10, tel. 33/13–44–11. Admission: 30 kr. Open Tues.–Sun. 10–5.*

4 Castle Island is dominated by the massive gray **Christiansborg Slot** (Christiansborg Castle). The complex, which contains the Folketinget (Parliament House) and the Royal Reception Chambers, is on the site of the city's first fortress, built by Bishop Absalon in 1167. While the castle was being built at the turn of the century, the National Museum excavated the ruins beneath the site. *Christiansborg ruins, tel. 33/92–64–92. Admission: 15 kr. Open May–Sept., daily 9:30–3:30; Oct.–Apr., Sun. and Tues.–Fri. 9:30–3:30. Folketinget: tel. 33/37–55–00. Admission free. Tour times vary; call ahead. Reception Chambers: Admission: 28 kr. Opening and tour times vary; call ahead. Closed Jan.*

5 The 19th-century Danish sculptor Bertel Thorvaldsen is buried at the center of the **Thorvaldsens Museum.** He was greatly influenced by the statues and reliefs of classical antiquity. In addition to his own works, there is a collection of paintings and drawings by other artists illustrating the influence of Italy on Denmark's Golden Age artists. *Porthusgade 2, tel. 33/32–15–32. Admission free. Open Tues.–Sun. 10–5.*

6 With its steep roofs, tiny windows, and gables, the **Børsen,** the old stock exchange, is one of Copenhagen's treasures. It is believed to be the oldest building still in use—although it functions only on special occasions. It was built by the 16th-century monarch King Christian IV, a scholar, warrior, and architect of much of

the city. The king is said to have had a hand in twisting the tails of the four dragons that form the structure's distinctive green copper spire. *Christiansborg Slotsplads. Not open to the public.*

7 **Amalienborg** has been the principal royal residence since 1784. Among the museum's highlights are the study of King Christian IX (1818–1906) and the drawing room of his wife, Queen Louise. The collection also includes Rococo banquet silver, highlighted by a bombastic Viking-ship centerpiece, and a small costume collection. *Amalienborg Place; museum, tel. 33/12–21–86. Admission: 35 kr. Open Mar.–late Oct., daily 11–4.*

8 The **Frihedsmuseet** (Liberty Museum) in Churchillparken gives an evocative picture of the heroic Danish Resistance movement during World War II, which managed to save 7,000 Jews from the Nazis by hiding them in homes and hospitals, then smuggling them across to Sweden. *Churchillparken, tel. 33/13–77–14. Admission free. Open Sept. 16–Apr., Tues.–Sat. 11–3, Sun. 11–4; May–Sept. 15, Tues.–Sat. 10–4, Sun. 10–5.*

Near the Langelinie, which on Sunday is thronged
9 with promenading Danes, is **Den Lille Havfrue** (Little Mermaid), the 1913 statue commemorating Hans Christian Andersen's lovelorn creation and the subject of hundreds of travel posters. *East on Langelinie.*

10 **Rosenborg Slot,** a Renaissance castle—built by Renaissance man Christian IV—houses the Crown Jewels, as well as a collection of costumes and royal memorabilia. Don't miss Christian IV's pearl-studded saddle. *Øster Voldgade 4A, tel. 33/15–32–86. Admission: 40 kr. Castle open late Oct.–Apr., Tues., Fri., and Sun. 11–2; treasury open daily 11–3. Both open May and Sept.–late Oct., daily 11–3; June–Aug., daily 10–4.*

The **Statens Museum for Kunst** (National Art Gallery) features a collection that ranges from modern Danish art to works by Rubens, Dürer, and the Impressionists. Particularly fine are the museum's 20 Matisses. *Sølvgade 48–50, tel. 33/91–21–26. Admission: 20 kr.–40 kr. (de-*

pending on exhibit). Open Tues.–Sun. 10–4:30, Wed. until 9 PM.

Shopping Strøget's pedestrian streets are synonymous with shopping. For glass, try **Holmegaard** (Æstergade 15, tel. 33/12–44–77), where handcrafted bowls, glasses, and vases are available. Just off the street is Pistolstræde, a typical old courtyard that has been lovingly restored and is filled with intriguing boutiques. **Magasin** (Kongens Nytorv 13, tel. 33/11–44–33), one of the largest department stores in Scandinavia, offers everything in terms of clothing and gifts, as well as an excellent grocery. **Illum** (Æstergade 52, tel. 33/14–40–02) is similar to Magasin, with another fine basement grocery and eating arcade. Don't confuse Illum with **Illums Bolighus** (Amagertorv 10, tel. 33/14–19–41), where designer furnishings, porcelain, quality clothing, and gifts are displayed in near-gallery surroundings. **Royal Copenhagen Porcelain** (Amagertorv 6, tel. 33/13–71–81) carries both old and new china and porcelain patterns and figurines. **Georg Jensen** (Amagertorv 4 and Æstergade 40, tel. 33/11–40–80) is one of the world's finest silversmiths and gleams with a wide array of silver patterns and jewelry. Don't miss the **Georg Jensen Museum** (Amagertorv 6, tel. 33/14–02–29), which showcases glass and silver beauties, ranging from tiny, twisted-glass shot glasses to an $85,000 silver fish dish.

Corfu, Greece

The northernmost of the seven major Ionian islands, Corfu has a lively history of conquest and counterconquest. All told, beginning with Classical times, Corfu has been ruled by the Corinthians, the tyrants of Syracuse, the kings of Epirus and of Macedonia, the Romans, the Norman and Angevin kings, the Venetians, and the British, and it was finally ceded to Greece in 1864. The climate of the island is rainy, which makes it green. Moderated by westerly winds, scored with fertile valleys, and punctuated by enormous, gnarled olive trees, the island is perhaps the most beautiful in Greece.

Currency The Greek monetary unit is the drachma (dr.). At press time, there were approximately 241 dr. to the U.S. dollar.

Telephones The country code for Greece is 30. Telephone kiosks are easy to find, although some can only be used for local calls. The easiest way to make a local or an international call is with a phone card, available at kiosks, convenience stores, or Hellenic Telecommunications Organization (OTE) offices. If you plan to make and pay for several international phone calls, go to an OTE office. For an **AT&T** long-distance operator, dial 00/800–1311; **MCI,** 00/800–1211; **Sprint,** 00/800–1411.

Shore Excursions The following are good choices in Corfu. They may not be offered by all cruise lines. Times and prices are approximate.

Paleokastritsa, Achilleion, and Corfu Town. Visit the pretty resort of Paleokastritsa and the 100-year-old Achilleion Palace, and drive past the major sights of the town. *4 hrs. Cost: $45.*

City tour with Achilleion and Kanoni. Visit the famed and funky Achilleion Palace, the village of Kanoni, and enjoy a walking tour of Corfu. *4 hrs. Cost: $43.*

Coming Ashore Most cruise ships dock at Corfu Town.

Getting Around Radio-dispatched taxis are available, and rates, set by the government, are reasonable. The bus network on the island is extensive, and buses tend to run fairly close to their schedules. Motorbike rentals are available, but caution is advised.

Exploring Corfu The **New Fortress** was built by the Venetians and added to by the French and the British. It was a Greek naval base until 1992, when it was opened to the public. Tourists can now wander through the fascinating maze of tunnels, moats, and fortifications. A classic British citadel stands at its heart, and there are stunning views of Corfu Town, the sea, and the countryside in all directions. The best times to come here are early morning and late afternoon. *Above the Old Port on north side of Corfu Town.*

The huge parade ground on the land side of the canal is the **Esplanade,** central to life in Corfu Town. It is bordered on the west by a street lined with a row of tall houses and arcades, called Liston, which was once the exclusive preserve of Corfiot nobility. Now the arcades are lively with cafés that spill out onto the square. Cricket matches are played on the northern side of the Esplanade.

The narrow streets that run west from the Esplanade lead to the medieval parts of the city, where Venetian buildings stand cheek-by-jowl with the 19th-century ones built by the British. This is a great shopping area—you can buy nearly anything on earth.

The **Archaeological Museum** displays artifacts from the excavation of Paleopolis. Note the Gorgon from the pediment of the 6th-century BC Temple of Artemis. *South of the Esplanade along Leoforos Dimokratias, tel. 0661/30680. Admission: 800 dr. Open daily 9–4:30.*

The village of **Analipis** crowns the site of the ancient town's Acropolis, and a path leads to a spring where Venetians watered their ships. Continue through the gardens and parks to the ruins of the Archaic Temple of Artemis and past the lagoon of Halikiopoulou to the tip of the peninsula, called Kanoni, one of the world's most beautiful spots.

The palace of **Achilleion** is a monument to bad taste redeemed by beautiful gardens stretching to the sea. The palace was built in the late 19th century by an Italian architect for Empress Elizabeth of Austria. The palace is a hodgepodge of a pseudo-Byzantine chapel, a pseudo-Pompeian room, and a pseudo-Renaissance dining hall, culminating in a hilariously vulgar fresco, *Achilles in His Chariot. 19 km/12 mi from Corfu Town, tel. 0661/56210. Admission: 700 dr. Open 8:30–7 in season.*

Shopping The downside of Corfu's popularity with tourists is that merchants have become greedy, at times charging outrageous prices in order to squeeze as much money as possible out of visitors. Ask your ship's cruise or shore-excursion director for the names of reputable shops.

Beaches The resort areas of Ermones and Glyfada, which are south of the popular resort area Paleokastritsa, offer good sunning. On the north coast, Roda and Sidari have good beaches.

Crete, Greece

The mountains, blue-gray and barren, split with deep gorges and honeycombed with caves, define both landscape and lifestyle in Crete. No other Greek island is so large and rugged. To Greeks, Crete is the Great Island, where rebellion was endemic for centuries—against Arab invaders, Venetian colonialists, Ottoman pashas, and German occupiers in World War II. Situated in the south Aegean, Crete was the center of Europe's earliest civilization, the Minoan, which flourished from about 2000 BC to 1200 BC. It was struck a mortal blow in about 1450 BC by some unknown cataclysm, now thought to be political.

Currency The Greek monetary unit is the drachma (dr.). At press time, there were approximately 241 dr. to the U.S. dollar.

Telephones The country code for Greece is 30. Telephone kiosks are easy to find, although some can only be used for local calls. The easiest way to make a local or an international call is with a phone card, available at kiosks, convenience stores, or Hellenic Telecommunications Organization (OTE) offices. Go to an OTE office for convenience and privacy if you plan to make several international calls. For an **AT&T** long-distance operator, dial 00/800–1311; **MCI,** 00/800–1211; **Sprint,** 00/800–1411.

Shore Excursions The following are good choices in Crete. They may not be offered by all cruise lines. Times and prices are approximate.

Knossos and the Museum. Minoan life is on display at the Archaeological Museum and Knossos, the largest Minoan palace. *4 hrs. Cost: $50.*

Chania and Akrotiri. This excursion explores the old town of Chania before heading to Akrotiri peninsula to see the tomb of Eleftherios Venizelos and the Ayia Triada Monastery. *Half day. Cost: $45.*

Coming Ashore Most ships dock at Heraklion. A few tie up at Souda Bay, which is about 15 minutes from Chania. Smaller vessels may dock at Ayios Nikolaos.

Getting Around You can rent cars, Jeeps, and motorbikes in all the island's towns. Bus companies offer regular service between main towns.

Exploring Crete The most important Minoan remains are housed in the **archaeological museum** in Heraklion, Crete's largest (and least attractive) city. The museum's treasures include the frescoes and ceramics from Knossos and Agia Triada depicting Minoan life and the Phaestos disc. *Xanthoudidou 1, Platia Eleftherias, tel. 081/226–092. Admission: 1,000 dr. Open Mon. 12:30–7 (12:30–5 in winter), Tues.–Sun. 8–7 (8–5 in winter).*

The partly reconstructed **Palace of Knossos** will give you a feeling for the Minoan world. Note the simple throne room, which contains the oldest throne in Europe, and the bathrooms with their efficient plumbing. The palace was the setting for the legend of the Minotaur, a monstrous offspring of Queen Pasiphae and a bull, which King Minos confined to the labyrinth under the palace. *Tel. 081/231–940. Admission: 1,250 dr. Open daily 8–7 (8–5 in winter).*

The town of **Ayios Nikolaos** on the Gulf of Mirabellow was built just a century ago by Cretans and is good for an afternoon of strolling and shopping. *24 km/15 mi from Heraklion.*

Beaches In addition to archaeological treasures, Crete can boast of beautiful mountain scenery and a large number of beach resorts along the north coast. One is **Mallia,** which contains the remains of another Minoan palace and has good sandy beaches. Two other beach resorts, **Ayios Nikolaos** and the nearby **Elounda,** are farther east. The south coast offers good beaches that are quieter.

Dublin, Ireland

Dublin is a small city with a population of just over 1 million. Even so, it has a distinctly cosmopolitan air, one that complements happily the individuality of the city and the courtesy and friendliness of its inhabitants. Originally a Viking settlement, Dublin is situated on the banks of the River Liffey, which divides the city north and south. The more lively and fashionable spots, such as the Grafton Street shopping area, are on the south side, although new construction is helping to reinvigorate the north side. Most of the city's historically interesting buildings date from the 18th century, and, although many of its finer Georgian buildings disappeared in the overenthusiastic redevelopment of the 1970s, enough remain, mainly south of the river, to recall the elegant Dublin of the past. Literary Dublin can still be recaptured by those who want to follow the footsteps of Leopold Bloom's progress, as described in James Joyce's *Ulysses*. And Trinity College—alma mater of Oliver Goldsmith, Jonathan Swift, and Samuel Beckett, among others—still provides a haven of tranquillity.

Currency The unit of currency in Ireland is the pound, or punt (pronounced poont), written as IR£ to avoid confusion with the pound sterling. The currency is divided into 100 pence (written *p*). Although the Irish pound is the only legal tender in the republic, U.S. dollars and British currency are often accepted in large hotels and shops licensed as bureaux de change. The rate of exchange at press time was 62 pence to the U.S. dollar.

Telephones The country code for the Republic of Ireland is 353. There are pay phones in all post offices and most hotels and bars, as well as in street booths. Telephone cards are available at all post offices and most newsagents. Booths accepting cards are equally common as coin booths. For calls to the United States and Canada, dial 001 followed by the area code. To reach an **AT&T** long-distance operator, dial 1–800/550–000; **MCI**, 1–800/551–001; **Sprint**, 1–800/552–001.

Shore Excursions The following is a good choice in Dublin. It may not be offered by all cruise lines. Time and price are approximate.

City Tour. Two of Dublin's main attractions, St. Patrick's Cathedral and Trinity College, are the highlight of this excursion, which passes other city sights, such as St. Stephen's Square, Georgian Dublin, the River Liffey, and the Customs House. *3½ hrs. Cost: $42.*

Coming Ashore Ships dock at the Ocean Pier in the city's industrial port area, about a 20-minute drive to downtown.

Getting Around Dublin is small as capital cities go—the downtown area is positively compact—and the best way to see the city and soak in the full flavor is on foot. Official licensed taxis, metered and designated by roof signs, do not cruise; they are located beside the central bus station, at train stations, at O'Connell Bridge, at St. Stephen's Green, at College Green, and near major hotels. They are not of a uniform type or color. Make sure the meter is on. The initial charge is IR£2; the fare is displayed in the cab. A 1½-km (1-mi) trip in city traffic costs about IR£3.50.

Exploring Dublin *Numbers in the margin correspond to points of interest on the Dublin map.*

1 **O'Connell Bridge** is the city's most central landmark. Look closely and you will notice a strange feature: The bridge is wider than it is long. The north side of O'Connell Bridge is dominated by an elaborate memorial to Daniel O'Connell, "the Liberator," erected as a tribute to the great 19th-century orator's achievement in securing Catholic emancipation in 1829.

Henry Street, a pedestrian-only shopping area, leads to the colorful **Moore Street Market,** where street vendors recall their most famous ancestor, Molly Malone, by singing their wares—mainly flowers and fruit—in the traditional Dublin style. *Open Mon.–Sat. 9–6.*

2 The **General Post Office,** known as the GPO, occupies a special place in Irish history. It was from the portico of its handsome classical facade that Padraig Pearse read the Proclamation of the Republic on Easter Monday 1916. You can still see the scars of bullets on its pillars from the fighting that ensued. The GPO remains the focal point for political rallies and demonstrations, and it is still a working post office, with an attractive two-story central gallery. *Henry St.*

Charlemont House, whose impressive Palladian facade dominates the top of Parnell Square, now
3 houses the **Hugh Lane Municipal Gallery of Modern Art.** Sir Hugh Lane, a nephew of Lady Gregory, who was Yeats's curious, high-minded

aristocratic patron, was a keen collector of Impressionist paintings. The gallery also contains some interesting works by Irish artists, including Yeats's brother Jack. *Parnell Sq., tel. 01/874–1903. Admission free. Open Tues.–Fri. 9:30–6, Sat. 9:30–5, Sun. 11–5.*

The Parnell Square area is rich in literary associations. They are explained and illustrated in

4 the **Dublin Writers Museum,** which opened in 1991 in two carefully restored 18th-century buildings. Paintings, letters, manuscripts, and photographs relating to Joyce, O'Casey, Shaw, Wilde, Yeats, Beckett, and others are on permanent display. There are also temporary exhibitions, lectures, and readings, as well as a bookshop. *18–19 Parnell Sq. N, tel. 01/872–2077. Admission: IR£2.75. Open Mon.–Sat. 10–5, Sun. 11:30–6.*

5 A must for every visitor is a stop at **Trinity College.** The college, familiarly known as TCD, was founded by Elizabeth I in 1592 and offered a free education to Catholics—provided that they accepted the Protestant faith. As a legacy of this condition, right up until 1966, Catholics who wished to study at Trinity had to obtain a dispensation from their bishop or face excommunication. Today more than 70% of Trinity's students are Catholics, a clear indication of how far away those days seem to today's generation. The college's facade, built between 1755 and 1759, consists of a magnificent portico with Corinthian columns. The design is repeated on the interior, so the views from outside the gates and from the quadrangle inside are the same. On the sweeping lawn in front of the facade are statues of two of the university's illustrious alumni—statesman Edmund Burke and poet Oliver Goldsmith. Other famous students include the philosopher George Berkeley (who gave his name to the northern California city), Jonathan Swift, Thomas Moore, Oscar Wilde, John Millington Synge, Henry Grattan, Wolfe Tone, Robert Emmet, Bram Stoker, Edward Carson, Douglas Hyde, and Samuel Beckett.

The 18th-century building on the left, just inside the entrance, is the chapel. There's an identical building opposite, which is the Examination Hall. The oldest buildings are the library in

Custom House, **15**
Dublin Castle, **11**
Dublin Writers Museum, **4**
Four Courts, **14**
Genealogical Office, **9**
General Post Office, **2**
Guinness Brewery, **12**
Hugh Lane Municipal Gallery of Modern Art, **3**
Irish Whiskey Corner, **13**
Leinster House, **7**
National Gallery of Ireland, **6**
National Museum, **8**
O'Connell Bridge, **1**
St. Patrick's Cathedral, **10**
Trinity College, **5**

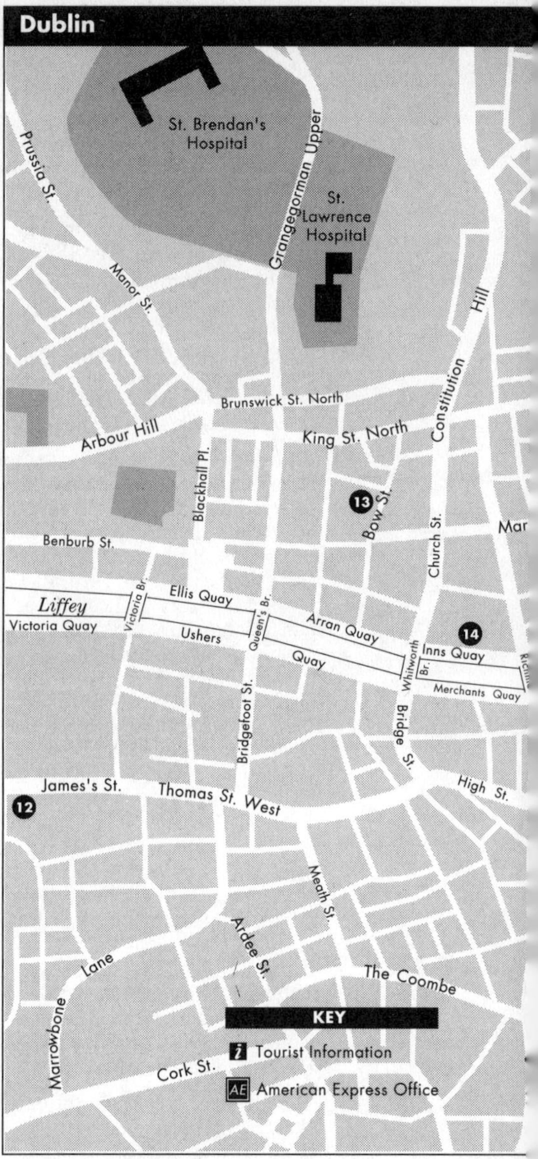

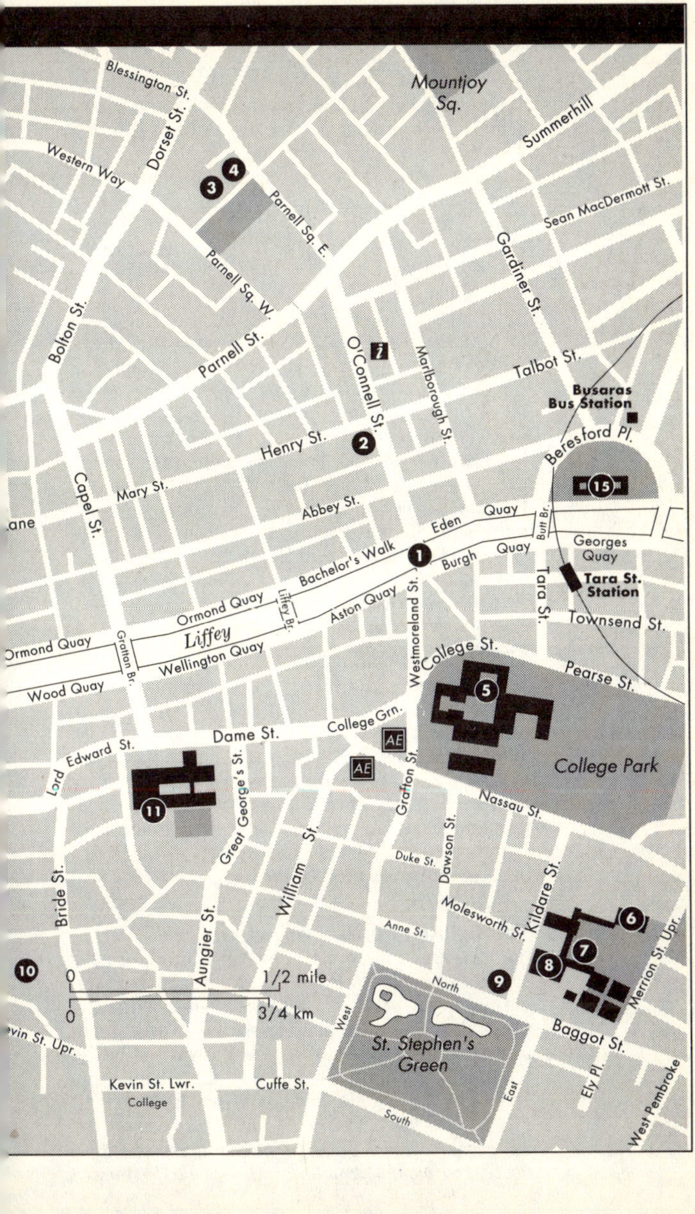
Blessington St.
Dorset St.
Western Way
Mountjoy Sq.
Summerhill
Sean MacDermott St.
Parnell Sq. E.
Parnell Sq. W.
Gardiner St.
Bolton St.
Parnell St.
O'Connell St.
Marlborough St.
Talbot St.
Busaras Bus Station
Beresford Pl.
Henry St.
Mary St.
Capel St.
Abbey St.
Eden Quay
Butt Br.
Georges Quay
Bachelor's Walk
Burgh Quay
Tara St. Station
Tara St.
Townsend St.
Ormond Quay
Liffey Br.
Aston Quay
Westmoreland St.
Liffey
Grattan Br.
Wellington Quay
Wood Quay
College St.
Pearse St.
College Grn.
Dame St.
Lord Edward St.
Great George's St.
Grafton St.
College Park
Nassau St.
William St.
Duke St.
Dawson St.
Kildare St.
Molesworth St.
Anne St.
Merrion St. Upr.
Bride St.
Aungier St.
1/2 mile
3/4 km
North
West
St. Stephen's Green
East
South
Baggot St.
Ely Pl.
West Pembroke
Kevin St. Lwr.
College
Cuffe St.

the far right-hand corner and a row of redbrick buildings known as the Rubrics, which contain student apartments; both date from 1712.

Ireland's largest collection of books and manuscripts is housed in the **Trinity College Library.** There are 3 million volumes gathering dust here; about 1 km (½ mi) of new shelving has to be added every year to keep pace with acquisitions. The library is entered through the library shop. Its principal treasure is the Book of Kells, a beautifully illuminated manuscript of the Gospels, dating from the 8th century. Only a few pages are displayed at a time, but there is an informative exhibit that reproduces many of them. At peak hours you may have to wait in line to enter the library. Apart from the many treasures it contains, the aptly named Long Room is impressive in itself, stretching for 213 ft and housing 200,000 of the library's volumes, mostly manuscripts and old books. Originally it had a flat plaster ceiling, but the perennial need for more shelving resulted in a decision to raise the level of the roof and add the barrel-vaulted ceiling and the gallery bookcases. *Tel. 01/608–2308. Admission: IR£3.50. Open Mon.–Sat. 9:30–5, Sun. noon–4:30.*

6 The **National Gallery of Ireland** is the first in a series of important buildings on the west side of Merrion Square. It is one of Europe's most agreeable and compact galleries, with more than 3,000 works on view, including a major collection of Irish landscape painting, 17th-century French works, paintings from the Italian and Spanish schools, and a collection of Dutch masters. *Merrion Sq. (West), tel. 01/661–5133. Admission free. Open Mon.–Sat. 10–5:30, Thurs. until 8:30, Sun. 2–5.*

7 The **Leinster House,** seat of the Irish Parliament, is an imposing 18th-century building with two facades: Its Merrion Square facade is designed in the style of a country house, while the other facade, in Kildare Street, is in the style of a town house. Visitors may be shown the house when Dáil Eireann (pronounced dawl Erin), the Irish Parliament, is not in session. *Kildare St., tel. 01/678–9911. Tours: Mon., Fri. by prior arrangement. Dáil visitors' gallery: Access with an introduction from a member of Parliament.*

8 The **National Museum** and the **National Library** each feature a massive, colonnaded rotunda entrance built in 1890. The museum houses a remarkable collection of Irish treasures from 6000 BC to the present, including the Tara Brooch, the Ardagh Chalice, and the Cross of Cong. Every major figure in modern Irish literature, from James Joyce onward, studied in the National Library at some point. In addition to a comprehensive collection of Irish authors, it contains extensive newspaper archives. *Kildare St., tel. 01/661–8811. National Museum: Admission free. Open Tues.–Sat. 10–5, Sun. 2–5. National Library: Admission free. Open Mon. 10–9, Tues.–Wed. 2–9, Thurs.–Fri. 10–5, Sat. 10–1.*

9 The **Genealogical Office**—the starting point for ancestor tracing—also incorporates the **Heraldic Museum,** which features displays of flags, coins, stamps, silver, and family crests that highlight the uses and development of heraldry in Ireland. *2 Kildare St., tel. 01/661–8811. Genealogical Office: Open weekdays 10–12:30, 2–4:30. Heraldic Museum: Admission free. Open Mon.–Wed., 10–8:30, Thurs.–Fri. 10–4:30, Sat. 10–12:30. Guided tours by appointment.*

Legend has it that St. Patrick baptized many
10 converts at a well on the site of **St. Patrick's Cathedral** in the 5th century. The building dates from 1190 and is mainly early English Gothic in style. At 305 ft, it is the longest church in the country. Its history has not always been happy. In the 17th century, Oliver Cromwell, dour ruler of England and no friend of the Irish, had his troops stable their horses in the cathedral. It wasn't until the 19th century that restoration work to repair the damage was begun. St. Patrick's is the national cathedral of the Protestant Church of Ireland and has had many illustrious deans. The most famous was Jonathan Swift, author of *Gulliver's Travels,* who held office from 1713 to 1745. Swift's tomb is in the south aisle, and Dean Swift's corner at the top of the north transept contains his pulpit, his writing table and chair, his portrait, and his death mask. Memorials to many other celebrated figures from Ireland's past line the walls of St. Patrick's. *Patrick St., tel. 01/475–4817. Admission:*

IR£1. Open May–Oct., weekdays 9–6, Sat. 9–5, Sun. 10–11, 12:30–3; Nov.–Apr., weekdays 9–6, Sat. 9–4, Sun. 10:30–11, 12:30–3.

Guided tours of the lavishly furnished state
11 apartments in **Dublin Castle** are offered every half hour and provide one of the most enjoyable sightseeing experiences in town. Only fragments of the original 13th-century building survive; the elegant castle you see today is essentially an 18th-century building. The state apartments were formerly the residence of the English viceroys and are now used by the president of Ireland to entertain visiting heads of state. The state apartments are closed when in official use, so phone first to check. *Off Dame St., tel. 01/677–7129. Admission: IR£2. Open weekdays 10–5, weekends 2–5.*

12 The **Guinness Brewery,** founded by Arthur Guinness in 1759 and covering 60 acres, dominates the area to the west of Christ Church. The brewery itself is closed to the public, but the Hop Store, part-museum and part-gift-shop, puts on an 18-minute audiovisual show. After the show, visitors get two complimentary glasses (or one pint) of the famous black stout. *Guinness Hop Store, Crane St., tel. 01/453–3645. Admission: IR£3. Open Apr.–Sept., Mon.–Sat. 9:30–5, Sun. 10:30–4:30.*

13 **Irish Whiskey Corner** is just behind St. Michan's. A 90-year-old warehouse has been converted into a museum to introduce visitors to the pleasures of Irish whiskey. There's an audiovisual show and free tasting. *Bow St., tel. 01/872–5566. Admission: IR£3. Tours: May–Oct., weekdays 11, 2:30, 3:30, Sat. 2:30, 3:30, Sun. 3:30.*

Off the River Liffey are two of Dublin's most famous landmarks, both of them the work of 18th-century architect James Gandon and both among the city's finest buildings. The first is the
14 **Four Courts,** surmounted by a massive copper-covered dome, giving it a distinctive profile. It is the seat of the High Court of Justice of Ireland. The building was completed between 1786 and 1802, then gutted in the Civil War of the 1920s; it has since been painstakingly restored. You will
15 recognize the same architect's hand in the **Custom House** (closed to the public), farther down

the Liffey. Its graceful dome rises above a central portico, itself linked by arcades to the pavilions at either end. *Four Courts: tel. 01/872–5555. Open daily 10:30–4.*

Shopping Although the rest of the country is well supplied with crafts shops, Dublin is the place to seek out more specialized items—antiques, traditional sportswear, haute couture, designer ceramics, books and prints, silverware and jewelry, and designer hand-knit items.

The city's most sophisticated shopping area is around **Grafton Street. St. Stephen's Green Center** contains 70 stores, large and small, in a vast Moorish-style glass-roof building on the Grafton Street corner. **Molesworth** and **Dawson streets** are the places to browse for antiques; **Nassau** and **Dawson streets,** for books; the smaller cross streets for jewelry, art galleries, and old prints. The pedestrian **Temple Bar** area, with its young, offbeat ambience, has a number of small art galleries, specialty shops (including music and books), and inexpensive and adventurous clothes shops. The area is further enlivened by buskers (street musicians) and street artists.

Tweeds and Woolens Ready-made tweeds for men can be found at **Kevin and Howlin** (on Nassau St.) and at **Cleo Ltd.** (on Kildare St.). The **Blarney Woollen Mills** (on Nassau St.) has a good selection of tweed, linen, and woolen sweaters in all price ranges. The **Woolen Mills** (at Ha'penny Bridge) has a good selection of hand-knits and other woolen sweaters at competitive prices.

Edinburgh/Leith, Scotland

Scotland and England *are* different—and let no Englishman tell you otherwise. Although the two nations have been united in a single state since 1707, Scotland retains its own marked political and social character, with, for instance, legal and educational systems quite distinct from those of England. And by virtue of its commanding geographic position, on top of a long-dead volcano, and the survival of a large number of outstanding buildings carrying echoes of the nation's history, Edinburgh ranks among the world's greatest capital cities. The key to understanding Edinburgh is to make the distinction between the Old and New Towns. Until the 18th century, the city was confined to the rocky crag on which its castle stands, straggling between the fortress at one end and the royal residence, the Palace of Holyroodhouse, at the other. In the 18th century, during a civilizing time of expansion known as the "Scottish Enlightenment," the city fathers fostered the construction of another Edinburgh, one a little to the north. This is the New Town, whose elegant squares, classical facades, wide streets, and harmonious proportions remain largely intact and are still lived in today.

Currency The British unit of currency is the pound sterling, divided into 100 pence (p). Scottish banks issue Scottish currency, of which all coins and notes—with the exception of the £1 notes—are accepted in England. At press time, exchange rates were approximately US$1.65 to the pound.

Telephones The United Kingdom's country code is 44. Public telephones are plentiful; other than on the street, the best place to find a bank of pay phones is in a hotel or large post office. The workings of coin-operated telephones vary, but there are usually instructions in each unit. Most take 10p, 20p, 50p, and £1 coins. A Phonecard is also available; it comes in denominations of 10, 20, 40, and 100 units and can be bought in a number of retail outlets. Cardphones, which are clearly marked with a special green insignia, will not accept coins. The cheapest way to make an overseas call is to dial it yourself. But be sure to have plenty of coins or phone cards close at hand. After you have inserted the coins or card, dial 010 (the international code), then the country code—for the United States it is 1—followed by the area code and local number. To reach an **AT&T** long-distance operator, dial 0500890011; **MCI,** 0800890222; **Sprint,** 0800890877 (from a British Telecom phone) or 0500890877 (from a Mercury Communications phone). To make a collect or other operator-assisted call, dial 155.

Shore Excursions The following is a good choice in Edinburgh. It may not be offered by all cruise lines. Time and price are approximate.

City Tour. Survey Old Town and New Town, visiting Edinburgh Castle. Pass by sights such as Princes Street, St. Giles Cathedral, the Royal Mile, and Holyroodhouse Palace. *4 hrs. Cost: $48.*

Coming Ashore Ships dock at Leith, the port for Edinburgh. It is about a 15-minute drive to Edinburgh from the pier.

Getting Around Walking is the best way to tour the old part of the city. It can be tiring, so wear comfortable shoes. Taxis are easily found; there are stands throughout the downtown area, most at the west end of Princes Street, South St. David Street and North St. Andrew Street (both just off St. Andrew Sq.), Waverley Market, Waterloo Place, and Lauriston Place.

Exploring Edinburgh *Numbers in the margin correspond to points of interest on the Edinburgh map.*

1 **Edinburgh Castle,** the brooding symbol of Scotland's capital and the nation's martial past, dominates the city center. The castle's attractions include the city's oldest building—the 11th-century St. Margaret's Chapel; the Crown Room, where the Regalia of Scotland are displayed; Old Parliament Hall; and Queen Mary's Apartments, where Mary, Queen of Scots, gave birth to the future King James VI of Scotland (who later became James I of England). In addition, military features of interest include the Scottish National War Memorial and the Scottish United Services Museum. *Castlehill, tel. 0131/668–8800. Admission: £5. Open Apr.–Sept., daily 9:30–5:15; Oct.–Mar., daily 9:30–4:15.*

2 **The Royal Mile,** the backbone of the Old Town, starts immediately below the Castle Esplanade, the wide parade ground that hosts the annual Edinburgh Military Tattoo—a grand military display staged during a citywide festival every summer. The Royal Mile consists of a number of streets, running into each other—Castlehill, Lawnmarket, High Street, and Canongate—leading downhill to the Palace of Holyroodhouse, home to the Royal Family when they visit Edinburgh. Tackle this walk in leisurely style; the many original Old Town "closes," narrow alleyways enclosed by high tenement buildings,

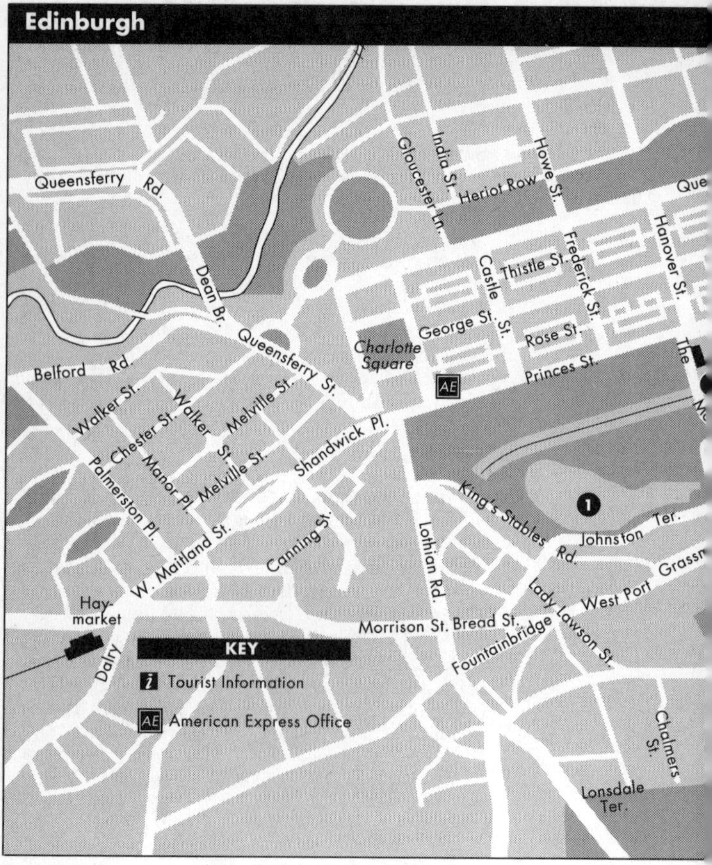

Edinburgh Castle, **1**

High Kirk of St. Giles, **5**

National Gallery of Scotland, **7**

Palace of Holyroodhouse, **6**

The Royal Mile, **2**

Scott Monument, **8**

Tolbooth, **4**

The Writers' Museum, **3**

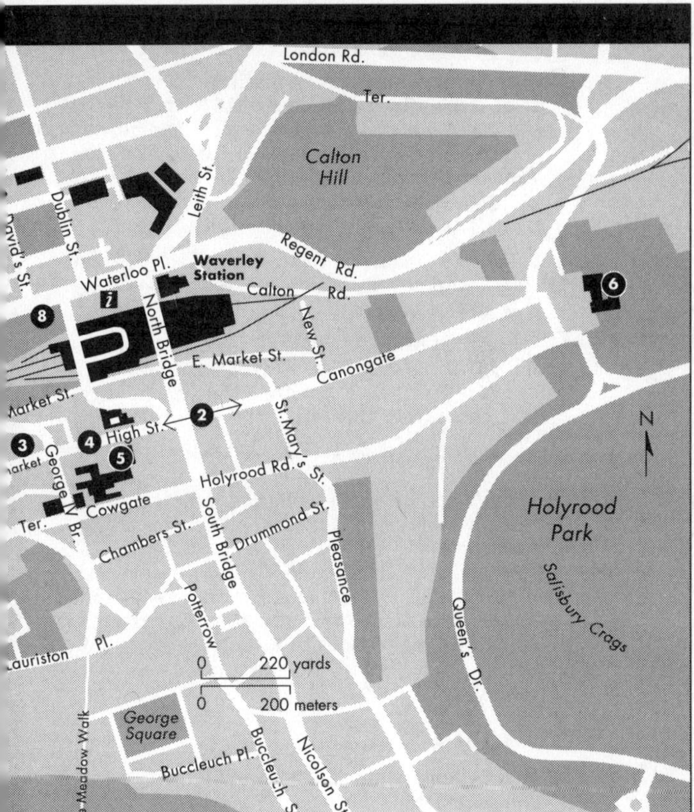
London Rd.
Ter.
Calton Hill
Leith St.
Dublin St.
David's St.
Regent Rd.
Waverley Station
Waterloo Pl.
Calton Rd.
New St.
North Bridge
E. Market St.
Canongate
Market St.
St. Mary's St.
High St.
George IV Br.
Holyrood Rd.
Cowgate
Ter.
Chambers St.
South Bridge
Drummond St.
Pleasance
Holyrood Park
Salisbury Crags
Queen's Dr.
Potterrow
Lauriston Pl.
0 220 yards
0 200 meters
George Square
Buccleuch Pl.
Buccleuch St.
Nicolson St.
Middle Meadow Walk
N

are rewarding to explore and give a real sense of the former life of the city.

3 **The Writers' Museum,** housed in Lady Stair's House, is a town dwelling of 1622 that recalls Scotland's literary heritage with exhibits on Sir Walter Scott, Robert Louis Stevenson, and Robert Burns. *Lady Stair's Close, Lawn market, tel. 0131/529–4901. Admission free. Open Mon.–Sat. 10–5, Sun. during festival 2–5.*

4 A heart shape set in the cobbles of High Street marks the site of the **Tolbooth,** the center of city life until it was demolished in 1817.

5 Near the former site of the Tolbooth stands the **High Kirk of St. Giles,** Edinburgh's cathedral; parts of the church date from the 12th century, the choir from the 15th. *High St. Admission free. Open Mon.–Sat. 9–5 (7 in summer), Sun. 1–5 and for services.*

6 The **Palace of Holyroodhouse,** still the Royal Family's official residence in Scotland, came into existence originally as a guest house for the Abbey of Holyrood, founded in 1128 by Scottish king David I. It was then extensively remodeled by Charles II in 1671. The state apartments, with their collections of tapestries and paintings, can be visited. *East end of Cannongate, tel. 0131/556–7371. Admission: £3.50. Open Apr.–Oct., Mon.–Sat. 9:30–5:15, Sun. 9:30–4:30; Nov.–Mar., daily 9:30–3:45.*

7 The **National Gallery of Scotland,** on the Mound, the street that joins the Old and New Towns, contains works by the old masters and the French Impressionists and has a good selection of Scottish paintings. This is one of Britain's best national galleries and is small enough to be taken in easily on one visit. *The Mound, tel. 0131/556–8921. Admission free; charge for special exhibitions. Open Mon.–Sat. 10–5, Sun. 2–5. Print Room weekdays 10–noon and 2–4 by arrangement.*

8 To the east along Princes Street is the unmistakable soaring Gothic spire of the 200-ft-high **Scott Monument,** built in the 1840s to commemorate the celebrated novelist of Scots history. There is a statue of Sir Walter and his dog within. The views from the top are well worth the 287-step

climb. *Princes Street, tel. 0131/529–4068. Currently closed for renovation.*

Florence/Livorno, Italy

Founded by Julius Caesar, Florence has the familiar grid pattern common to all Roman colonies. Except for the major monuments, which are appropriately imposing, the buildings are low and unpretentious. It is a small, compact city of ocher and gray stone and pale plaster; its narrow streets open unexpectedly into spacious squares populated by strollers and pigeons. At its best, it has a gracious and elegant air, though it can at times be a nightmare of mass tourism. Plan, if you can, to visit Florence in early spring or late fall to avoid the crowds.

A port call in Florence is a visit to the birthplace of the Italian Renaissance, and the city bears witness to the proud spirit and unparalleled genius of its artists and artisans. In fact, there is so much to see that it is best to savor a small part rather than attempt to absorb it all in a muddled vision.

Currency The unit of currency in Italy is the lira (plural, lire). At press time, the exchange rate was about 1,595 lire to the U.S. dollar. When your purchases run into hundreds of thousands of lire, beware of being shortchanged, a dodge that is practiced at ticket windows and cashiers' desks, as well as in shops and even banks. Always count your change before you leave the counter.

Telephones The country code for Italy is 39. Most local calls cost 200 lire for two minutes. Pay phones take either 100-, 200-, or 500-lire coins or *schede telefoniche* (phone cards), purchased in bars, tobacconists, post offices, and TELECOM offices in either 5,000-, 10,000-, or 15,000-lire denominations. To place international calls, many travelers go to the Telefoni telephone exchange (usually marked TELECOM), where the operator assigns you a booth, can help place your call, and will collect payment when you have finished. To dial an international call, insert a phone card, dial 00, then the country code, area code, and phone number. For **AT&T,** dial access number 172–1011; **MCI,** 172–1022; **Sprint,** 172–1877. You

will be connected directly with an operator in the United States.

Shore Excursions

The following is a good choice in Florence. It may not be offered by all cruise lines. Time and price are approximate.

City and Coastal Tour. See many of Florence's major civic and religious sights on this whirlwind day of sightseeing—plus a stop along the way to see the Leaning Tower of Pisa. *10 hrs. Cost: $145, including lunch.*

Coming Ashore

Ships dock at Livorno, which is a little more than an hour from Florence. Most cruise lines sell bus transfers to Florence for independent sightseeing for about $70.

Getting Around

Once in the city, you can see most of Florence's major sights on foot, as they are packed into a relatively small central area. Wear comfortable shoes and wander to your heart's content: It is easy to find your way around in Florence. The system of street addresses is unusual, with commercial addresses (those with an *r* in them, meaning *rosso,* or red) and residential addresses numbered separately (32/r might be next to or a block away from plain 32).

Taxis wait at stands. Use only authorized cabs, which are white with a yellow stripe or rectangle on the door. The meter starts at 4,000 lire. To call a taxi, phone 055/4798 or 055/4390.

Exploring Florence

The best place to begin a tour of Florence is **Piazza del Duomo,** where the cathedral, bell tower, and baptistery stand in the rather cramped square.

The lofty **Duomo** (or Cattedrale of Santa Maria del Fiore) cathedral is one of the longest in the world. Begun by master sculptor and architect Arnolfo di Cambio in 1296, its construction took 140 years to complete. Inside, the church is cool and austere, a fine example of the architecture of the period. Among the sparse decorations, take a good look at the frescoes on the left wall and on the dome. The dome itself is a great architectural and technical achievement and was the inspiration of such later domes as the one for St. Peter's in Rome and even the Capitol in Washington. You can climb to the cupola gallery,

463 fatiguing steps up between the two skins of the double dome, for a fine view of Florence and the surrounding hills. *Piazza del Duomo, tel. 055/2302885. Admission to dome: 8,000 lire. Open weekdays 10–5 (1st Sat. of month 10–3:30), Sun. 1–5. Cupola (entrance in left aisle of cathedral) open weekdays 8:30–6:20, Sat. 9:30–5 (1st Sat. of month 9:30–3:20).*

Next to the Duomo is Giotto's 14th-century **Campanile** (bell tower), richly decorated with colored marble and sculpture reproductions (the originals are in the Museo dell'Opera del Duomo). The 414-step climb to the top is less strenuous than that to the cupola. *Piazza del Duomo. Admission: 8,000 lire. Open Apr.–Oct., Mon.–Sat. 9–6:30; Nov.–Mar., daily 9–4:20.*

In front of the cathedral is the **Battistero** (Baptistery), one of the city's oldest and most beloved edifices, where, since the 11th century, Florentines have baptized their children. The most famous of the baptistery's three portals is Ghiberti's east doors (facing the Duomo), dubbed the "gates of Paradise" by Michelangelo; gleaming copies now replace the originals, which have been removed to the Museo dell'Opera del Duomo (Cathedral Museum). *Admission: 3,000 lire. Open Mon.–Sat. 1:30–6:30, Sun. 8:30–12:30.*

Along Via Calzaiuoli you'll come upon **Piazza della Signoria,** the heart of Florence and the city's largest square. In the center of the square a slab marks the spot of the 1497 "burning of the vanities," when reformist monk Savonarola urged the Florentines to burn their pictures, books, musical instruments, and other worldly objects. On the same spot, a year later, he was hanged and then burned at the stake as a heretic. Copies of several famous statues are found in the square or the adjoining loggia, including a copy of Michelangelo's *David* and a copy of Cellini's *Perseus Holding the Head of Medusa.*

The **Galleria degli Uffizi** (Uffizi Gallery) houses Italy's most important collection of paintings. The palace was built to house the administrative offices of the Medicis, onetime rulers of the city ("uffizi" is Italian for "offices"). Later their fabulous art collection was arranged in the Uffizi Gallery on the top floor, which was opened to the public in the 17th century—making this the world's first public gallery of modern times. The emphasis is on Italian art of the Gothic and Renaissance periods. Make sure you see the works by Giotto, and look for the Botticellis in Rooms X–XIV, Michelangelo's *Holy Family* in Room XXV, and the works by Raphael next door. In addition to its art treasures, the gallery offers a magnificent close-up view of Palazzo Vecchio's tower from the little coffee bar at the end of the corridor. Authorities have done wonders in repairing the damage caused by a bomb in 1993. *Loggiato Uffizi 6, tel. 055/23885. Admission: 12,000 lire. Open Tues.–Sat. 8:30–6:50, Sun. 8:30–1:50.*

The **Galleria dell'Accademia** (Accademia Gallery) houses Michelangelo's famous *David*. Skip the works in the exhibition halls leading to the main attraction; they are of minor importance, and you'll gain a length on the tour groups. Michelangelo's statue is a tour de force of artistic conception and technical ability, for he was using a piece of stone that had already been worked on by a lesser sculptor. Take time to see the forceful *Slaves*, also by Michelangelo; the rough-hewn, unfinished surfaces contrast dramatically with the highly polished, meticulously carved *David*. Michelangelo left the *Slaves* "unfinished" as a symbolic gesture: to accentuate the figures' struggle to escape the bondage of stone. *Via Ricasoli 60, tel. 055/214375. Admission: 12,000 lire. Open Tues.–Sat. 8:30–6:50, Sun. 8:30–1:50.*

The remarkable **Cappelle Medicee** (Medici Chapels) contain the tombs of practically every member of the Medici family, and there were a lot of them, for they guided Florence's destiny from the 15th century to 1737. Cosimo I, a Medici whose acumen made him the richest man in Europe, is buried in the crypt of the Chapel of the Princes, and Donatello's tomb is next to that of his patron. The chapel upstairs is decorated in a dazzling array of colored marble. In Michelangelo's New Sacristy, his tombs of Giuliano and Lorenzo de' Medici bear the justly famed statues of *Dawn* and *Dusk*, and *Night* and *Day*. *Piazza Madonna degli Aldobrandini, tel. 055/213206. Admission: 10,000 lire. Open daily*

8:30–1:50. Closed 2nd and 4th Sun. and 1st, 3rd, and 5th Mon. of month.

Don't be put off by the grim look of Bargello, a fortresslike palace that served as residence of Florence's chief magistrate in medieval times, and later as a prison. It now houses Florence's **Museo Nazionale del Bargello** (National Museum), a treasure-house of Italian Renaissance sculpture. In a historically and visually interesting setting, it displays masterpieces by Donatello, Verrocchio, Michelangelo, and many other major sculptors. This museum is on a par with the Uffizi, so don't shortchange yourself on time. *Via del Proconsolo 4, tel. 055/238–8606. Admission: 8,000 lire. Open Tues.–Sun. 9–2.*

The **Ponte Vecchio** (Old Bridge) is Florence's oldest bridge. It seems to be just another street lined with goldsmiths' shops until you get to the middle and catch a glimpse of the Arno flowing below. Spared during World War II by the retreating Germans (who blew up every other bridge in the city), it also survived the 1966 flood. It leads into the Oltrarno District, which has its own charm and still preserves much of the atmosphere of old-time Florence, full of fascinating craft workshops. *East of Ponte Santa Trinita and west of Ponte alle Grazie.*

The church of **Santo Spirito** is important as one of Brunelleschi's finest architectural creations, and it contains some superb paintings, including a Filippino Lippi *Madonna.* Santo Spirito is the hub of a colorful neighborhood of artisans and intellectuals. An outdoor market enlivens the square every morning except Sunday; in the afternoon, pigeons, pet owners, and pensioners take over. *Piazza Santo Spirito. Open Thurs.–Tues. 8–noon and 4–5:30; Wed. 8–noon.*

Shopping Florence offers top quality for your money in leather goods, linens and upholstery fabrics, gold and silver jewelry, and cameos. Straw goods, gilded wooden trays and frames, hand-printed paper desk accessories, and ceramic objects make good inexpensive gifts. Many shops offer fine old prints.

The most fashionable streets in Florence are **Via Tornabuoni** and **Via della Vigna Nuova.**

Goldsmiths and jewelry shops can be found on and around the **Ponte Vecchio.**

The **monastery of Santa Croce** houses a leather-working school and showroom (entrances at Via San Giuseppe 5/r, Piazza Santa Croce 16). The entire Santa Croce area is known for its leather workshops and inconspicuous shops selling gold and silver jewelry at prices much lower than those of the elegant jewelers near Ponte Vecchio.

Outside the Church of San Lorenzo, you'll find yourself in the midst of the sprawling **San Lorenzo Market,** dealing in everything and anything, including some interesting leather items. *Piazza San Lorenzo, Via dell'Ariento. Open Tues.–Sat. 8–7.*

French Riviera

Few places in the world have the same pull on the imagination as France's fabled Riviera, the Mediterranean coastline stretching from St-Tropez in the west to Menton on the Italian border. Cooled by the Mediterranean in the summer and warmed by it in winter, the climate is almost always pleasant. Avoid the area in July and August, however, unless you love crowds.

Although the Riviera's coastal resorts seem to live exclusively for the tourist trade and have often been ruined by high-rise blocks, the hinterlands remain relatively untarnished. The little villages perched high on the hills behind medieval ramparts seem to belong to another century. One of them, St-Paul-de-Vence, is the home of the Maeght Foundation, one of the world's leading museums of modern art. Artists, attracted by the light, have played a considerable role in popular conceptions of the Riviera, and their presence is reflected in the number of modern art museums: the Musée Picasso at Antibes, the Musée Renoir and the Musée d'Art Moderne Mediterranée at Cagnes-sur-Mer, and the Musée Jean Cocteau near the harbor at Menton. Wining and dining are special treats on the Riviera, especially if you are fond of garlic and olive oil. Bouillabaisse, a spicy fish stew, is the most popular regional specialty.

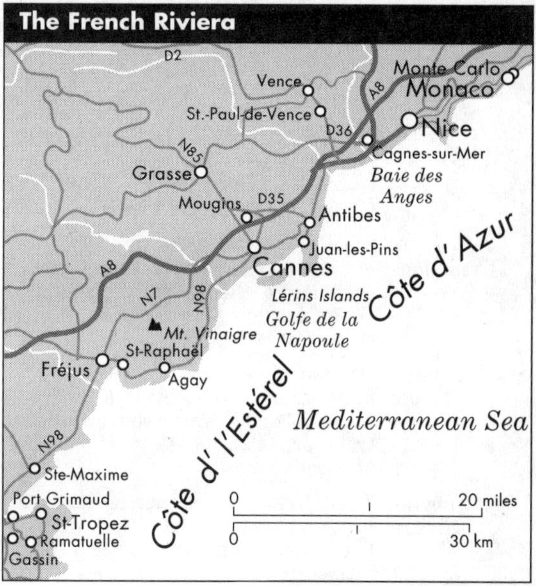

The tiny principality of Monaco, which lies between Nice and Menton, is included in this section, despite the fact that it is a sovereign state. Although Monaco has its own army and police force, its language, food, and way of life are French.

Currency The unit of French currency is the franc (fr), subdivided into 100 centimes. At press time, the U.S. dollar bought 5.5 francs.

Telephones The country code for France is 33. In 1996, two digits were added to all phone numbers. The digits are determined by zone: for the southeast, the code is 04. (Drop the zero if you are calling France from a foreign country.) Though there is no frontier between France and Monaco, Monaco is a different country; when dialing numbers from outside the country, even if calling from France, you must prefix the call with "377." Phone booths are plentiful; they are nearly always available at post offices and cafés. Some French pay phones take 1-, 2-, and 5-franc coins (1-fr minimum), but most phones are now operated by *télécartes* (phone cards), which can be used for both local and international calls. The cards are sold in post offices, métro stations, and cafés sporting a red TABAC (tobacco) sign outside (cost: 40 frs for 50 units; 96 frs for 120 units). To call abroad, dial 19 and wait for the tone, then dial the country code, area code, and number. To reach an **AT&T** long-distance operator, dial 19–0011; **MCI,** 19–0019; **Sprint,** 19–0087. Dial 12 for local operators.

Shore Excursions The best way to spend time in the French Riviera is to wander the city streets, lunch at a café, or head to the beach. Depending on where you're docked, your cruise line may offer excursions to other nearby towns.

Coming Ashore Only small ships dock at St-Tropez or Monaco. Most larger ones will dock or drop anchor at Nice or Cannes, where you can hire a car, catch a train, or take a shore excursion to St-Tropez or Monaco.

Exploring the Riviera The towns of the French Riviera are easily and best seen on foot. Only if you wish to travel between towns will you need additional transportation.

St-Tropez Between the old and new ports is the **Musée de l'Annonciade,** set in a cleverly converted chapel, which houses paintings by artists drawn to St-Tropez between 1890 and 1940—including Paul Signac, Matisse, Derain, and Van Dongen. *Quai de l'Épi, tel. 04–94–97–04–01. Admission: 25 frs. Open June–Sept., Wed.–Mon. 10–noon and 3–7; Oct.–May, Wed.–Mon. 10–noon and 2–6.*

A long climb up to the **Citadelle** (citadel) is rewarded by a splendid view over the old town and across the gulf to Ste-Maxime, a quieter, more working-class family resort with a decent beach.

Cannes Cannes is for relaxing—strolling along the seafront on the **Croisette** and getting tanned on the beaches. Near the eastern end of La Croisette is the Parc de la Roserie, where some 14,000 roses nod their heads in the wind.

The **Palais des Festivals** is where the famous film festival is held each May, and it is near the Cannes harbor.

Only a few steps inland is the old town, known as the **Suquet,** with its steep, cobbled streets and its 12th-century watchtower.

Nice The **place Masséna** is the logical starting point for an exploration of Nice. This fine square was built in 1815 to celebrate a local hero: one of Napoléon's most successful generals.

The **Promenade des Anglais,** built by the English community here in 1824, is only a short stroll past the fountains and the **Jardin Albert Ier**. It now carries heavy traffic but still forms a splendid strand between town and sea.

Just up rue de Rivoli is the **Palais Masséna,** a museum concerned with the Napoleonic era. *65 rue de France, tel. 04–93–88–11–34. Admission free. Open Dec.–Oct., Tues.–Sun. 10–noon and 2–5; May–Sept. 3–6.*

Farther west, along rue de France and right up avenue des Baumettes, is the **Musée des Beaux-Arts Jules-Chéret,** Nice's fine-arts museum, built in 1878 as a palatial mansion for a Russian princess. The rich collection of paintings includes works by Renoir, Degas, and Monet; Oriental prints; sculptures by Rodin; and ceramics by Picasso. *33 av. des Baumettes, tel. 04–93–44–53–72. Admission: 25 frs. Open May–Sept., Tues.–Sun. 10–noon and 3–6; Oct.–April, Tues.–Sun. 10–noon and 2–5.*

The narrow streets in the old town are the prettiest part of Nice: Take the rue de l'Opéra to see the ornate **St-François-de-Paule** church (1750) and the **opera house.** At the northern extremity of the old town lies the vast **place Garibaldi**—all yellow-ocher buildings and formal fountains.

The **Musée Chagall** is just off the boulevard de Cimiez, near the Roman ruins. The museum was built in 1972 to house the Chagall collection, including the 17 huge canvases of *The Message of the Bible,* which took 13 years to complete. *Av. du Dr-Ménard, tel. 04–93–81–75–75. Admission: 28 frs. Open July–Sept., Wed.–Mon. 10–7; Oct.–June, Wed.–Mon. 10–12:30 and 2–5:30.*

A 17th-century Italian villa amid the Roman remains contains two museums: the **Musée Archéologique** (Archaeological Museum), with a plethora of ancient objects, and the renovated **Musée Matisse,** with paintings and bronzes by Henri Matisse (1869–1954). *164 av. des*

Arènes-de-Cimiez. Musée Matisse: tel. 04-93-81-08-08. Admission 25 fr. Open Apr.-Sept. Wed.-Mon. 1-7. Musée Archéologique: tel. 04-93-81-08-08. Open Dec.-Oct., Tues.-Sat. 10-noon and 2-5, Sun. 2-5.

Monaco For more than a century Monaco's livelihood was centered in its splendid copper-roof **casino.** The oldest section dates from 1878 and was conceived by Charles Garnier, architect of the Paris opera house. It's as elaborately ornate as anyone could wish, bristling with turrets and gold filigree and masses of interior frescoes and bas-reliefs. There are lovely sea views from the terrace, and the gardens out front are meticulously tended. The main activity is in the American Room, where beneath the gilt-edged ceiling, busloads of tourists feed the one-armed bandits. *Pl. du Casino, tel. 92-16-21-21. Persons under 21 not admitted. Admission: European rooms, 50 frs; English Club and Monte-Carlo Sporting Club rooms, 100 frs.; American room, free. Open daily noon-4 AM; closed May 1.*

The **Musée National des Automates et Poupées d'Autrefois** (Museum of Antique Dolls and Automatons, sometimes simply called the Musée National) has a compelling collection of 18th- and 19th-century dolls and mechanical figures, the latter shamelessly showing off their complex inner workings. It's magically set in a 19th-century seaside villa (designed by Garnier). *17 av. Princesse-Grace, tel. 93-30-91-26. Admission: 28 frs. Open daily except holidays: Easter-Aug., 10-6:30; Sept.-Easter, 10-12:15 and 2:30-6:30.*

Monaco Town, the principality's old quarter, has many vaulted passageways and exudes an almost tangible medieval feel. The magnificent **Palais du Prince** (Prince's Palace), a grandiose Italianate structure with a Moorish tower, was largely rebuilt in the last century. Here, since 1297, the Grimaldi dynasty has lived and ruled. The spectacle of the Changing of the Guard occurs each morning at 11:55; inside, guided tours take visitors through the state apartments and a wing containing the **Palace Archives** and **Musée Napoléon** (Napoleonic Museum). *Pl. du Palais, tel. 93-25-18-31. Palace admission: 40 frs. Open June-Oct., daily 9:30-12:30 and 2-6:30.*

In case you want to see the world.
At American Express, we're here to make your journey a smooth one. So we have over 1,700 travel service locations in over 120 countries ready to help. What else would you expect from the world's largest travel agency?
do more
AMERICAN EXPRESS
Travel
http://www.americanexpress.com/travel

5 CENTS
CANADA
PESOS
LIBERTY
VINGT
FRANCS
FB 747022 T

Musée Napoléon and Palace Archives admission: 20 frs. Open Tues.–Sun. 9:30–6:30.

Monaco's **cathedral** is a late-19th-century neo-Romanesque confection in which Philadelphia-born Princess Grace lies entombed in splendor along with past members of the Grimaldi dynasty. *4 rue Colonel Bellando de Castro.*

Next to the St-Martin Gardens—which contain an evocative bronze monument in memory of Prince Albert I (Prince Rainier's great-grandfather, the one in the sou'wester and flying oilskins, benignly guiding a ship's wheel)—is the **Musée Océanographique** (Oceanography Museum and Aquarium). This museum is also an internationally renowned research institute, founded by the very Prince Albert who is remembered outside as an eminent marine biologist; the well-known underwater explorer Jacques Cousteau was its director until his death in 1997. The aquarium is the undisputed highlight, however, where a collection of the world's fish and crustacea—some colorful, some drab, some the stuff of nightmares—live out their lives in public. *Av. St-Martin, tel. 93–15–36–00. Admission: 70 frs. Open July–Aug., daily 9–8; Sept.–June, daily 9:30–7 (6 in winter).*

Before heading back inland, take a stroll to the eastern tip of the rock, to the **Fort Antoine Theater** (av. de la Quarantaine, tel. 93–30–19–21), a converted 18th-century fortress that certainly looks a lot prettier now than it would have in more warlike times, covered as it is in ivy and flowering myrtle and thyme. In the summer, this is an open-air theater that seats 350.

The Moneghetti area is the setting for the **Jardin Exotique** (Garden of Exotic Plants), where 600 varieties of cacti and succulents cling to the rock face, their improbable shapes and sometimes violent coloring further testimony that Mother Nature will try anything once. Your ticket also allows you to explore the caves next to the gardens and to visit the adjacent **Museum of Prehistoric Anthropology.** *Blvd. du Jardin Exotique, tel. 93–15–80–06. Admission: 39 frs. Open mid-May–mid-Sept., daily 9–7.*

Beaches
In Cannes Many of Cannes's beaches are private, but that doesn't mean you can't use them, only that you must pay for the privilege. The Croisette offers splendid views of the Napoule Bay.

In St-Tropez Close to town are **Plage des Greniers** and the **Bouillabaisse,** but most people prefer a 10-km (6-mi) sandy crescent at **Les Salins** and **Pampellone.** These beaches are about 3 km (2 mi) from town.

Gibraltar

The Rock of Gibraltar acquired its name in AD 711 when it was captured by the Moorish chieftain Tarik at the start of the Arab invasion of Spain. It became known as Jebel Tariq (Rock of Tariq), later corrupted to Gibraltar. After successive periods of Moorish and Spanish domination, Gibraltar was captured by an Anglo-Dutch fleet in 1704 and ceded to the British by the Treaty of Utrecht in 1713. This tiny British colony, whose impressive silhouette dominates the straits between Spain and Morocco, is a rock just 4⁄5 km (3⅗ mi) long, ¾ km (½ mi) wide, and 1,394 ft high.

Currency Gibraltar's official language is English and the currency is the British pound sterling. At press time, a U.S. dollar bought £1.54.

Shore Excursions The following is a good choice in Gibraltar. It may not be offered by all cruise lines. Time and price are approximate.

The Rock. By taxi, you'll climb the 1,394-ft-high Rock of Gibraltar for a panoramic view of the town and harbor. Includes a visit to Apes' Den, home of Barbary apes. *1½ hrs. Cost: $32.*

Coming Ashore Cruise ships dock at Gibraltar's pier. From here, you can walk or take a taxi or shuttle to the center of town.

Getting Around Since Gibraltar is not quite 6 km (3⅗ mi) long and only ¾ km (½ mi) wide, getting around is not a major problem.

Exploring Gibraltar **Punta Grande de Europa** (Europa Point) is the Rock's most southerly tip. Stop here to admire the view across the Straits to the coast of Morocco, 22½ km (14 mi) away. You are standing on what in ancient times was called one of the two

Pillars of Hercules. Across the water in Morocco, a mountain between the cities of Ceuta and Tangier formed the second pillar. Plaques explain the history of the gun installations here, and, nearby on Europa Flats, you can see the Nun's Well, an ancient Moorish cistern, and the Shrine of Our Lady of Europe, venerated by sailors since 1462.

Jews Gate is an unbeatable lookout point over the docks and Bay of Gibraltar to Algeciras in Spain. From here you can gain access to the Upper Nature Preserve, which includes St. Michael's Cave, the Apes' Den, and the Great Siege Tunnel. *Engineer Rd. Admission to preserve, including all sights: £5, plus £1.25 per vehicle. Open daily 10–6.*

St. Michael's Cave, a series of underground chambers adorned with stalactites and stalagmites, provides an admirable setting for concerts, ballet, and drama.

Apes' Den, near the Wall of Charles V, is where you'll find the famous Barbary apes, a breed of cinnamon-colored, tailless monkeys, natives of the Atlas Mountains in Morocco. Legend holds that as long as the apes remain, the British will continue to hold the Rock. Winston Churchill himself issued orders for the maintenance of the ape colony when its numbers began to dwindle during World War II. *Old Queen's Rd.*

The **Great Siege Tunnel** (Old Queen's Rd.) is found at the northern end of the Rock. These huge galleries were carved out during the Great Siege of 1779–83. Here, in 1878, the governor, Lord Napier of Magdala, entertained former president Ulysses S. Grant at a banquet in St. George's Hall. From here, the Holyland Tunnel leads out to the east side of the Rock above Catalan Bay.

The recently refurbished **Gibraltar Museum**'s exhibits recall the history of the Rock throughout the ages. *Bomb House La., tel. 9567–74289. Admission: £1.75. Open weekdays 10–6, Sat. 10–2.*

Greek Islands

The islands of the Aegean have colorful legends—the Minotaur in Crete; the lost con-

The Greek Islands

tinent of Atlantis, which some believe was Santorini; and the Colossus of Rhodes, to name a few. Each island has its own personality. Mykonos has windmills, dazzling whitewashed buildings, hundreds of tiny churches and chapels on golden hillsides, and small fishing harbors. Visitors to volcanic Santorini sail into what was once a vast volcanic crater and anchor near the island's forbidding cliffs. In Rhodes, a bustling modern town surrounds a walled town with a medieval castle.

Currency The Greek monetary unit is the drachma (dr.). At press time, there were approximately 241 dr. to the U.S. dollar.

Telephones The country code for Greece is 30. Telephone kiosks are easy to find, although some can only be used for local calls. The easiest way to make a local or an international call is with a phone card, available at kiosks, convenience stores, or Hellenic Telecommunications Organization (OTE) offices. Go to an OTE office for convenience and privacy if you plan to make several international calls. For an **AT&T** long-distance operator, dial

00/800–1311; **MCI,** 00/800–1211; **Sprint,** 00/800–1411.

Shore Excursions The following excursions are good choices in the Greek Islands. They may not be offered by all cruise lines. Times and prices are approximate.

In Mykonos The best way to explore Mykonos is on your own, wandering through the narrow whitewashed streets. Some lines may offer excursions to the neighboring island of Delos.

In Santorini **Akrotiri & Wine Tasting.** Visit the excavated town of Akrotiri, and then continue on your bus to a winery for a tasting. *4 hrs. Cost: $60.*

Oia. By motor coach, ride to the cliff-top village of Oia, where there will be time to wander through the town. *4 hrs. Cost: $30.*

In Rhodes **Mount Philerimos and Rhodes Town.** Visit the Church of Our Lady on the plateau of Philerimos and walk through the old walled portion of Rhodes Town to the Palace of Grand Masters. *4½ hrs. Cost: $49.*

Lindos. Drive 50 km (30 mi) to Lindos Village and up the summit of the Acropolis to see ruins and to shop in the village. *4 hrs. Cost: $45.*

In Lesbos **Island Tour.** Breeze through the island's highlights, including the Church of Taxiarches, Theofilos Museum, Theriade Museum, and Agiassos village. *4 hrs. Cost: $36.*

Coming Ashore Depending on which Greek Islands your ship visits—and how many port calls it makes—you may dock, tender, or both.

In Mykonos Ships tender passengers to the main harbor area along the Esplanade in Mykonos Town.

In Santorini Ships drop anchor in the harbor off Thira or call at the port of Athinios. Passengers coming ashore below Thira can take the cable car to town, or, if you like a little more adventure, try the donkey service. Passengers who come ashore at Athinios will be met by buses and taxis. The bus ride into Thira takes about a half hour, and from there you can make connections to Oia.

In Rhodes Ships dock at Mandraki Harbor, once the ancient port of Rhodes. Rhodes Town stretches in front of the port.

In Lesbos Cruise ships visiting Lesbos tender passengers to the main town of Mytilini, where most of the town's sights are clustered.

Getting Around Most port cities in the Greek Islands are compact enough to explore on foot. There are, however, several outlying towns worth visiting; for these you'll need to hire a driver or rent a car.

In Mykonos Mykonos Town is well suited to walking. Taxis and buses will take you to other points of interest. Motorbikes also can be rented.

In Santorini Buses and taxis will take you around town. Many people rent mopeds, but they're not recommended as a safe means of traveling about the island.

In Rhodes It is possible to tour the island in one day only if you rent a car. Walking is advisable in Rhodes Town. Taxis can take you to other nearby sights and beaches.

In Lesbos A car is handy on Lesbos if you want to explore the island, and rentals cost around $60 a day. Bus service is relatively expensive and infrequent.

Exploring the Greek Islands
Mykonos Besides their sun-kissed beaches, the Greek Islands offer a diverse mix of historical, architectural, and cultural attractions. A visit to the **archaeological museum** is a good way to get a sense of the island's history; the most significant local find is a 7th-century BC *pithos* (storage jar) showing the Greeks emerging from the Trojan Horse. *North end of port, tel. 0289/22325. Admission: 400 dr. Open Tues.–Sun. 8:30–3.*

The most famous of the island's churches is the **Church of Paraportiani.** The sloping, whitewashed conglomeration of four chapels, mixing Byzantine and vernacular idioms, has been described as a "confectioner's dream gone mad," and its position on a promontory facing the sea sets off the unique architecture. *Anargon St.*

Venetia (Little Venice) is a neighborhood where a few old houses have been turned into bars. In the distance across the water are the famous windmills. *Southwest end of the port.*

The **Old Folk Museum** is housed in an 18th-century house and features one bedroom furnished and decorated in the fashion of the period. On display are looms and lace-making devices, Cycladic costumes, old photographs, and Mykoniot musical instruments. *Near Little Venice, tel. 0289/22591 or 0289/22748. Admission free. Open Mon.–Sat. 5:30–8:30, Sun. 6:30–8:30.*

About 40 minutes by boat from Mykonos and its 20th-century holiday pleasures is the ancient isle of **Delos**—the legendary sanctuary of Apollo. Its Terrace of the Lions, a remarkable group of nine Naxian marble sculptures from the 7th century BC, is a must. Worth seeing, too, are some of the houses of the Roman period, with their fine floor mosaics.

The best of the mosaics from Delos's ruins are in the island's **archaeological museum.** *Tel. 0289/22–259. Admission to archaeological site (including entrance to museum): 1,200 dr. Open Tues.–Sun. 8:30–3.*

Santorini Santorini's volcano erupted during the 15th century BC, destroying its Minoan civilization. At **Akrotiri,** on the south end of the island, the remains of a Minoan city buried by volcanic ash are being excavated. The site, believed by some to be part of the legendary Atlantis, should be a must on your sightseeing list. *13 km/8 mi from Fira, tel. 0286/81–366. Admission: 1,200 dr. Open Tues.–Sun. 8:30–3.*

Oia, the serene town at the northern tip, is charming and has spectacular views despite being packed with visitors in the summer. This is the place, if your time ashore allows, to watch the sunset. Oia, 14 km (8½ mi) from Thira, has the usual souvenir and handicrafts shops and several reasonably priced jewelry shops. Be sure to try the local wines. The volcanic soil produces a unique range of flavors, from light and dry to rich and aromatic.

The capital, **Fira,** midway along the west coast of the east rim, is no longer just a picturesque town but a major tourist center, overflowing with discos, shops, and restaurants.

At **Ancient Thira,** a cliff-top site on the east coast of the island, a well-preserved ancient town includes a theater and agora, houses, fortifications, and ancient tombs. *Take taxi partway up Mesa Vouna then hike to summit, no phone. Admission free. Open Tues.–Sun. 8:30–3.*

For an enjoyable but slightly unnerving excursion, take the short boat trip to the island's still-active small offshore volcanoes, called the **Kamenes** (Burnt Ones). You can descend into a small crater, hot and smelling of sulfur, and swim in the nearby water, which has been warmed by the volcano.

Rhodes The fascinating **old walled city,** near the harbor, was built by crusaders—the Knights of St. John—on the site of an ancient city. The knights ruled the island from 1309 until they were defeated by the Turks in 1522.

Within the fine medieval walls, on the Street of the Knights, stands the Knights' Hospital. Behind it, the **archaeological museum** houses ancient pottery and sculpture, including two famous statues of Aphrodite. *Platia Mouseou (Museum Square), reached by the wide staircase from the hospital, tel. 0241/27–657. Admission: 800 dr. Open Tues.–Fri. 8:30–7, weekends and holidays 8:30–3.*

Another museum that deserves your attention is the restored and moated medieval **Palati ton Ippoton** (Palace of the Knights). Destroyed in 1856 by a gunpowder explosion, the palace was renovated by the Italians as a summer retreat for Mussolini. Note its splendid Hellenistic and Roman floor mosaics. *Street of the Knights, tel. 0241/23–359. Admission: 1,200 dr. Open Tues.–Fri. 8–7, weekends 8:30–3.*

The walls of Rhodes's **Old Town** are among the greatest medieval monuments in the Mediterranean. For 200 years the knights strengthened them, making them up to 40 ft thick in places and curving the walls to deflect cannonballs. You can take a guided walk on about half of the 4-km (2½-mi) road along the top of the fortifications. *Old town, tel. 0241/21–954; 0241/23–359 tour information. Tours Tues. and Sat. 2:45 (arrive at least 15 mins early); departure from palace entrance.*

The enchanting village of **Lindos** is about 60 km (37 mi) down the east coast from Rhodes Town. Take a donkey from the village center and ride or put on your comfortable shoes and walk up the steep hill to the ruins of the ancient **Akropoli tis Archaias Lindou** (Acropolis of Lindos), which is slowly being restored. The sight of its beautiful colonnade with the sea far below is unforgettable. Look for little St. Paul's Harbor, beneath the cliffs of the Acropolis; seen from above, it appears to be a lake, as the tiny entrance from the sea is obscured by the rocks. *Above town, tel. 0244/31–258. Admission: 1,200 dr. Open Tues.–Sun. 8:30–2:45.*

Lesbos Above **Mytilini** looms the stone castle built by the Byzantines on a 600 BC temple of Apollo. It was repaired by Francesco Gateluzzi of the famous Genoese family. Inside there's only a crumbling prison and a Roman cistern, but a visit is worth it for the fine views. *Tel. 0251/27297. Admission: 400 dr. Open daily sunrise–sunset.*

One of Greece's best art museums is at **Varia,** home of the early 20th-century painter Theofilos. Eighty of his paintings can be seen. *4 km/2½ mi south of Mytilini, tel. 0251/28179. Admission: 250 dr. Open Tues.–Sun. 9–1 and 4:30–8.*

The **Theriade Library and Museum of Modern Art** includes Theriade's publications "Minotaure" and "Verved" and his collection of works, mostly lithographs, by Picasso, Matisse, Chagall, and Miró. *Next to Varia, tel. 0251/28179. Admission: 500 dr. Open Tues.–Sun. 9–2 and 5–8.*

The 18th-century monastery **Taxiarchis Michail** is famous for its black icon of Archangel Michael. Visitors used to make a wish and press a coin to the archangel's forehead; if it stuck, the wish would be granted. Owing to wear and tear on the icon, the practice is now forbidden. *In town of Mandamados, 37 km/23 mi northwest of Mytilini.*

At the foot of Mt. Olympus, the island's highest peak, sits **Agiassos** village. It remains a lovely settlement, with gray stone houses, cobblestone lanes, a medieval castle, and the church of

Panayia Vrefokratousa. The latter was founded in the 12th century to house an icon believed to be the work of St. Luke.

In the main town of **Mytilini** there is a traditional Lesbos house, restored and furnished in 19th-century style, that people are permitted to visit. Call to arrange a time with owner Marika Vlachou. *Mitropleos 6, tel. 0251/28550. Admission free by appointment only.*

Shopping
In Mykonos Mykonos is the best of the Greek Islands for shopping. The main shopping street in Mykonos runs perpendicular to the harbor and is lined with jewelry stores, clothing stores, boutiques, cafés, and candy stores.

In Santorini For locally made items head to Oia, where you will find the best art galleries, antiques shops, craft shops, and stores that sell Byzantine reproductions. Boutiques abound in Thira as well.

In Rhodes Many attractive souvenir and handicrafts shops are in the Old Town, particularly on Sokratous Street, and just outside the walls vendors sell decorative Rhodian pottery, local embroidery, sea sponges, and relatively inexpensive jewelry.

In Lesbos Lesbos is famous for its chestnuts, olive oil, and ouzo. Agiassos is known for its wood crafts.

Beaches
In Mykonos Within walking distance of Mykonos Town are **Tourlos, Ayios Stefanos,** and **Ayios Ioannis. Psarou,** on the south coast, protected from wind by hills and surrounded by restaurants, offers a wide selection of water sports and is considered the finest beach.

In Santorini There is a red-sand beach below Akrotiri on the southwest shore. Long black-sand/volcanic beaches are found in Kamari and Perissa.

In Rhodes Rhodes Town and the more sheltered east coast have exquisite stretches of beach, while the west side can be choppy. **Elli** beach in town has fine sand. Much of the coast is developed, so you can reach the best beaches only through the hotels that occupy them. There also is a long nice stretch of beach between Haraki and Vlicha Bay.

In Lesbos Some of the most spectacular beaches are sandy coves in the southwest, including the stretch from Skala Eressou to Sigri. **Vatera,** one of the island's best beaches, lies southwest of Agiassos on the southeast side of the island.

Helsinki, Finland

Helsinki is a city of the sea, built on peninsulas and islands along the Baltic shoreline. Streets curve around bays, bridges arch over the nearby islands, and ferries carry traffic to destinations farther offshore. The smell of the sea hovers over the city, while the huge ships that ply the Baltic constantly come and go from the city's harbors. Helsinki has grown dramatically since World War II and now accounts for about one-sixth of the Finnish population. The city covers a total of 698 km (433 square mi) and includes 315 islands. Most of the city's sights, hotels, and restaurants, however, are on one peninsula—forming a compact hub of special interest to cruise passengers.

Currency The unit of currency in Finland is the Finnish mark, divided into 100 penniä. At press time, the exchange rate was about FIM 4.75 to the U.S. dollar. Credit cards are widely accepted, even in many taxicabs. Traveler's checks can be changed only in banks.

Telephones The country code for Finland is 358. Local calls can be made from public pay phones; have some FIM 1 and FIM 5 coins ready. Some pay phones only accept a phone card, the Tele kortti or HPY kortti, available at post offices, R-kiosks, and some grocery stores. They come in increments of FIM 30, 50, 100, and 150. You can dial North America directly from anywhere in Finland. To make a direct international phone call from Finland, dial 00, then the appropriate country code and phone number. For an **AT&T** long-distance operator, dial 9800–10010; **MCI,** 9800–10280; **Sprint,** 9800–10284.

Shore Excursions The following is a good choice in Helsinki. It may not be offered by all cruise lines. Time and price are approximate.

Heart of Helsinki. Take in the major sights, including the Senate Square, the Esplanade, and other Helsinki landmarks on this quick tour of the town. *2½ hrs. Cost: $30.*

Coming Ashore Ships calling at Helsinki dock harborside near Market Square. From here, you can easily spend the day exploring the city center on foot.

Getting Around If you want to use public transportation, your best buy is the Helsinki Card, which gives unlimited travel on city public transportation, as well as free entry to many museums, a free sightseeing tour, and a variety of other discounts. A one-day pass costs FIM 105; you can buy it at some hotels and travel agencies, Stockmann's department store, and the Helsinki City Tourist Office. Streetcars can be very handy and route maps and schedules are posted at most downtown stops. Single tickets are sold on board for FIM 7 (one ride without transfers) or FIM 9 (one ride with transfers). Taxis are all marked TAKSI. The meters start at FIM 30, with the fare rising on a kilometer basis. A listing of all taxi companies appears in the white pages under *Taksi*—try to choose one that is located nearby, because they charge from point of dispatch. The main phone number for taxi service is 700–700. Many accept credit cards.

Exploring Helsinki *Numbers in the margin correspond to points of interest on the Helsinki map.*

1 The **Kauppatori** (Market Square) is frequented by locals and tourists alike. Under bright orange tents you'll find stalls selling everything from colorful, freshly cut flowers to ripe fruit to vegetables trucked in from the hinterland to handicrafts made in small villages. Look at the fruit stalls—mountains of strawberries, raspberries, blueberries, and, if you're lucky, cloudberries. Watching over it all is the unmissable, curvaceous Havis Amanda statue. *At South Harbor, harborside at Eteläranta and Pohjoisesplanadi. Open year-round, Mon.–Sat. 7–2, and also arts and crafts 3:30–8 June–Aug.*

On the Pohjoisesplanadi (North Esplanade) is
2 the **Presidentinlinna** (President's Palace), built as a private home in 1818 and converted for use by the czars in 1843. It was the official residence of Finnish presidents from 1919 to 1993. It still houses the presidential offices and is the scene of official receptions. Visitors are not allowed inside. *Pohjoisesplanadi 1, tel. 09/641–200.*

At the district of **Katajanokka,** 19th-century brick warehouses are slowly being renovated to form a complex of boutiques, arts-and-crafts studios, and restaurants. You'll find innovative designs at these shops, and the restaurants tend to offer lighter fare, which can make this a tempting area in which to stop for lunch.

3 **Senaatintori** (Senate Square), the heart of neoclassical Helsinki, is dominated by the domed
4 **Tuomiokirkko** (Lutheran cathedral). The square is the work of Carl Ludvig Engel. The harmony created with the Tuomiokirkko, the main building of Helsinki University, and the State Council Building places you amid one of the purest styles of European architecture. Senaatintori has a dignified, stately air, enlivened in summer by sun worshipers who gather on the wide steps leading up to Tuomiokirkko and throughout the year by the bustle around the Kiseleff Bazaar on the square's south side. *North of City Hall. Tuomiokirkko open June–Aug., weekdays 9–5, Sat. 9–7, Sun. 9–8; Sept.–May, weekdays 10–4, Sat. 10–7, Sun. 10–4.*

5 Worth taking a look at is the old brick **Vanha Kauppahalli** (Old Market Hall)—with its voluminous displays of meat, fish, and other gastronomic goodies. *Eteläranta, along the South Harbor. Open weekdays 8–5, Sat. 8–2.*

6 The **Rautatieasema** (railway station) and its square form the bustling commuting hub of the city. The station's huge red-granite figures are by Emil Wikström, but the solid building they adorn was designed by Eliel Saarinen, one of the founders of the early 20th-century National Romantic style. *Kaivokatu, tel. 09/7071.*

7 The **Valtion Taidemuseo Ateneum** (Finnish National Gallery) houses both the Ateneum Museum of Finnish Art and the Museum of Contemporary Art, while the latter awaits its own building, which at press time was slated to open in spring 1998. *Kaivokatu 2–4, tel. 09/173–361. Admission: FIM 20. Open Tues. and Fri. 9–6, Wed. and Thurs. 9–9, weekends 11–5.*

In front of the main post office, west of the rail-
8 way station, is the **Mannerheimin patsas** (statue of Marshal Mannerheim), gazing down Mannerheimintie, the major thoroughfare named in his

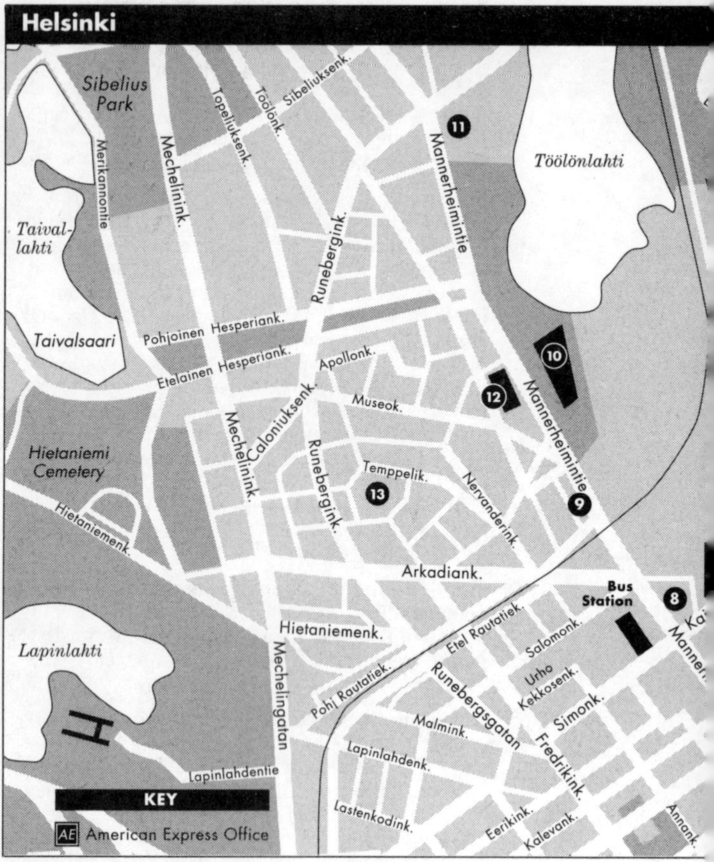

Eduskantatalo, **9**
Finlandiatalo, **10**
Kauppatori, **1**
Mannerheimin patsas, **8**
Presidentin-linna, **2**
Rautatieasema, **6**
Senaatintori, **3**
Suomen Kansallis-museo, **12**
Suomen Kansallis-ooppera, **11**
Temppeliaukion kirkko, **13**
Tuomiokirkko, **4**
Valtion Taidemuseo Ateneum, **7**
Vanha Kauppahalli, **5**

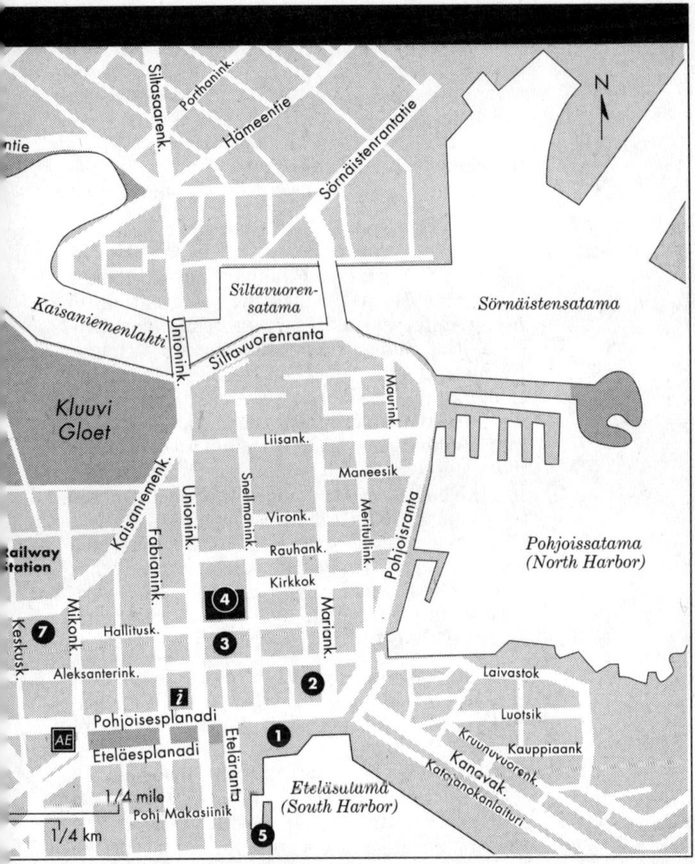

N
Siltasaarenk.
Porthanink.
Hämeentie
Sörnäistenrantatie
ntie
Siltavuoren-
satama
Sörnäistensatama
Kaisaniemenlahti
Unionink.
Siltavuorenranta
Kluuvi
Gloet
Maurink.
Liisank.
Maneesik
Kaisaniemenk.
Unionink.
Snellmanink.
Vironk.
Merituliink.
Pohjoisranta
Rauhank.
Fabianink.
Kirkkok
Pohjoissatama
(North Harbor)
ailway
tation
Mikonk.
Keskusk.
Hallitusk.
Mariank.
Aleksanterink.
Laivastok
Luotsik
Pohjoisesplanadi
AE
Eteläesplanadi
Eteläranta
Kruunuvuorenk.
Kauppiaank
Kanavak.
Katajanokanlaituri
Eteläsatama
(South Harbor)
1/4 mile
Pohj Makasiinik
1/4 km

honor. Perhaps no man in Finnish history is so revered as Baron Carl Gustaf Mannerheim, the military and political leader who guided Finland through much of the turbulent 20th century. When he died in Switzerland on January 28, 1951, his body was flown back to lie in state in the cathedral. For three days, young war widows, children, and soldiers filed past his bier.

About 1 km (½ mi) along, past the colonnaded
9 red-granite **Eduskantatalo** (Parliament House;
10 tel. 09/4321), stands **Finlandiatalo** (Finlandia
Hall; tel. 09/40241), one of the last creations of
Alvar Aalto, and, a bit farther up Mannerheim-
11 intie, the **Suomen Kansallisooppera** (Finnish
National Opera; tel. 09/4030–2350), a striking
example of Scandinavian architecture. If you
can't make it to a concert there, take a guided
tour. Behind the hall and the opera house lies
the inland bay of Töölönlahti, and almost oppo-
12 site the hall stands the **Suomen Kansallismuseo**
(National Museum), another example of National Romantic exotica in which Eliel Saarinen played a part. The museum, which normally has international cultural exhibits, is closed for renovation until December 1999. *Mannerheimintie 34, tel. 09/405–0470.*

Tucked away in a labyrinth of streets to the west
13 of the Opera is the strikingly modern **Temppel-**
iaukion kirkko (Temple Square Church). Carved out of solid rock and topped with a copper dome, this landmark is a center for church services and concerts. (From here it's only a short distance back to Mannerheimintie, where you can pick up any streetcar for the downtown area.) *Lutherinkatu 3, tel. 09/494–698. Open weekdays 10–8, Sat. 10–6, Sun. 11:45–1:45 and 3:30–5:45. Closed Tues. 1–2* PM *and during concerts and services.*

Shopping Helsinki's prime shopping districts run along **Pohjoisesplanadi** (North Esplanade) and **Aleksanterinkatu** in the city center. Along Pohjoisesplanadi and Eteläesplanadi, you'll find Finland's design houses, while antiques shops cluster in the neighborhood behind Senate Square, called **Kruununhaka.** The **Forum** (Mannerheimintie 20) is a modern, multistory shopping center with a wide variety of stores, including clothing, gifts, books, and toys. You can also make purchases until 10 PM daily in the shops along the Tunneli underpass underneath the railway station. Some shops in the **Kiseleff Bazaar Hall** (Aleksanterinkatu 22–28), which once housed Stockmann's and now has shops selling handicrafts, toys, and knitwear, are open on Sunday from noon to 4 in the summer. **Kalevala Koru** (Unioninkatu 25) has jewelry based on ancient Finnish designs.

Ibiza, Spain

Settled by the Carthaginians in the 5th century BC, Ibiza in the 20th century has been transformed by tourism. From a peasant economy, it became a wild, anything-goes gathering place for the international jet set and for the hippies of the 1960s—only to enter the 1990s with its principal resort, Sant Antoni, regarded as one of the most boorish, noisy, and brash on the Mediterranean. And yet, of the islands, only on Ibiza (and Formentera, the tiny island just off Ibiza's southern tip) will you find women in the fields dressed in the simple country costume of long black skirt and wide-brimmed straw hat, gathering almonds in their aprons or herding errant goats.

Currency The unit of currency in Spain is the peseta (pta.). At press time, the exchange rate was about 145 ptas. to the U.S. dollar.

Telephones The country code for Spain is 34. Pay phones generally take the new, smaller 5- and 25-pta. coins; the minimum charge for short local calls is 25 ptas. Area codes always begin with a 9 and are different for each province. If you're dialing from outside the country, drop the 9. Calling abroad can be done from any pay phone marked TELÉFONO INTERNACIONAL. Use 50-pta. (or 100-pta. if the phone takes them) coins initially, then coins of any denomination to prolong your call. Dial 07 for international, wait for the tone to change, then dial 1 for the United States or 0101 for Canada. For lengthy international calls, go to the *telefónica*, a telephone office, where an operator assigns you a private booth and collects payment at the end of the call; this is the least expensive and by far the easiest way of phoning abroad. **AT&T** (tel. 900/99–00–11); **MCI** (tel. 900/99–00–14); **Sprint** (tel. 900/99–00–13).

Shore Excursions The following is a good choice in Ibiza. It may not be offered by all lines. Time and price are approximate.

Sanctuaries of Ibiza. Explore Ibiza's Old World treasures from a 15th-century church to the fortified upper town. *4 hrs. Cost: $40.*

Coming Ashore Ships calling at Ibiza dock in the harbor at Eivissa. You can explore the town on foot, but to see the outlying areas of the island you will need to take a taxi or bus.

Exploring Ibiza Once a quiet fisherman's quarter, **Sa Penya** is the part of Eivissa that turned into a tourist mecca in the 1960s and it is full of restaurants and shops.

Dalt Vila, the walled upper town, is entered through Las Tablas, its main gate. On each side of the gate stands a statue, Roman in origin; both are now headless.

Inside the upper town, a ramp continues to the right and opens onto a long, narrow plaza lined with cafés. At the top of the hill lies the **cathedral,** which sits on the site of religious constructions from each of the cultures that have ruled Eivissa since the Phoenicians. Built in the 13th and 14th centuries and renovated in the 18th century, the cathedral has a Gothic tower and a baroque nave. The painted panels above a small vault adjoining the sacristy depict souls in purgatory being consumed by flames and tortured by devils while angels ascend to heaven. *At top of Carrer Major. Admission: 250 ptas. Open Sun.–Fri. 10–1 and 4–6:30, Sat. 10–1.*

The **Museu Dalt Vila** (Museum of Archaeology) in the upper town has a collection of Phoenician, Punic, and Roman artifacts. *Plaça Catedral 3, tel. 971/30–12–31. Admission: 450 ptas. Open Mon.–Sat. 10–1.*

A passageway leads between the cathedral and castle to the **Bastion of Sant Bernardo.** (There's a great view here of the wide bay.)

A Punic necropolis, with more than 3,000 tombs, has been excavated at **Puig des Molins.**

Many of the artifacts can be seen at the Museu Puig d'Es Molins (Punic Archaeological Museum), adjacent to the site. *Via Romana 31, tel. 971/30-17-71. Admission: 450 ptas. Open Mon.-Sat. 10-1.*

The **Museu d'Art Comtemporani** (Museum of Contemporary Art) is housed in the gateway's arch. *Ronda Pintor Narcis Putget s/n, tel. 971/130-27-23. Admission: 350 ptas. Open daily 10:30-1 and 6-8:30.*

Irish Coast and Cork

Hilly Cork is Ireland's second-largest city. The road to Cork City passes through the beautiful wooded glen of Glanmire and along the banks of the River Lee. In the center of Cork, the Lee divides in two, giving the city a profusion of picturesque quays and bridges. The name Cork derives from the Irish *corcaigh* (pronounced corky), meaning a marshy place. The city received its first charter in 1185 and grew rapidly in the 17th and 18th centuries with the expansion of its butter trade. It is now the major metropolis of the south, with a population of about 133,250.

Currency The unit of currency in Ireland is the pound, or punt (pronounced poont), written as IR£ to avoid confusion with the pound sterling. The currency is divided into 100 pence (written *p*). Although the Irish pound is the only legal tender in the republic, U.S. dollars and British currency are often accepted in large hotels and shops licensed as bureaux de change. The rate of exchange at press time was 62 pence to the U.S. dollar and 95 pence to the British pound sterling.

Telephones The country code for the Republic of Ireland is 353. There are pay phones in all post offices and most hotels and bars, as well as in street booths. Telephone cards are available at all post offices and most newsagents. Booths accepting cards are equally common as coin booths. For calls to the United States and Canada, dial 001 followed by the area code. To reach an **AT&T** long-distance operator, dial 1-800/550-000; **MCI**, 1-800/551-001; **Sprint**, 1-800/552-001.

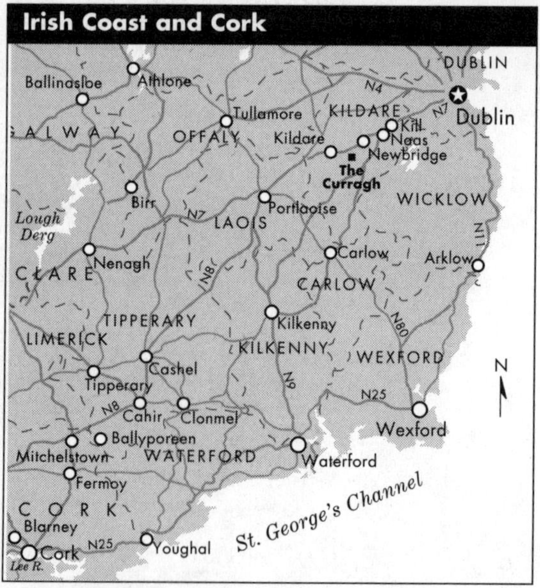

Shore Excursions The following are good choices in Cork. They may not be offered by all cruise lines. Times and prices are approximate.

Cork City and Blarney Tour. This is a good choice for passengers who want to visit Blarney. Upon reaching the village, you'll walk up the castle's steps to reach the famous Blarney stone. The tour also includes highlights of Cork city. *4 hrs. Cost: $42.*

Cobh Island and Whiskey Distillery. Drive through the seaside resort town of Cobh, the countryside, and Cork to reach Midleton for a visit to the Jameson Irish Whiskey Heritage Center. *4 hrs. Cost: $42.*

Coming Ashore Ships dock at the harbor of Cobh, which is around 24 km (15 mi) from the main district of Cork.

Getting Around Once in the compact main district of Cork, the best way to see the city and soak in its full flavor is on foot.

Exploring Cork Patrick Street is the focal point of Cork and its major shopping district (*see below*). In the hilly area to the north is the famous 120-ft **Shandon Steeple,** the bell tower of St. Anne's Church. It is shaped like a pepper pot and houses the bells immortalized in the song *The Bells of Shandon.* Visitors can climb the tower; read the inscriptions on the bells; and, on request, have them rung over Cork. *Admission: IR£1, with bell tower IR£1.50. Open May–Oct., Mon.–Sat. 9:30–5; Nov.–Apr., Mon.–Sat. 10–3:30.*

Cobh is an attractive hilly town dominated by its 19th-century **cathedral.** It was the first and last European port of call for transatlantic liners, one of which was the ill-fated *Titanic*. Cobh has other associations with shipwrecks: It was from here that destroyers were sent out in May 1915 to search for survivors of the *Lusitania,* torpedoed by a German submarine with the loss of 1,198 lives.

Cobh's maritime past and its links with emigration are documented in a IR£2 million heritage center known as the **Queenstown Project,** which opened in the town's old railway station in 1993. *Tel. 021/813–591. Admission: IR£3.50. Open Feb.–Nov., daily 10–6.*

Most visitors to Cork want to kiss the famous **Blarney Stone** in the hope of acquiring the "gift of the gab." Blarney itself, 8 km (5 mi) from Cork City, should not, however, be taken too seriously as an excursion. All that is left of Blarney Castle is its ruined central keep containing the celebrated stone. This is set in the battlements, and to kiss it, you must lie on the walk within the walls, lean your head back, and touch the stone with your lips. Nobody knows how the tradition originated, but Elizabeth I is credited with giving the word *blarney* to the language when, commenting on the unfulfilled promises of Cormac MacCarthy, Lord Blarney of the time, she remarked, "This is all Blarney; what he says, he never means." In Blarney village there are several good crafts shops, and the outing provides a good opportunity to shop around for traditional Irish goods at competitive prices. *Tel. 021/385–252. Admission: IR£3. Open Mon.–Sat. 9 to sundown, Sun. 9–5:30.*

Shopping Patrick Street is the main shopping area of Cork, and there you will find the city's two major department stores, **Roches** and **Cash's.** Cash's has a good selection of Waterford crystal. The liveliest place in town to shop is just off Patrick Street, to the west, near the city-center parking lot, in the pedestrian-only **Paul Street** area. **Mendows & Byrne** of Academy Street stocks the best in modern Irish design, including tableware, ceramics, knitwear, handwoven tweeds, and high fashion. The **Donegal Shop,** in Paul Street Piazza, specializes in made-to-order tweed suits and rainwear.

At the top of Paul Street is the **Crawford Art Gallery,** which has an excellent collection of 18th- and 19th-century views of Cork and mounts adventurous exhibitions by modern artists. *Emmet Pl., tel. 021/273–377. Admission free. Open weekdays 10–5, Sat. 9–1.*

Istanbul, Turkey

Turkey is one place to which the phrase "East meets West" really applies, both literally and figuratively. It is in Turkey's largest city, Istanbul, that the continents of Europe and Asia meet, separated only by the Bosporus, which flows 29 km (18 mi) from the Black Sea to the Sea of Marmara. On the vibrant streets of this city of 12 million people, miniskirts and trendy boots mingle with head scarves and prayer beads. People from as far away as Ghana, Sri Lanka, and the Philippines and as nearby as the central Asian republics and the former Soviet Union make their way to Istanbul in search of better lives.

Istanbul is noisy, chaotic, and exciting. Spires and domes of mosques and medieval palaces dominate the skyline. At dawn, when the muezzin's call to prayer rebounds from ancient minarets, many people are making their way home from the nightclubs and bars, while others are kneeling on their prayer rugs, facing Mecca. Day and night, Istanbul has a schizophrenic air to it. Women in jeans, business suits, or elegant designer outfits pass women wearing the long skirts and head coverings that villagers have worn for generations. Donkey-drawn carts vie with old Chevrolets and Pontiacs or shiny Toyotas and BMWs for dominance of the loud, narrow streets, and the world's most fascinating Oriental bazaar competes with Western boutiques for the time and attention of both tourists and locals.

Currency The monetary unit is the Turkish lira (TL). At press time, the exchange rate was 116,060 TL to the U.S. dollar. These rates are subject to wide fluctuation, so check close to your departure. Be certain to retain your original exchange slips when you convert money into Turkish lira—you will need them to reconvert the money. Because the Turkish lira is worth a lot less than most currencies, it's best to convert only what you plan to spend.

Telephones All telephone numbers in Turkey now have seven local digits plus three-digit city codes. Intercity calls are preceded by 0. Pay phones are yellow, push-button models. Most take *jetons* (tokens) although an increasing number, particularly in large cities, take phone cards. Multilingual directions are posted in phone booths. For all international calls dial 00, then dial the country code, area or city code, and the number. You can reach an international operator by dialing 132. To reach an **AT&T** long-distance operator, dial 00800–12277; **MCI,** 00800–11177; **Sprint,** 00800–14477.

Shore Excursions The following are good choices in Istanbul. They may not be offered by all lines. Times and prices are approximate.

Bazaar Sights. Visit the major city sights, including the Hippodrome, Blue Mosque, and Hagia Sophia, and shop at the Grand Bazaar, which should be a must on anyone's list of things to do. *4½ hrs. Cost: $40.*

Coming Ashore Ships dock on the Bosporus in Istanbul on the newer Asian side of the city. Across the Galata Bridge lie the city's main attractions.

Getting Around The best way to get around all the magnificent monuments in Sultanahmet in Old Istanbul is to walk. They're all within easy distance of one another. To get to other areas, you can take metered taxis, which are plentiful, inexpensive, and more comfortable than city buses. A tram

Arkeoloji Müzesi, **4**
Aya Irini, **2**
Çiçek Pasaji, **10**
Dolmabahçe Palace, **11**
Galata Tower, **9**
Hagia Sophia, **5**
Hippodrome, **7**
Merasim Avlusu, **3**
Sultan Ahmet Cami, **6**
Topkapı Saray, **1**
Türk Ve Islam Eserleri Müzesi, **8**

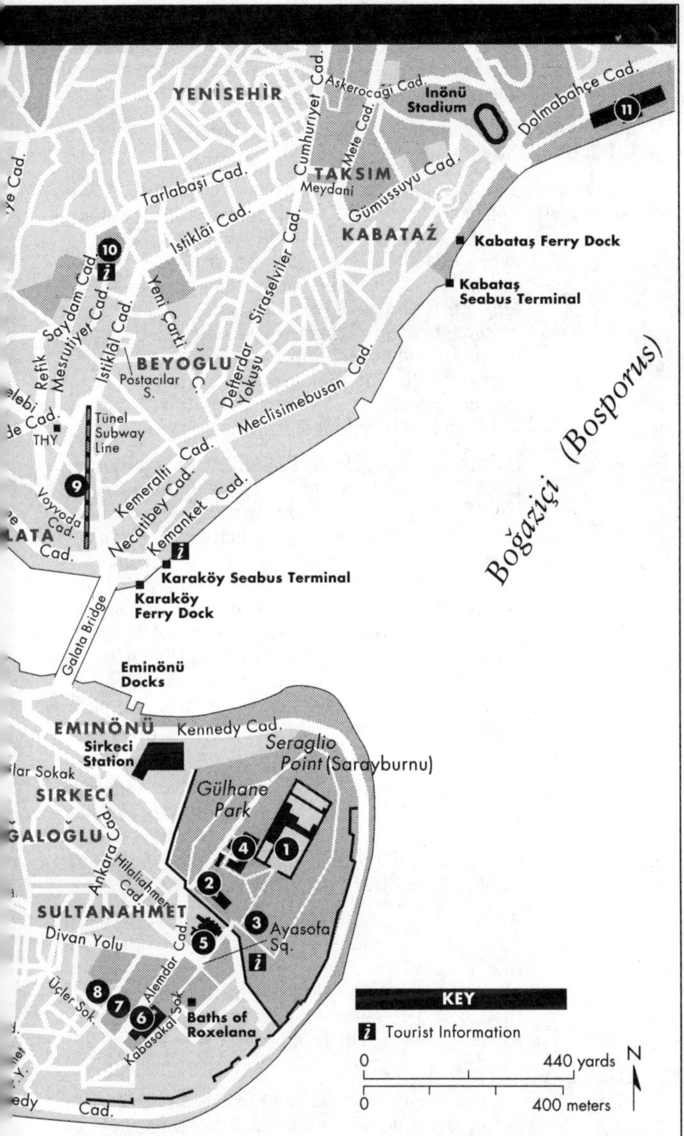
YENİSEHİR
Askerocaği Cad.
Inönü Stadium
Dolmabahçe Cad.
11
Cumhuriyet Cad.
Mete Cad.
TAKSIM Meydani
Gümüssuyu Cad.
Tarlabaşi Cad.
Istiklâi Cad.
KABATAŹ
Kabataş Ferry Dock
Kabataş Seabus Terminal
10
Saydam Cad.
Mesrutiyet Cad.
Istiklâl Cad.
Yeni Carti
Siraselviler Cad.
Refik
BEYOĞLU
Postacılar S.
Defterdar Yokuşu
Cad.
Meclisimebusan Cad.
Tünel Subway Line
THY
9
Voyvoda Cad.
Kemeralti Cad.
Necatibey Cad.
Kemanket Cad.
Cad.
Karaköy Seabus Terminal
Karaköy Ferry Dock
Galata Bridge
Boğaziçi (Bosporus)
Eminönü Docks
EMINÖNÜ
Kennedy Cad.
Sirkeci Station
Seraglio Point (Sarayburnu)
Sokak
SIRKECI
Gülhane Park
Ankara Cad.
4
1
Hilaliahmer Cad.
2
SULTANAHMET
3
Ayasofa Sq.
Divan Yolu
5
Alemdar Cad.
Üçler Sok.
8
7
6
Kabasakal Sok.
Baths of Roxelana
Cad.
KEY
Tourist Information
0
440 yards
0
400 meters
N

system runs from Topkapí, via Sultanahmet, to Sirkeci. Nostalgic trams run the length of İstiklâl Caddesi from Taksim to Tünel and cost about 25¢.

Exploring Istanbul

Numbers in the margin correspond to points of interest on the Istanbul map.

Old Istanbul (Sultanahmet)

1 The number one attraction in Istanbul is **Topkapí Saray** (Topkapí Palace), on Seraglio Point in Old Istanbul, known as Sultanahmet. The palace, which dates from the 15th century, was the residence of a number of sultans and their harems until the mid-19th century. To avoid the crowds, try to get there by 9 AM, when the gates open. If you're arriving by taxi, tell the driver you want the Topkapí Saray in Sultanahmet, or you could end up at the remains of the former Topkapí bus terminal on the outskirts of town.

Sultan Mehmet II built the first palace during the 1450s, shortly after the Ottoman conquest of Constantinople. Over the centuries, sultan after sultan added ever more elaborate architectural fantasies, until the palace eventually ended up with more than four courtyards and some 5,000 residents, many of them concubines and eunuchs. Topkapí was the residence and center of bloodshed and drama for the Ottoman rulers until the 1850s, when Sultan Abdül Mecit moved with his harem to the European-style Dolmabahçe Palace, farther up the Bosporus coast.

2 In Topkapí's outer courtyard are the **Aya Irini** (Church of St. Irene), open only during festival
3 days for concerts, and the **Merasim Avlusu** (Court of the Janissaries), originally for members of the sultan's elite guard.

Adjacent to the ticket office is the **Bab-i-Selam** (Gate of Salutation), built in 1524 by Suleyman the Magnificent, who was the only person allowed to pass through it. In the towers on either side, prisoners were kept until they were executed beside the fountain outside the gate in the first courtyard.

In the second courtyard, amid the rose gardens, is the **Divan-i-Humayun,** the assembly room of the council of state, once presided over by the grand vizier (prime minister). The sultan would sit behind a latticed window, hidden by a curtain so no one would know when he was listening, although occasionally he would pull the curtain aside to comment.

One of the most popular tours in Topkapí is the **Harem,** a maze of nearly 400 halls, terraces, rooms, wings, and apartments grouped around the sultan's private quarters on the west side of the second courtyard. Forty rooms are restored and open to the public. Next to the entrance are the quarters of the eunuchs and about 200 of the lesser concubines, who were lodged in tiny cubicles, as cramped and uncomfortable as the main rooms of the harem are large and opulent. Tours begin every half hour; because of the crowds during the height of the tourist season, buy a ticket for the harem tour soon after entering the palace.

In the third courtyard is the **Hazine Dairesi** (Treasury), four rooms filled with jewels, including two uncut emeralds, each weighing 3½ kilograms (7.7 pounds), that once hung from the ceiling. Here, too, you will be dazzled by the emerald dagger used in the movie *Topkapí* and the 84-carat "Spoonmaker" diamond, which according to legend, was found by a pauper and traded for three wooden spoons.

In the fourth and last courtyard of the Topkapí Palace are small, elegant summerhouses, mosques, fountains, and reflecting pools scattered amid the gardens on different levels. Here you will find the **Rivan Kiosk,** built by Murat IV in 1636 to commemorate the successful Rivan campaign. In another kiosk in the gardens, called the **Iftariye** (Golden Cage), the closest relatives of the reigning sultan lived in strict confinement under what amounted to house arrest. The custom began during the 1800s after the old custom of murdering all possible rivals to the throne had been abandoned. The confinement of the heirs apparently helped keep the peace, but it deprived them of any chance to prepare themselves for the formidable task of ruling a great empire. *Topkapí Palace, tel. 212/512–0480. Admission: $4.25, harem $1. Open Wed.–Mon. 9:30–5.*

To the left as you enter the outer courtyard of Topkapí Palace, a lane slopes downhill to three
4 museums grouped together: the **Arkeoloji Müzesi** (Archaeological Museum), which houses a fine collection of Greek and Roman antiquities, including finds from Ephesus and Troy; the **Eski Şark Eserleri Müzesi** (Museum of the Ancient Orient), with Sumerian, Babylonian, and Hittite treasures; and the **Çinili Köşkü** (Tiled Pavilion), which houses ceramics from the early Seljuk and Osmanli empires. *Tel. 212/520–7740. Admission: $2 includes all 3 museums. Open Tues.–Sun. 9:30–5.*

5 Just outside the walls of Topkapí Palace is **Hagia Sophia** (Church of the Divine Wisdom), one of the world's greatest examples of Byzantine architecture. Built in AD 532 under the supervision of Emperor Justinian, it took 10,000 men six years to complete. Hagia Sophia is made of ivory from Asia, marble from Egypt, and columns from the ruins of Ephesus. The dome was the world's largest until the dome at St. Peter's Basilica was built in Rome 1,000 years later. Hagia Sophia was the cathedral of Constantinople for 900 years, surviving earthquakes and looting Crusaders until 1453, when it was converted into a mosque by Mehmet the Conqueror. Minarets were added by succeeding sultans. Hagia Sophia originally had many mosaics depicting Christian scenes, which were plastered over by Suleyman I, who felt they were inappropriate for a mosque. In 1935, Atatürk converted Hagia Sophia into a museum. Shortly after that, American archaeologists discovered the mosaics, which were restored and are now on display.

According to legend, the **Sacred Column,** in the north aisle, "weeps water" that can work miracles. It's so popular that, over the centuries, believers have worn a hole through the marble and brass column with their constant caresses. You can stick your finger in it and make a wish. *Ayasofya Meyd., Sultanahmet, tel. 212/522–1750. Admission: $4.50. Open Tues.–Sun. 9:30–5.*

6 Across from Hagia Sophia is the **Sultan Ahmet Cami** (Blue Mosque), with its shimmering blue

tiles, 260 stained-glass windows, and six minarets, as grand and beautiful a monument to Islam as Hagia Sophia was to Christianity. Mehmet Ağa, also known as Sedefkar (Worker of Mother of Pearl), built the mosque during the reign of Sultan Ahmet I in eight years, beginning in 1609, nearly 1,100 years after the completion of Hagia Sophia. His goal was to surpass Justinian's masterpiece, and many believe he succeeded.

Press through the throngs and enter the mosque at the side entrance that faces Hagia Sophia. Remove your shoes and leave them at the entrance. Immodest clothing is not allowed, but an attendant will lend you a robe if he feels you are not dressed appropriately. *Sultanahmet Sq., no phone. Admission free. Open daily 9–5.*

The **Hünkar Kasri** (Carpet and Kilim museums) are in the mosque's stone-vaulted cellars and upstairs at the end of a stone ramp, where the sultans rested before and after their prayers. *Tel. 212/518–1330. Admission: $1.50. Call for hrs.*

7 The **Hippodrome** is a long park directly in front of the Blue Mosque. As a Roman stadium with 100,000 seats, it was once the focal point for city life, including chariot races, circuses, and public executions. Disputes between fans of rival chariot teams often degenerated into violence. In 531, 30,000 people died in the Hippodrome in what came to be known as the Nike riots. What remain today are the **Dikilitas** (Egyptian Obelisk), the **Örme Sütun** (Column of Constantinos), and the **Yilanli Sütun** (Serpentine Column), taken from the Temple of Apollo at Delphi in Greece. *Atmeydanı, Sultanahmet. Admission free.*

On the western side of the Hippodrome is **Ibrahim Paşa Palace,** the grandiose residence of the son-in-law and grand vizier of Suleyman the Magnificent. Ibrahim Paşa was executed when he became too powerful for Suleyman's liking.
8 The palace now houses the **Türk Ve Islâm Eserleri Müzesi** (Museum of Turkish and Islamic Arts), which gives superb insight into the lifestyles of Turks of every level of society, from the 8th century to the present. *Şifahane Sok, across*

from the Blue Mosque, in line with the Serpentine Column, tel. 212/518–1385 or 212/518–1805. Admission: $2. Open Tues.–Sun. 9:30–5.

New Town New Town is the area on the northern shore of the Golden Horn, the waterway that cuts through Istanbul and divides Europe from Asia. The area's most prominent landmark is the

9 **Galata Tower,** built by the Genoese in 1349 as part of their fortifications. In this century, it served as a fire lookout until 1960. Today it houses a restaurant and nightclub, and a viewing tower. *Büyük Hendek Cad., tel. 212/245–1160. Admission: $1. Open daily 9–8.*

10 North of the tower is the **Çiçek Pasaji** (Flower Arcade), off İstiklâl Caddesi, a lively blend of tiny restaurants, bars, and street musicians. Strolling farther on İstiklâl Caddesi is an experience in itself. The busy pedestrian road is lined with shops, restaurants, banks, and cafés in turn-of-the-century buildings. The restored original 19th-century tram still carries people from Tünel to Taksim Square. On the side streets you'll find Greek and Armenian churches, bars, and other establishments; in the narrow, poorer residential alleys, you'll see laundry hanging between the old buildings, as you dodge through the children at play.

11 The **Dolmabahçe Palace** was built in 1853 and, until the declaration of the modern republic in 1923, was the residence of the last sultans of the Ottoman Empire. It was also the residence of Atatürk, who died here in 1938. The palace, floodlit at night, is an extraordinary mixture of Hindu, Turkish, and European styles of architecture and interior design. Queen Victoria's contribution to the lavishness was a chandelier weighing 4½ tons. Guided tours of the palace take about 80 minutes. *Gümüssuyu Cad., tel. 212/258–5544. Admission: $10 for long tour, $5.50 for short tour. Open Apr.–Oct. 9–4; Nov.–Mar. 9–3. Closed Mon. and Thurs.*

Shopping The **Kapalı Çarşışı** (Grand Bazaar) is what it sounds like: a smattering of all things Turkish—carpets, brass, copper, jewelry, textiles, and leather goods. A shopper's paradise, it lies about ½ km (¼ mi) northwest of the Hippodrome (*see* Exploring, *above*), a 15-minute walk or five-minute taxi ride. Also called the Covered Bazaar, this maze of 65 winding, covered streets hides 4,000 shops, tiny cafés, and restaurants. Originally built by Mehmet the Conqueror in the 1450s, it was ravaged by two modern-day fires, one in 1954 that virtually destroyed it, and a smaller one in 1974. In both cases, the bazaar was quickly rebuilt. It's filled with thousands of curios, including carpets, fabrics, clothing, brass ware, furniture, icons, and gold jewelry. *Yeniçeriler Cad. and Fuatpaşa Cad. Admission free. Open Apr.–Oct., Mon.–Sat. 8:30–7; Nov.–Mar., Mon.–Sat. 8:30–6:30.*

Tünel Square, a quick, short metro ride up from Karaköy, is a quaint group of stores with old prints, books, and artifacts.

Bargaining The best part of shopping in Turkey is visiting the *bedestans* (bazaars), all brimming with copper and brass items, hand-painted ceramics, alabaster and onyx goods, fabrics, richly colored carpets, and relics and icons trickling in from the former Soviet Union. The key word for shopping in the bazaars is "bargain." You must be willing to bargain, and bargain hard. It's great fun once you get the hang of it. As a rule of thumb, offer 50% less after you're given the initial price and be prepared to go up by about 25% to 30% of the first asking price. It's both bad manners and bad business to underbid grossly or to start bargaining if you're not serious about buying. Part of the fun of roaming through the bazaars is having a free glass of *çay* (tea), which vendors will offer you whether you're a serious shopper or just browsing. Outside the bazaars prices are usually fixed. Beware of antiques: Chances are you will end up with an expensive fake, but even if you do find the genuine article, it's illegal to export antiques of any type.

Limassol, Cyprus

The Mediterranean island of Cyprus was once a center for the cult of Aphrodite, the Greek goddess who is said to have risen naked and perfect from the sea near what is now the beach resort of Paphos.

The influence of diverse cultures adds to the island's appeal to cruise passengers. Many fortifications built by the Crusaders and the Venetians still stand. The tomb of the Prophet Mohammed's aunt (Hala Sultan Tekke), on the shores of the great salt lake near Larnaca, is one of Islam's most important shrines. A piece of the true cross is said to exist in the Monastery of Stavrovouni, and Paphos has the remains of a pillar to which St. Paul was allegedly tied and beaten for preaching Christianity.

The upheavals are not over. Following independence from the British in 1960, the island became the focus of Greek-Turkish contention. Currently nearly 80% of the population are Greek Cypriots and 18% are Turkish Cypriots. Since 1974 Cyprus has been divided by a thin buffer zone—occupied by United Nations (UN) forces—between the Turkish Cypriot north and the Greek Cypriot south. The zone cuts right through the capital city of Nicosia. Talks aimed at uniting the communities into one bizonal federal state have been going on for years. The U.S. government is now involved in trying to resolve the dispute, and with the Republic of Cyprus anxious to join the European Union, governments from that organization's member countries are taking a greater interest, too.

Currency The monetary unit in the Republic of Cyprus is the Cyprus pound (C£), which is divided into 100 cents. At press time, the rate of exchange was C£0.46 to the U.S. dollar.

Telephones To reach an **AT&T** long-distance operator, dial 080–90010; **MCI,** 080–90000; **Sprint,** 080–90001. Public phones may require a deposit of a coin or phone card when you call these services.

Shore Excursions The following are good choices in Limassol. They may not be offered by all cruise lines. Times and prices are approximate.

Paphos Castle. A drive along the southwest of Cyprus leads to vineyards, coastal scenery, and the Paphos castle for a tour. *4½ hrs. Cost: $35.*

Kolossi Castle and Curium Ruins. Visit a Crusader castle and Cyprus's Greek and Roman ruins after a drive through the countryside. *3 hrs. Cost: $36.*

Village Tour. Journey through the country to explore three quaint villages—Omodos, Platres, and Lania. *3½ hrs. Cost: $36.*

Coming Ashore

Ships dock at Limassol, a commercial port and wine-making center on the south coast. The city is a bustling, cosmopolitan town popular with tourists. Luxury hotels, apartments, and guest houses stretch along 12 km (7 mi) of seafront. The nightlife is lively. In central Limassol, the elegant modern shops of Makarios Avenue contrast with those of the old part of town, where you'll discover local handicrafts.

Getting Around

Shared taxis accommodate four to seven passengers and are a cheap, fast, and comfortable way of traveling. Seats must be booked by phone, and passengers may embark/disembark anywhere within the town boundaries. The taxis run every half hour Monday–Saturday 5:45 AM–6:30 PM. Sunday service is less frequent and rides must be booked one day ahead. Drivers are bound by law to use and display a meter. In-town journeys range from C£1.50 to about C£3.

Exploring Limassol

Near the old port is **Limassol Fort,** a 14th-century castle built on the site of an earlier Byzantine fortification. According to tradition, Richard the Lionhearted married his future queen of England here in 1191. *Near old port.*

The **Cyprus Medieval Museum** at Limassol Fort displays a variety of medieval armor and relics. *Near old port, tel. 05/330132. Admission: 50¢. Open weekdays 7:30–5, Sat. 9–5, Sun. 10–1.*

For a glimpse of Cypriot folklore, visit the **Folk Art Museum** on St. Andrew's Street. The collection includes national costumes and fine examples of the island's crafts and woven materials. *St. Andrews St., tel. 05/362303. Admission: 30¢. Open Mon. and Wed.–Fri. 8:30–1:30 and 4–7:30, Tues. 8:30–1:30.*

The **Troodos Mountains,** north of Limassol, are popular in summer for the shade of their cedar and pine forests and the coolness of their springs. Small, painted churches in the Troodos and Pitsilia foothills are rich examples of a rare indigenous art form. Asinou Church and St. Nicholas of the Roof, south of Kakopetria, are especially noteworthy. Nearby is the Tall Trees Trout Farm, a shady oasis serving delicious fresh fish meals. Be sure to visit the Kykko Monastery, whose prized icon of the Virgin is reputed to have been painted by St. Luke.

Curium (Kourion), west of Limassol, has numerous Greek and Roman ruins. There is an amphitheater, where actors occasionally present classical and Shakespearean drama. Next to the theater is the Villa of Eustolios, a summerhouse that belonged to a wealthy Christian. A nearby Roman stadium has been partially rebuilt. Three kilometers (2 miles) farther along the main Paphos road is the Sanctuary of Apollo Hylates (Apollo of the Woodlands), an impressive archaeological site. *Admission: C£1. Open daily 7:30–sunset.*

Other places to visit include **Kolossi Castle,** a Crusader fortress of the Knights of St. John, a 15-minute drive outside Limassol; and the fishing harbor of **Latchi** on the west coast, 32 km (20 mi) north of Paphos. Near Latchi are the **Baths of Aphrodite,** where the goddess of love is said to have seduced swains. The wild and undeveloped Akamas Peninsula is perfect for a hike.

Lisbon, Portugal

Portugal's capital presents unending treats for the eye. Its wide boulevards are bordered by black-and-white mosaic sidewalks made of tiny cobblestones called *calçada*. Modern, pastel-color apartment blocks vie for attention with art nouveau houses faced with decorative tiles. Winding, hilly streets provide scores of *miradouros*, natural vantage points that offer spectacular views of the river and the city. Lisbon is not easy to explore on foot. The steep inclines of many streets present a tough challenge to cruise passengers, and places that appear to be close to one another on a map are sometimes on different levels. Yet the effort is worthwhile—judicious use of trams, the funicular railway, and the majestic city-center vertical lift (also called the *elevador*) make walking tours enjoyable even on the hottest summer day.

Currency The unit of currency in Portugal is the escudo, which can be divided into 100 centavos. At press time, the exchange rate was about 150$00 to the U.S. dollar. Owing to the complications of dealing in millions of escudos, 1,000$00 is always called a *conto*.

Telephones The country code for Portugal is 351. Public telephones are easily found; older models accept coins, while phones marked CREDIFONE take phone cards (available at post offices and tobacconists). International and collect calls can be made from most public telephones as well as from main post offices, which almost always have a supply of phone cabins—you'll be assigned a booth and payment will be collected at the end of the call. Access numbers to reach American long-distance operators are: for **AT&T,** 050–171288; **MCI,** 050–171234; **Sprint,** 050–171877.

Shore Excursions The following are good choices in Lisbon. They may not be offered by all cruise lines. Times and prices are approximate.

Lisbon Highlights. If you'd rather not do a lot of walking, sign up for this tour of Lisbon's many moods. *4 hrs. Cost: $40.*

Walking the City. Tour the Alfama district on foot, visiting St. George's Castle, Santa Justa Elevator, Rossio Square, and Black Horse Square. *4 hrs. Cost: $32.*

Coming Ashore Ships dock at the Fluvial terminal, adjacent to Praça do Comércio. Lisbon is a hilly city, and the sidewalks are paved with cobblestones, so walking can be tiring, even when you're wearing comfortable shoes.

Getting Around Lisbon's tram service is one of the best in Europe, and buses go all over the city. A Tourist Pass for unlimited rides on the tram, bus, metro, or the *elevador* (funicular railway system) costs 430$00 for one day's travel. Cabs can be easily recognized by a lighted sign on green roofs. There are taxi stands in the main squares, and you can usually catch one cruising by, though this can be difficult late at night. Taxis are metered and take up to four passengers at no extra charge. Rates start at 300$00.

Alfama, **2**
Castelo de São Jorge, **1**
Fundação Calouste Gulbenkian , **7**
Igreja de São Roque, **9**
Instituto do Vinho do Porto, **8**
Museu de Artes Decorativas, **3**
Parque Eduardo VII, **6**
Rossío, **5**
Sé, **4**

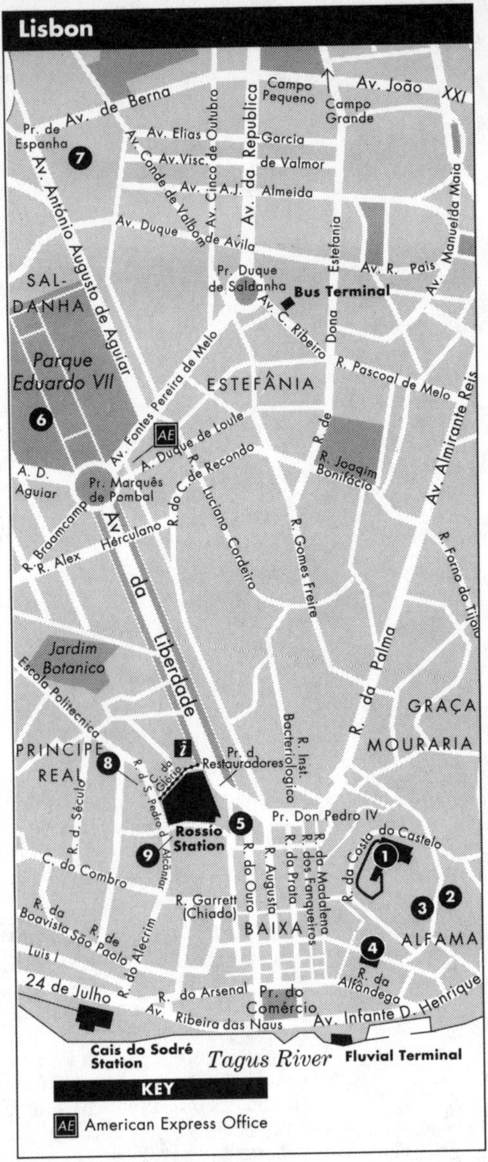

Numbers in the margin correspond to points of interest on the Lisbon map.

Exploring Lisbon

The Moors, who imposed their rule on most of the southern Iberian Peninsula during the 8th century, left their mark on Lisbon in many ways. The most visible examples are undoubt-
1 edly the imposing **Castelo de São Jorge** (St. George's Castle), set on one of the city's highest hills, and the Alfama, a district of narrow, twisting streets that wind their way up toward the castle. The best way to tour this area of Lisbon is to take a taxi to the castle and walk down.

Although the Castelo de São Jorge is Moorish in construction, it stands on the site of a fortification used by the Visigoths in the 5th century. The castle walls enclose the ruins of a Muslim palace that was the residence of the kings of Portugal until the 16th century; there is also a small village with a surviving church, a few simple houses, and souvenir shops. Inside the main gate are terraces offering panoramic views of Lisbon; be wary of slippery footing. *No phone. Admission free. Open Apr.–Sept., daily 9–9; Oct.–Mar., daily 9–7.*

2 **Alfama,** a warren of streets below St. George's Castle, is a jumble of whitewashed houses, with their flower-laden balconies and red-tile roofs resting on a foundation of dense bedrock. It's a notorious place for getting lost, but it's relatively compact, and you'll keep coming upon the same main squares and streets.

3 The **Museu de Artes Decorativas** (Museum of Decorative Arts) is housed in an 18th-century mansion. More than 20 workshops teach rare handicrafts—bookbinding, ormolu, carving, and cabinetmaking. *Largo das Portas do Sol 2, tel. 01/886–2183. Admission: 500$00. Open Wed., and Fri.–Sun. 10–5, Tues. and Thurs. 10–8.*

4 The **Sé** (cathedral), founded in 1150 to commemorate the defeat of the Moors three years earlier, has an austere Romanesque interior enlivened by a splendid 13th-century cloister. *Largo da Sé, no phone. Admission to cathedral free,*

cloister 100$00, sacristy 300$00. Open daily 9–noon and 2–6.

5 **Rossío** (officially, Praça Dom Pedro IV), Lisbon's principal square, which in turn opens on its northwestern end into the Praça dos Restauradores, can be considered the beginning of modern Lisbon. Here the broad, tree-lined Avenida da Liberdade begins its northwesterly ascent; it ends just over 1½ km (1 mi) away at the green expanses of the Parque Eduardo VII.

6 In the **Parque Eduardo VII,** rare flowers, trees, and shrubs thrive in the *estufa fria* (cold greenhouse) and the *estufa quente* (hot greenhouse). *Parque Eduardo VII, tel. 01/388–2278. Admission to greenhouses: 75$00. Open winter, daily 9–5; summer, daily 9–6.*

7 The renowned **Fundação Calouste Gulbenkian** is a cultural trust whose museum houses treasures collected by Armenian oil magnate Calouste Gulbenkian (1869–1955) and donated to the people of Portugal. There are superb examples of Greek and Roman coins, Persian carpets, Chinese porcelain, and paintings by such old masters as Rembrandt and Rubens, as well as Impressionist and pre-Raphaelite works. *Av. de Berna 45, tel. 01/795–0236. Admission: 200$00, free Sun. Open June–Sept., Tues., Thurs., Fri., and Sun. 10–5, Wed. and Sat. 2–7:30; Oct.–May, Tues.–Sun. 10–5.*

8 In the cozy, clublike lounge at the **Instituto do Vinho do Porto** (Port Wine Institute), visitors can sample from more than 300 types and vintages of Portugal's most famous beverage—from the extra-dry white varieties to the older ruby-red vintages. *Rua S. Pedro de Alcântara 45, tel. 01/342–3307. Admission free. Prices of tastings vary, starting at 200$00. Open Mon.–Sat. 10–10.*

9 The highly decorative **Igreja de São Roque** (Church of St. Roque) is best known for the flamboyant 18th-century Capela de São João Baptista (Chapel of St. John the Baptist), but it is nonetheless a showpiece in its own right. Adjoining the church is the Museu de Arte Sacra (Museum of Sacred Art). *Largo Trinidade*

Coelho, tel. 01/346–0361. Church open daily 8:30–6. Museum admission: 150$00, free Sun. Open Tues.–Sat. 10–noon and 1–5, Sun. 1–5.

To see the best examples of that uniquely Portuguese, late-Gothic architecture known as Manueline, head for **Belém,** at the far southwestern edge of Lisbon.

The **Mosteiro dos Jerónimos** (Jerónimos Monastery), in the Praça do Império, is an impressive structure conceived and planned by King Manuel I at the beginning of the 16th century to honor the discoveries of Vasco da Gama. Construction began in 1502 and was largely financed by treasures brought back from the so-called *descobrimentos*—the "discoveries" made by the Portuguese in Africa, Asia, and South America. Don't miss the stunning double cloister with its arches and pillars heavily sculpted with marine motifs. *Praça do Império, tel. 01/362–0034. Admission to church free, cloisters: 400$00, free Sun. Open June–Sept., Tues.–Sun. 10–6:30; Oct.–May, Tues.–Sun. 10–1 and 2:30–5.*

The **Museu de Marinha** (Maritime Museum) is at the west end of the Mosteiro dos Jerónimos monastery. Its huge collection reflects Portugal's long seafaring tradition, and exhibits range from early maps, model ships, and navigational instruments to entire fishing boats and royal barges. *Praça do Império, tel. 01/362–0010. Admission: 250$00, free Sun. 10–1. Open Tues.–Sun. 10–6.*

The **Torre de Belém** (Belém Tower) is another fine example of Manueline architecture, with openwork balconies, loggia, and domed turrets. Although it was built in the early 16th century on an island in the middle of the River Tagus, today the tower stands near the north bank—the river's course has changed over the centuries. *Av. de India, tel. 01/301–6892. Admission: 400$00 June–Sept., 250$00 Oct.–May. Open June–Sept., Tues.–Sun. 10–6; Oct.–May, Tues.–Sun. 10–1 and 2:30–5.*

Shopping

The **Baixa** (Rua Augusta between the Rossío and the River Tagus), one of Lisbon's main shopping and banking districts, features a small crafts market, some of the best shoe shops in

Europe, glittering jewelry stores, and a host of delicatessens selling anything from game birds to *queijo da serra*—a delicious mountain cheese from the Serra da Estrela range north of Lisbon.

On Avenida Engeneiro Duarte Pacheco, west of Parque Eduardo VII, the blue-and-pink towers of the **Amoreiras,** a huge modern shopping center, dominate the Lisbon skyline. *Open daily 9 AM–11 PM.*

The ***Feira da Ladra*** (flea market) is held on Tuesday morning and all day Saturday in the Largo de Santa Clara behind the Church of São Vicente, near the Alfama district.

London/Southampton, England

Southampton—a traditional terminal port for transatlantic crossings and the starting point for many historic voyages, including that of the *Mayflower*—is the port for ships calling at London, a city with a vibrant artistic, cultural, and commercial life. Modern London began to evolve in the Middle Ages, more than 600 years ago, and still standing is much of the work of Christopher Wren, the master architect chiefly responsible for reconstruction after the disastrous Great Fire of 1666. Traditionally London has been divided between the City, to the east, where its banking and commercial interests lie, and Westminster to the west, the seat of the royal court and of government. Today the distinction between the two holds good, and even the briefest exploration will reveal each area's distinct atmosphere. It is also in these two areas that you will find most of the grand buildings that have played a central role in British history: the Tower of London and St. Paul's Cathedral, Westminster Abbey and the Houses of Parliament, Buckingham Palace, and the older royal palace of St. James's.

Currency The British unit of currency is the pound sterling, divided into 100 pence (p). At press time, exchange rates were approximately U.S.$1.65 to the pound.

Telephones The United Kingdom's country code is 44. If calling the United Kingdom from abroad, drop the initial zero from the area code. Phone booths are not hard to find; other than on the street, the best place to find a bank of pay phones is in a hotel or large post office. The workings of coin-operated telephones vary, but there are usually instructions in each unit. Most take 10p, 20p, 50p, and £1 coins. A Phonecard is also available; it comes in denominations of 10, 20, 40, and 100 units and can be bought in a number of retail outlets. Cardphones, which are clearly marked with a special green insignia, will not accept coins. The cheapest way to make an overseas call is to dial it yourself—but be sure to have plenty of coins or phone cards close at hand. After you have inserted the coins or card, dial 010 (the international code), then the country code—for the United States, it is 1—followed by the area code and local number. To reach an **AT&T** long-distance operator, dial 0500890011; **MCI,** 0800890222; for **Sprint,** 0800890877 (from a British Telecom phone) or 0500890877 (from a Mercury Communications phone). To make a collect or other operator-assisted call, dial 155.

Shore Excursions Most cruise lines use Southampton as an embarkation or disembarkation point. Your best bet is to add a few days to your cruise to visit London. You can either arrange your own package or book a line's pre- or post-cruise package.

The following is a good choice should you want to tour sights near Southampton. It may not be offered by all cruise lines. Time and price are approximate.

Salisbury and Stonehenge. An hour from Southampton lies Salisbury Cathedral, which was built in AD 1220. After a walk through town and lunch, continue to Stonehenge. *Full day. Cost: $90.*

Coming Ashore Ships dock at the Southampton terminal. Southampton's attractions are a short drive from the pier; London is about an hour and a half from Southampton by bus. Places such as Winchester, Stonehenge, Salisbury, and Bath are not far from Southampton.

Getting Around London, although not simple of layout, is a rewarding walking city, and this remains the best way to get to know its nooks and crannies. If you want, you can take "the tube," London's extensive Underground system, which is by far the most widely used form of city transportation. Trains run both beneath and above the ground out into the suburbs, and all stations are clearly marked with the London Underground circular symbol. (A SUBWAY sign refers to an under-the-street crossing.)

There are 13 Underground lines—all named and identifiable by color. The latest is the Docklands Light Railway, which runs from Bank, in the City, and Stratford, east London, to Island Gardens at the edge of the Docklands. This connects to Greenwich thanks to the old foot tunnel under the River Thames, used by dockers in days gone by. The Central, District, Northern, Metropolitan, and Piccadilly lines all have branches, so be sure to note which branch is needed for your particular destination. Electronic platform signs tell you the final stop and route of the next train, and most signs also indicate how many minutes you'll have to wait for the train to arrive. A pocket map of the entire tube network is available free from most Underground ticket counters. One-day Travelcards are a good buy. These allow unrestricted travel on the tube, most buses, and British Rail trains in the Greater London zones and are valid weekdays after 9:30 AM, weekends, and all public holidays. They cannot be used on airbuses, night buses, or for certain special services. The price is £2.80–£3.80.

London's black taxis are famous for their comfort and for the ability of their drivers to remember the mazelike pattern of the capital's streets. Hotels and main tourist areas have ranks (stands) where you wait your turn to take one of the taxis that drive up. You can also hail a taxi if the flag is up or the yellow FOR HIRE sign is lighted. Fares start at £1.40; surcharges of 40p–60p are a tricky addition, used for extra passengers, bulky luggage, and the like.

Exploring London

Numbers in the margin correspond to points of interest on the London map.

Westminster is the royal backyard—the traditional center of the royal court and of government. Here, within a kilometer or so of one another, are virtually all of London's most celebrated buildings (St. Paul's Cathedral and the Tower of London excepted). Generations of kings and queens and their offspring have lived here since the end of the 11th century—including the current monarch. The Queen resides at Buckingham Palace through most of the year; during summer periods when she visits her country estates, the palace is partially open to visitors.

1 **Trafalgar Square** dates from about 1830. In short, it is London's most famous and festive square, as it presides over many a political demonstration, a raucous New Year's party, and the highest concentration of bus stops and pigeons in the capital. A statue of Lord Nelson, victor over the French in 1805 at the Battle of Trafalgar, at which he lost his life, stands atop a column. Huge stone lions guard the base of the column, which is decorated with four bronze panels depicting naval battles against France and cast from French cannons captured by Nelson. The bronze equestrian statue on the south side of the square is of the unhappy Charles I; he is looking down Whitehall toward the spot where he was executed in 1649.

2 In the **National Gallery,** which occupies the long neoclassical building on the north side of Trafalgar Square, is a comprehensive collection of paintings, with works from virtually every famous artist and school from the 14th to the 19th century. The gallery is especially strong on Flemish and Dutch masters, Rubens and Rembrandt among them, and on Italian Renaissance works. The Sainsbury Wing houses the early Renaissance collection. *Trafalgar Sq., tel. 0171/839–3321; 0171/839–3526 recorded information. Admission free; charge for special exhibitions. Open Mon.–Sat. 10–6, Sun. 2–6; June–Aug., also Wed. until 8.*

3 At the foot of Charing Cross Road is a second major art collection, the **National Portrait Gallery,** which contains portraits of well-known (and not so well-known) Britons, including monarchs, statesmen, and writers. *2 St. Martin's Pl., at foot of Charing Cross Rd., tel. 0171/930–*

London

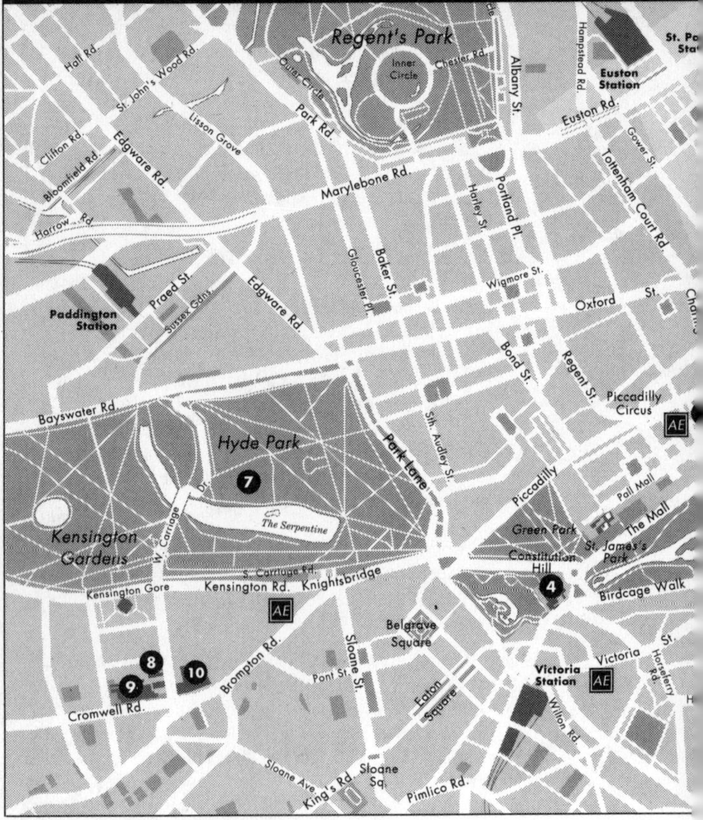

British Museum, **11**

Buckingham Palace, **4**

Hyde Park, **7**

Lloyd's of London, **13**

National Gallery, **2**

National Portrait Gallery, **3**

Natural History Museum, **9**

Parliament Square, **5**

St. Paul's Cathedral, **12**

Science Museum, **8**

Tower of London, **14**

Trafalgar Square, **1**

Victoria and Albert Museum, **10**

Westminster Abbey, **6**

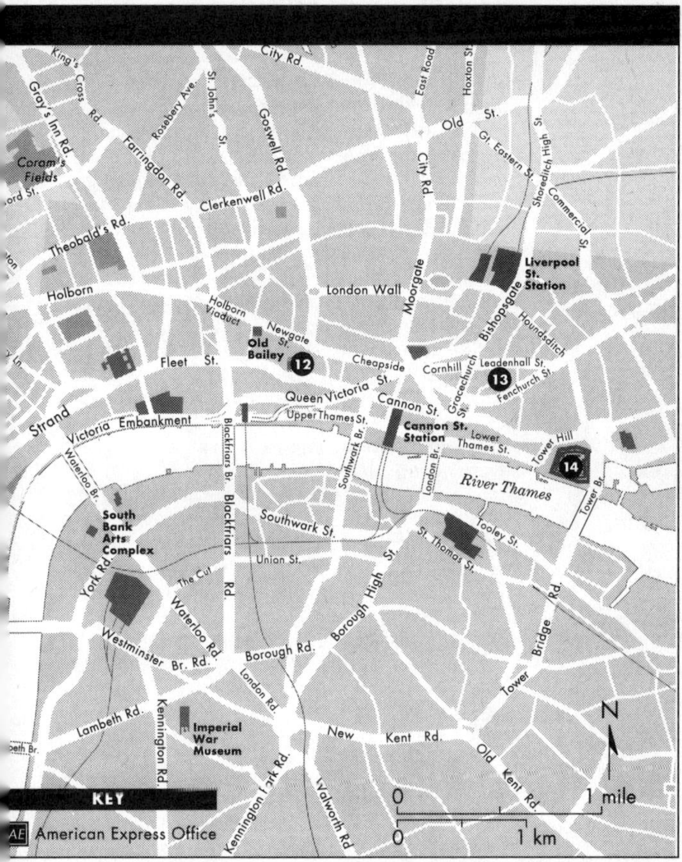
City Rd.
King's Cross Rd.
Gray's Inn Rd.
Coram's Fields
Rosebery Ave.
St. John's St.
Goswell Rd.
Farringdon Rd.
Clerkenwell Rd.
Theobald's Rd.
Holborn
Holborn Viaduct
Newgate St.
Old Bailey
12
Fleet St.
Strand
Victoria Embankment
London Wall
Moorgate
East Road
Hoxton St.
Old St.
City Rd.
Gt. Eastern St.
Shoreditch High St.
Commercial St.
Liverpool St. Station
Bishopsgate
Houndsditch
Cheapside
Cornhill
Gracechurch St.
Leadenhall St.
13
Fenchurch St.
Queen Victoria St.
Cannon St.
Upper Thames St.
Cannon St. Station
Lower Thames St.
Tower Hill
14
Blackfriars Br.
Southwark Br.
London Br.
River Thames
Tower Br.
Waterloo Br.
South Bank Arts Complex
Blackfriars Rd.
Southwark St.
Union St.
Tooley St.
St. Thomas St.
Borough High St.
York Rd.
The Cut
Waterloo Rd.
Westminster Br. Rd.
Borough Rd.
London Rd.
Tower Bridge Rd.
Lambeth Rd.
Kennington Rd.
Imperial War Museum
New Kent Rd.
Old Kent Rd.
Kennington Park Rd.
Walworth Rd
N
0
1 mile
0
1 km
KEY
AE American Express Office

1552. Admission free. Open weekdays 10–5, Sat. 10–6, Sun. 2–6.

4 **Buckingham Palace** is the London home of the queen and the administrative hub of the entire royal family. When the queen is in residence (normally on weekdays except in Jan., Aug., Sept., and part of June), the royal standard flies over the east front. Inside there are dozens of splendid state rooms used on such formal occasions as banquets for visiting heads of state. The private apartments of Queen Elizabeth and Prince Philip are in the north wing. Behind the palace lie some 40 acres of private gardens, a wildlife haven. The ceremony of the Changing of the Guard takes place in front of the palace at 11:30 daily, May through July, and on alternate days during the rest of the year. It's advisable to arrive early, since people are invariably stacked several deep along the railings, whatever the weather. Parts of Buckingham Palace are open to the public during August and September; the former chapel, bombed during World War II, rebuilt in 1961, and now the Queen's Gallery, shows paintings from the vast royal art collections. *Buckingham Palace Rd., tel. 0171/839–1377. Admission: £8.50. Open early Aug.–early Oct. (confirm specific dates, which are subject to the queen's mandate), daily 9:30–4. Queen's Gallery, tel. 0171/799–2331. Admission: £3. Open Tues.–Sat. and bank holidays 10–5, Sun. 2–5.*

5 **Parliament Square** is flanked, on the river side, by the Palace of Westminster. Among the statues of statesmen long since dead are those of Churchill, Abraham Lincoln, and Oliver Cromwell, the Lord Protector of England during the country's brief attempt at being a republic (1648–60).

6 **Westminster Abbey** is the most ancient of London's great churches and the most important, for it is here that Britain's monarchs are crowned. The abbey dates largely from the 13th and 14th centuries, although Henry VII's Chapel, an exquisite example of the heavily decorated late-Gothic style, was not built until the early 1600s, and the twin towers over the west entrance are an 18th-century addition. There is

much to see inside, including the touching tomb of the Unknown Warrior, a nameless World War I soldier buried, in memory of the war's victims, in earth brought with his corpse from France; and the famous Poets' Corner, where England's great writers—Milton, Chaucer, Shakespeare, et al.—are memorialized, and some are actually buried. Behind the high altar are the royal tombs, including those of Queen Elizabeth I; Mary, Queen of Scots; and Henry V. In the Chapel of Edward the Confessor stands the Coronation Chair. Among the royal weddings that have taken place here are those of the present queen and most recently, in 1986, the (ill-starred) duke and duchess of York. *Broad Sanctuary, tel. 0171/222–5152. Admission to the nave is free; to Poets' Corner and Royal Chapels £4 (Royal Chapels free Wed. 6–7:45 PM). Open Mon., Tues., Thurs., and Fri. 9–4, Wed. 9–8; Sat. 9–2 and 3:45–5; Sun. all day for services only; museum and cloisters open Sun.; closed weekdays to visitors during services; chapels closed Sun. No photography except Wed. 6–8 PM.*

7 **Hyde Park,** which covers about 340 acres, was originally a royal hunting ground, while Kensington Gardens, which adjoins it to the west, started life as part of the royal Kensington Palace. These two parks contain many fine trees and are a haven for wildlife. Rotten Row, the sandy track that runs along the south edge of the parks, has been a fashionable riding trail for centuries. It was Henry VIII's royal path to the hunt—hence the name, a corruption of *route du roi.* It's still used by the Household Cavalry, the queen's guard. You can see them leave, in full regalia, plumed helmets and all, at around 10:30, or await the return of the exhausted ex-guard about noon. The neighboring Kensington Gardens are a little more formal than Hyde Park. First laid out as palace grounds, they adjoin Kensington Palace. There is boating and swimming in the Kensington's Serpentine, an S-shape lake formed by damming a stream that used to flow here. Refreshments are served at the lakeside tearooms, and the Serpentine Gallery (tel. 0171/402–6075) holds noteworthy exhibitions of modern art. *Bounded by the*

Ring, Bayswater Rd., Park Lane, and Knightsbridge.

8 London's **Science Museum** is the leading national collection of science and technology, with extensive hands-on exhibits on outer space, astronomy, computers, transportation, and medicine. *Exhibition Rd., tel. 0171/938–8000 or 0171/938–8123 (recorded information). Admission: £5. Open Mon.–Sat. 10–6, Sun. 11–6.*

9 The **Natural History Museum** is housed in an ornate late-Victorian building with striking modern additions. As in the Science Museum, its displays on topics such as human biology and evolution are designed to challenge visitors to think for themselves. *Cromwell Rd., tel. 0171/938–9123 or 0142/692–7654 (recorded information). Admission: £5.50; free weekdays 4:30–5:50. Open Mon.–Sat. 10–6, Sun. 2:30–6.*

10 The **Victoria and Albert Museum** (or V&A) originated in the 19th century as a museum of decorative art. It has extensive collections of costumes, paintings, jewelry, and crafts from every part of the globe; the collections from India, China, and the Islamic world are especially strong. *Cromwell Rd., tel. 0171/938–8500 or 0171/938–8441 (recorded information). Admission: £5; free after 4:30, except Wed. Open Mon. noon–5:50, Tues.–Sun. 10–5:50.*

11 The **British Museum** ("Mankind's attic") houses a vast and priceless collection of treasures, including Egyptian, Greek, and Roman antiquities; Renaissance jewelry; pottery; coins; glass; and drawings from virtually every European school since the 15th century. It's best to pick out one section that particularly interests you—to try to see everything would be an overwhelming and exhausting task. Some of the highlights are the Elgin Marbles, sculptures that formerly decorated the Parthenon in Athens; the Rosetta stone, which helped archaeologists interpret Egyptian script; and a copy of the Magna Carta, the charter signed by King John in 1215 to which is ascribed the origins of English liberty. *Great Russell St., tel. 0171/636–1555 or 0171/580–1788 (recorded information). Admission free. Open Mon.–Sat. 10–5, Sun. 2:30–6.*

The City, the traditional commercial center of London, is the most ancient part of the capital, having been the site of the great Roman city of Londinium. Since those days, the City has been built and rebuilt several times. The wooden buildings of the medieval City were destroyed in the Great Fire of 1666. There were further waves of reconstruction in the 19th century, and then again after World War II to repair the devastation wrought by air attacks. The 1980s saw the construction of many mammoth office developments, some undistinguished, others incorporating adventurous and exciting ideas. Throughout all these changes, the City has retained its unique identity and character. The lord mayor and Corporation of London are still responsible for the government of the City, as they have been for many centuries. Commerce remains the lifeblood of the City, which is a world financial center rivaled only by New York, Tokyo, and Zurich. The biggest change has been in the City's population. Until the first half of the 19th century, many of the merchants and traders who worked in the City lived there, too. Today, despite its huge daytime population, scarcely 8,000 people live in the 677 acres of the City. Try, therefore, to explore the City on a weekday morning or afternoon. On weekends its streets are deserted, and many of the shops and restaurants, and even some of the churches, are closed.

12 Following the Great Fire, **St. Paul's Cathedral** was rebuilt by Sir Christopher Wren, the architect who was also responsible for designing 50 City parish churches to replace those lost in the Great Fire. St. Paul's is Wren's greatest work. Fittingly, he is buried in the crypt under a simple Latin epitaph, composed by his son, which translates as: "Reader, if you seek his monument, look around you." The cathedral has been the site of many famous state occasions, including the funeral of Winston Churchill in 1965 and the ill-fated marriage of the Prince and Princess of Wales in 1981. The greatest architectural glory of the cathedral is the dome. This consists of three distinct elements: an outer, timber-frame dome covered with lead; an interior dome built of brick and decorated with frescoes of the life of

St. Paul by the 18th-century artist Sir James Thornhill; and, in between, a brick cone that supports and strengthens both. There is a good view of the church from the Whispering Gallery, high up in the inner dome. The gallery is so called because of its remarkable acoustics, whereby words spoken on one side can be clearly heard on the other, almost 115 ft away. *St. Paul's Churchyard, Paternoster Sq., tel. 0171/248–2705. Admission to cathedral free; ambulatory (American Chapel), crypt, and treasury: £3.50; galleries: £3; combined ticket: £6. Cathedral open for visits Mon.–Sat. 8:30–4:30; ambulatory, crypt, and galleries open Mon.–Sat. 9:30–4:15.*

13 One of the most striking pieces of contemporary City architecture is the headquarters of **Lloyd's of London,** designed by the modernist architect Richard Rogers, whose other famous work is Paris's Pompidou Center. The underwriters of Lloyd's provide insurance for everything imaginable, from oil rigs to a pianist's fingers, though they suffered a crash in 1993, with most of the so-called Names, whose millions formed Lloyd's backbone, losing major money. *1 Lime St., tel. 0171/623–7100. Admission free.*

The spectacular **Shakespeare's Globe** theater is a replica of Shakespeare's open-roofed Globe Playhouse (built in 1599; incinerated in 1613), where most of the playwright's great plays premiered. It stands 200 yards from the original site, overlooking the Thames. Built with authentic Elizabethan materials, down to the first thatched roof in London since the Great Fire, the theater stages its works in natural light (and sometimes rain), to 1,000 people on wooden benches in the "bays," plus 500 "groundlings," standing on a carpet of filbert shells and clinker, just as they did nearly four centuries ago. The theater season is only from June through September; throughout the year, you can tour the Globe through admission to the museum devoted to Shakespeare and his times on the premises. *New Globe Walk, Bankside (South Bank), tel. 0171/928–6406. Open daily 10–5. Call for performance schedule.*

14 The **Tower of London** is one of London's most famous sights and one of its most crowded, too.

Come as early in the day as possible and head for the Crown Jewels, so you can see them before the crowds arrive. They are a breathtakingly splendid collection of regalia, precious stones, gold, and silver; the Royal Scepter contains the largest cut diamond in the world. The tower served the monarchs of medieval England as both fortress and palace. Every British sovereign from William the Conqueror in the 11th century to Henry VIII in the 16th lived here, and it remains a royal palace, in name at least. Look for the ravens whose presence at the tower is traditional. It is said that if they leave, the tower will fall and England will lose her greatness. *Tower Hill, tel. 0171/709–0765. Admission: £3.30. Open Mar.–Oct., Mon.–Sat. 9:30–6, Sun. 10–6; Nov.–Feb., Mon.–Sat. 9:30–5, Sun. 10–5. Yeoman Warder guides conduct tours daily from Middle Tower, no charge, but tips are generally given. Subject to weather and availability of guides, tours are conducted about every 30 mins until 3:30 in summer, 2:30 in winter.*

Shopping Shopping is one of London's great pleasures. Different areas retain their traditional specialties. **Chelsea** centers on the King's Road; once synonymous with ultrafashion, it still harbors some designer boutiques, plus antiques and home-furnishings stores. **Covent Garden** is a something-for-everyone neighborhood, with clothing chain stores and top designers, stalls selling crafts, and shops selling gifts of every type—bikes, kites, herbs, beads, hats, you name it.

Knightsbridge has Harrods, of course, but also Harvey Nichols, the top clothes shop, and many expensive designers' boutiques along Sloane Street, Walton Street, and Beauchamp Place.

Piccadilly is a busy street lined with some grand and very English shops (including Hatchards, the booksellers; Swaine, Adeney Brigg, the equestrian outfitters; and Fortnum and Mason, the department store that supplies the queen's groceries).

Napoli Coast, Italy

Campania (the region of Naples, the Amalfi coast, and other sights) is where most people's preconceived ideas of Italy become a reality. You'll find lots of sun, good food that relies heavily on tomatoes and mozzarella, acres of classical ruins, and gorgeous scenery.

Currency The unit of currency in Italy is the lira (plural, lire). At press time, the exchange rate was about 1,595 lire to the U.S. dollar. When your purchases run into hundreds of thousands of lire, beware of being shortchanged, a dodge that is practiced at ticket windows and cashiers' desks, as well as in shops and even banks. Always count your change before you leave the counter.

Telephones The country code for Italy is 39. Most local calls cost 200 lire for two minutes. Pay phones take either 100-, 200-, or 500-lire coins or *schede telefoniche* (phone cards), purchased in bars, tobacconists, post offices, and TELECOM offices in either 5,000-, 10,000-, or 15,000-lire denominations. To place international calls, many travelers go to the Telefoni telephone exchange, where the operator assigns you a booth, can help place your call, and will collect payment when you have finished. Telefoni exchanges (usually marked TELECOM) are found in all cities. To dial an international call, insert a phone card, dial 00, then the country code, area code, and phone number. The cheaper and easier option, however, will be to use your AT&T, MCI, or Sprint calling card. For **AT&T,** dial access number 172–1011; **MCI,** 172–1022; **Sprint,** 172–1877. You will be connected directly with an operator in the United States.

Shore Excursions The following are good choices on the Napoli Coast. They may not be offered by all cruise lines. Times and prices are approximate.

In Naples **Pompeii.** It's a 45-minute motor-coach ride to the ruins at Pompeii, a place where time has stood still since AD 79, when Mt. Vesuvius erupted. *4 hrs. Cost: $49.*

Herculaneum and Naples. The well-preserved ruins at Heraklion and downtown Naples are the focus of this two-town tour. *3½ hrs. Cost: $49.*

In Sorrento **Excavations at Pompeii.** Here's another chance to see the ruins at Pompeii. *4½ hrs. Cost: $50.*

In Capri Capri is a place to wander, not tour. Cruise lines will arrange round-trip tickets on the public jetfoil for passengers wishing to visit Capri.

In Amalfi Cruise lines often offer excursions featuring the Amalfi coast, from Naples or Sorrento. You can also arrange to hire a car, often through the ship's tour desk.

Coming Ashore Ships calling on the Napoli Coast generally drop anchor offshore. Nearby towns are easily reached from the major ports of call.

In Naples Ships calling at Naples tender passengers to shore from Naples Bay. You'll probably do a lot of walking in Naples, since the buses are crowded and taxis get stalled in traffic. Keep a firm grip on your pocketbook and camera.

In Sorrento Ships calling at Sorrento tender passengers to shore from the town's harbor. Sorrento is best explored on foot, since motor coaches must remain in designated areas.

In Capri The trip on the public jetfoil to Capri is about a 20-minute ride from Sorrento or about a 40-minute ride from Naples. A cog railway or bus service takes you up to the town of Capri from the marina.

In Amalfi Amalfi is within driving distance of Naples or Sorrento. Once in town, you will want to wander around on foot.

Exploring the Napoli Coast

Naples The 17th-century **Palazzo Reale** (Royal Palace), built during the rule of the Bourbons, is still furnished in the lavish baroque style that suited the Bourbons so well. *Piazza del Plebiscito, tel. 081/580–8111. Admission: 8,000 lire. Open Apr.–Oct., Tues.–Sun. 9–7:30; Nov.–Mar., Tues.–Sun. 9–1:30.*

The massive stone **Castel Nuovo** was built by the city's Aragon rulers in the 13th century. The decorative triumphal arch that forms the entrance was erected during the Renaissance; set incongruously into the heavy castle walls, the arch is one of the finest of its kind. The castle also has some rooms displaying sculptures and frescoes that date from the 14th and 15th centuries. *Piazza Municipio. Admission: 7,000 lire. Open Mon.–Sat. 9–7, Sun. 9–1.*

A favorite Neapolitan song celebrates the quiet beauty of the church of **Santa Chiara,** which was built in the early 1300s in Provençal Gothic style. Directly across is the oddly faceted stone facade and elaborate baroque interior of the church of the **Gesù** (Via Benedetto Croce). *Piazza Gesù Nuovo. Admission free. Open daily 7–noon and 4–7 (until 6 in winter).*

The museum in the **Certosa di San Martino,** a Carthusian monastery restored in the 17th century, contains an eclectic collection of Neapolitan landscape paintings, royal carriages, and *presepi* (Christmas crèches). Check out the view from the balcony off Room 25. *Certosa di San Martino, tel. 081/578–1769. Admission: 8,000 lire. Open Tues.–Sun. 9–2.*

The **Museo Archeologico Nazionale** (National Archaeological Museum) is dusty, unkempt, and undergoes perpetual renovations, but it holds one of the world's great collections of antiquities. Greek and Roman sculptures, vividly colored mosaics, countless objects from Pompeii and Herculaneum, and an equestrian statue of the Roman emperor Nerva are all worth seeing. *Piazza Museo, tel. 081/440166. Admission: 12,000 lire. Open Aug.–Sept., Mon.–Sat. 9–7, Sun. 9–1; Oct.–July, Wed.–Mon. 9–2.*

The **Museo di Capodimonte,** housed in an 18th-century palace built by Bourbon king Charles III, is surrounded by a vast park that must have been lovely when it was better cared for. In the picture gallery are some fine Renaissance paintings; climb the stairs to the terrace for a magnificent view of Naples and the bay. Downstairs you can visit the State Apartments and see the extensive collection of porcelain, much of it produced in the Bourbons' own factory right here on the grounds. *Parco di Capodimonte, tel. 081/744–1307. Admission: 8,000 lire. Open Apr.–Oct., Tues.–Sun. 9–7:30; Nov.–Mar., Tues.–Sat. 9–6, Sun. 9–2.*

Near Naples is **Pompeii,** where an estimated 2,000 residents were entombed on that fateful August day when Mt. Vesuvius erupted in AD 79. The ancient city of Pompeii was much larger than nearby Herculaneum, and excavations have progressed to a much greater extent (though the remains are not as well preserved, owing to some 18th-century scavenging for museum-quality artwork, most of which you are able to see at Naples's Museo Archeologico Nazionale; *see above*). This prosperous Roman city had an extensive forum, lavish baths and temples, and patrician villas richly decorated with frescoes. It's worth buying a detailed guide of the site to give meaning and understanding to the ruins and their importance. Be sure to see the Villa dei Misteri, whose frescoes are in mint condition. Perhaps that is a slight exaggeration, but the paintings are so rich with detail and depth of color that one finds it difficult to believe that they are more than 1,900 years old. Have lots of small change handy to tip the guards at the more important houses so they will unlock the gates for you. *Pompeii Scavi, tel. 081/861–0744. Admission: 12,000 lire. Open daily 9–1 hr before sunset (ticket office closes 2 hrs before sunset).*

Sorrento The **Museo Correale,** an attractive 18th-century villa, houses an interesting collection of decorative arts (furniture, china, and so on) and paintings of the Neapolitan school. *Via Correale. Admission: 8,000 lire; gardens only 2,000 lire. Open Apr.–Sept., Mon. and Wed.–Sat. 9–12:30 and 5–7, Sun. 9–12:30; Oct.–Mar., Mon. and Wed.–Sat. 9–11:30 and 3–5, Sun. 9–11:30.*

Capri No matter how many day-trippers crowd onto the island, no matter how touristy certain sections have become, Capri remains one of Italy's loveliest places. Stroll the **Piazzetta,** a choice place from which to watch the Capri town action, and window-shop expensive boutiques or browse in souvenir shops along Via Vittorio Emanuele on your way to the **Giardini di Augusto** (Gardens of Augustus), which have gorgeous views. The town of Capri is deliberately commercial and self-consciously picturesque.

To get away from the crowds, hike to **Villa Jovis,** one of the many villas that Roman emperor Tiberius built on the island, at the end of a lane that climbs steeply uphill. The walk takes about 45 minutes, with pretty views all the way and a final spectacular vista of the entire Bay of Naples and part of the Gulf of Salerno. *Villa Jovis,*

Via Tiberio. Admission: 4,000 lire. Open daily 9–1 hr before sunset.

In Anacapri, the island's only other town, there is the little church of **San Michele,** off Via Orlandi, where a magnificent hand-painted majolica-tile floor shows you an 18th-century vision of the Garden of Eden. (You'll need to take a bus or open taxi to Anacapri from Capri town.) *Off Via Orlandi. Open Easter–Oct., daily 7–7; Nov.–Easter, daily 10–3.*

Villa San Michele is the charming former home of Swedish scientist-author Axel Munthe. *Via Axel Munthe. Admission: 6,000 lire. Open May–Sept., daily 9–6; Nov.–Feb., daily 10:30–3:30; Mar., daily 9:30–4:30; Apr. and Oct., daily 9:30–5.*

Amalfi The main historical attraction is the **Duomo,** or Cathedral of St. Andrew, which shows a mix of Moorish and early Gothic influences. The interior is a 10th-century Romanesque skeleton in an 18th-century baroque dress. *Admission free. Open daily 7:30–9 in summer.*

The village of **Ravello,** 8 km (5 mi) north of Amalfi, is not actually on the coast, but on a high mountain bluff overlooking the sea. The road up to it is a series of switchbacks, and the village itself clings precariously on the mountain spur. The village flourished during the 13th century and then fell into a tranquillity that has remained unchanged for the past six centuries.

The center of Ravello is **Piazza Duomo,** with its cathedral, founded in 1087. Note the fine bronze 12th-century doors and, inside, two pulpits richly decorated with mosaics: one depicting the story of Jonah and the whale; the other—more splendid—carved with fantastic beasts and resting on a pride of lions.

The 11th-century **Villa Rufolo** in Ravello is where the composer Richard Wagner once stayed, and there is a Wagner festival every summer on the villa's garden terrace. There is a Moorish cloister with interlacing pointed arches, beautiful gardens, an 11th-century tower, and a belvedere with a fine view of the coast. *Piazza del Duomo. Admission: 3,000 lire. Open summer, daily 9–8; winter, daily 9–6 or sunset.*

At the entrance to the **Villa Cimbrone** is a small cloister that looks medieval but was actually built in 1917, with two bas-reliefs: one representing nine Norman warriors, the other illustrating the seven deadly sins. Then, the long avenue leads through peaceful gardens scattered with grottoes, small temples, and statues to a belvedere and terrace, where, on a clear day, the view stretches out over the Mediterranean Sea. *Admission: 5,000 lire. Open daily 8:30–1 hr before sunset.*

Norwegian Coast and Fjords

Norway's Far North, land of the summertime midnight sun, offers picturesque scenery and quaint towns. The fjords continue northward from Bergen all the way to Kirkenes, at Norway's border with Finland and Russia. Norway's Far North is for anyone eager to hike, climb, fish, bird-watch for seabirds, see Samiland (land of the Sami, or "Lapps"), or experience the unending days of nighttime sun in June and July.

The major towns north of Bergen are Ålesund, Trondheim, Bodø, Narvik, Tromsø, Hammerfest, and Kirkenes. The best way to reach these places is by ship.

Currency The unit of currency in Norway is the krone, written as Kr. on price tags but officially written as NOK (bank designation), NKr, or kr. The exchange rate at press time was NKr 6.42 to the U.S. dollar.

Telephones The country code for Norway is 47. Norway's phone system is not as expensive as one might fear. International calls can be made from any pay phone. For calls to North America, dial 095–1, then the area code and number. You will need to dial 00 for an international connection. To reach an **AT&T** long-distance operator, dial 80019011; **MCI,** 180019912; **Sprint,** 180019877.

Shore Excursions The following are good choices in the towns along Norway's coast. They may not be offered by all cruise lines. Times and prices are approximate.

In Trondheim **City Tour.** A visit to an open-air folk museum is the highlight of this tour, which also visits Nidaros Cathedral—built on the grave of St. Olav, who founded the city in AD 997. *3 hrs. Cost: $38.*

City View with Ringve Museum. You'll drive through the city on your way to the Ringve Museum of Musical Instruments, which is housed in a manor overlooking the fjord. *3 hrs. Cost: $45.*

In Bodø **Tour of Kjerringoy.** From Bodø, head off for Kjerringoy, which gained independence from Norway in 1800. Once there, you'll have time to wander the city's Central Square and streets. *Half day. Cost: $15.*

In Tromsø **Views of the City.** Tour the Tromsø Museum before driving around the island of Tromsø. Pass Lake Prestvatn, where the Northern Lights Observatory is located, to reach Tromsø Bridge for a visit to Tromsdalen Church, known as the Arctic Cathedral. The tour includes a ride on the cable car to Mt. Storsteinen for panoramic views of the city. *3 hrs. Cost: $34.*

Northern Lights. Visit the Northern Lights Planetarium, which opened in 1989, where you'll see a film on a 360-degree screen about, of course, the Aurora Borealis. A must for amateur astronomers. *3 hrs. Cost: $42.*

Coming Ashore Ships calling at Tromsø, Bodø, and Trondheim dock in the harbor, which is the lifeline of all the towns along the Norwegian coast.

Getting Around Attractions are close by the pier, and the best way to explore these ports is on foot.

Exploring Trondheim Construction of Scandinavia's largest medieval building, **Nidaros Domkirke** (cathedral), started in 1320 but was not completed until the early 1920s. For centuries, Niadaros Domkirke drew religious pilgrims. Norwegian kings were crowned here, and the crown jewels are still on display. *Kongsgården 2, tel. 73/52–52–33. Admission: NKr 12. Open mid-June–mid-Aug. weekdays 9–5:30, weekends 9–2; mid-Aug.–mid-Sept. weekdays 9–3; mid-Sept.–mid-Apr. weekdays noon–2:30, weekends 11:30–11:30–2; May–mid-June, weekdays 9–3, weekends 9–2.*

Scandinavia's two largest wooden buildings are in Trondheim. One is the rococo **Stiftsgården,** a royal palace built in 1774. The other is a student dormitory. *Tel. 73/52–13–11. Admission: NKr 30. Open early June, Tues.–Sat. 10–3, Sun. noon–5; late June–mid-Aug., Tues.–Sat. 10–5, Sun. noon–5; late Aug.–May, open one day per month.*

Exploring Bodø Bodø was bombed by the Germans in 1940. The stunning, contemporary **Bodø Cathedral,** its spire separated from the main building, was built after the war. Inside are rich, modern tapestries; outside is a war memorial.

The **Nordland County Museum** depicts the life of the Sami, as well as regional history. *Prinsengt. 116, tel. 75526128. Admission free. Open weekdays 9–3, weekends noon–3.*

Exploring Tromsø Be sure to see the spectacular **Ishavskatedral** (Arctic Cathedral), with its eastern wall made entirely of stained glass, across the long stretch of Tromsø bridge. Coated in aluminum, the bridge's triangular peaks make a bizarre mirror for the midnight sun. *Tel. 77/63–76–11. Admission: NKr 10. Open June–Aug., Mon.–Sat. 10–6, Sun. 1:30–6. Times may vary according to church services.*

Be sure to walk around old Tromsø (along the waterfront) and to visit the **Tromsø Museum,** which concentrates on science, the Sami, and northern churches. *Lars Thøringsvei 10, Folkeparken, tel. 77645000; take Bus 27 or 22. Admission: NKr 10. Open June–Aug., daily 9–9; Sept.–May, weekdays 8:30–3:30, Sat. noon–3, Sun. 11–4.*

Oslo, Norway

Although it's one of the world's largest capital cities by land area, Oslo has only about 480,000 inhabitants. The foundations for modern Norwegian culture were laid here in the 19th century, during the period of union with Sweden, which lasted until 1905. Oslo blossomed at this time, and Norway produced its three greatest men of arts and letters: composer Edvard Grieg (1843–1907), dramatist Henrik Ibsen (1828–1906), and painter Edvard Munch (1863–1944). The polar explorers Roald Amundsen and Fridtjof Nansen also lived during this period.

In recent years, the city has become more lively: Shops are open later, and pubs, cafés, and restaurants are crowded at all hours. The downtown area is compact, but the city limits include forests, fjords, and mountains, giving Oslo a pristine airiness that complements its urban dignity. Explore downtown on foot, or if you've been here before, venture beyond via bus, streetcar, or train.

Currency The unit of currency in Norway is the krone, written as Kr. on price tags but officially written as NOK (bank designation), NKr, or kr. The exchange rate at press time was NKr 6.42 to the U.S. dollar.

Telephones The country code for Norway is 47. Public telephones accept small-denomination coins; for dialing instructions (in English), check the Oslo phone book. Norway's phone system is not as expensive as one might fear. International calls can be made from any pay phone. For calls to North America, dial 095–1, then the area code and number. You will need to dial 00 for an international connection. To reach an **AT&T** long-distance operator, dial 80019011; **MCI,** 180019912; **Sprint,** 180019877.

Shore Excursions The following are good choices in Oslo. They may not be offered by all cruise lines. Times and prices are approximate.

Sculpture and Skiing. See how master sculptor Gutav Vigeland has populated Frogner park with human figures made of stone, iron, and bronze, and the ski jump where in winter some of the world's top athletes compete and where in summer you can get a great view of Oslo and the fjords. *3 hrs. Cost: $36.*

Munch Museum and Scandinavian Design. Art lovers won't want to miss this tour, which takes in the Munch Museum and the Museum of Scandinavian Design, with its diverse collection of arts and crafts from AD 600 to the present. *3 hrs. Cost: $34.*

Coming Ashore Ships dock in Oslo's harbor. You can walk right into the main part of the city from the pier. The waterfront toward the central harbor is the heart of Oslo and head of the fjord. Aker Brygge, a quayside shopping and cultural center, with a theater, cinemas, and galleries among the shops, restaurants, and cafés, is a great place to hang out. You don't have to buy anything—just sit amid the fountains and statues and watch the activities.

Getting Around A taxi is available if the roof light is on. There are taxi stands at Oslo Central Station and usually alongside Narvesen newsstands, or call 22388090; during peak hours, though, you may have to wait. The city has good public transportation.

Exploring Oslo *Numbers in the margin correspond to points of interest on the Oslo map.*

Oslo's main street, **Karl Johans Gate,** runs right through the center of town, from Oslo Central Station uphill to the Royal Palace. Half its length is closed to traffic, and it is in this section that you will find many of the city's shops and outdoor cafés.

1 The **Slottet** (Royal Palace) is the king's residence. The neoclassical palace, completed in 1848, is as sober, sturdy, and unpretentious as the Norwegian character. The surrounding park is open to the public, though the palace is not. The changing of the guard happens daily at 1:30. When the king is in residence—signaled by a red flag—the Royal Guard strikes up the band.

2 The **Universitet** (University) is made up of three big buildings. The main hall of the university is decorated with murals by Edvard Munch, Norway's most famous artist. The *aula* (hall) is open only during July. The Nobel Peace Prize is presented there each year on December 10. *Karl Johans Gate 47. Admission to hall free. Open July, weekdays noon–2:45.*

3 **Nasjonalgalleriet** (the National Gallery) is Norway's largest public gallery. It has a small but high-quality selection of paintings by European artists, but of particular interest is the collection of works by Scandinavian Impressionists. Edvard Munch is represented here, although most of his work is in the Munch Museum (*see below*). *Universitetsgt. 13, tel. 22/20–04–04. Admission free. Open Mon., Wed., Fri., and Sat. 10–4, Thurs. 10–8, Sun. 11–3.*

Oslo

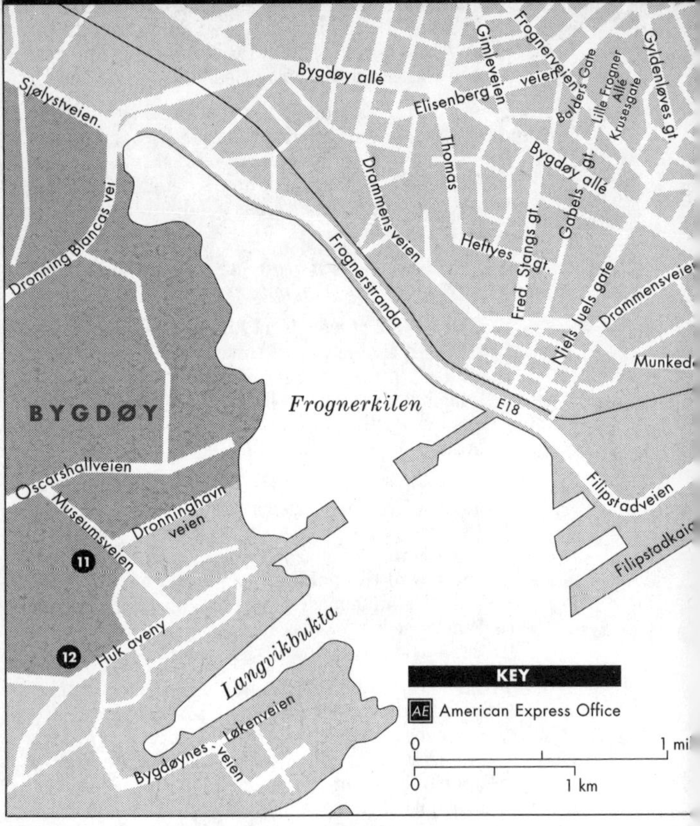

Akershus Slott, **8**
Forsvarsmuseet and Hjemmefrontmuseum, **9**
Historisk Museum, **4**
Munchmuseet, **13**
Nasjonalgalleriet, **3**
Nationaltheatret, **5**
Norsk Folkemuseum, **11**
Oslo Domkirke, **7**
Rådhuset, **10**
Slottet, **1**
Stortinget, **6**
Universitet, **2**
Vikingskipshuset, **12**

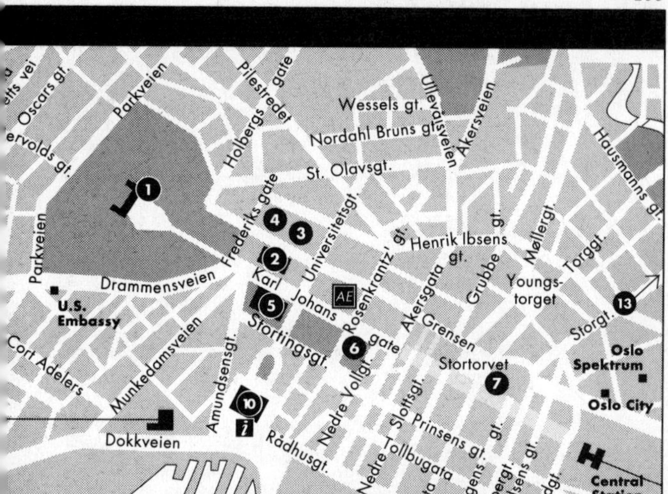
Oscars gt.
Parkveien
Pilestredet
Holbergs gate
Wessels gt.
Nordahl Bruns gt.
Ullevålsveien
Akersveien
Hausmanns gt.
St. Olavsgt.
Frederiks gate
Universitetsgt.
Henrik Ibsens gt.
Grubbe gt.
Møllergt.
Torggt.
Parkveien
Drammensveien
Karl Johans gate
Rosenkrantz' gt.
Akersgata
Youngs-torget
Storgt.
U.S. Embassy
Stortingsgt.
Grensen
Oslo Spektrum
Cort Adelers
Munkedamsveien
Nedre Vollgt.
Stortorvet
Oslo City
Amundsensgt.
Slottsgt.
Prinsens gt.
Dokkveien
Rådhusgt.
Nedre Tollbugata
Dronningens gt.
Skippergt.
Fred Olsens gt.
Strandgt.
Central Station
Kirkegata
Pipervika
Akershusstranda
Mynt gt.
Kongens gate
Bjørvika
Akerselva
Skippergt.
Oslofjorden

4 The **Historisk Museum** (Historical Museum) is in back of the National Gallery. In addition to displays of daily life and art from the Viking period, the museum has an ethnographic section with a collection related to the great polar explorer Roald Amundsen, the first man to reach the South Pole. *Frederiksgt. 2, tel. 22/85–99–12. Admission free. Open summer, Tues.–Sun. 11–3.*

5 The **Nationaltheatret** (National Theater) is watched over by the statues of Bjørnstjerne Bjørnson and Henrik Ibsen. Bjørnson was the nationalist poet who wrote Norway's anthem. Internationally lauded playwright Ibsen wrote *Peer Gynt* (he personally requested Edvard Grieg's musical accompaniment), *A Doll's House*, and *Hedda Gabler*, among others. He worried that his plays, packed with allegory, myth, and sociological and emotional angst, might not have appeal outside Norway. Instead, they were universally recognized and changed the face of modern theater. *Stortingsgt. 15, tel. 22/41–27–10.*

6 The **Stortinget** (Parliament) is a bowfront, yellow-brick building that stretches across the block. It is open to visitors by request when Parliament is not in session: A guide will take you around the frescoed interior and into the debating chamber. *Karl Johans Gate 22, tel. 22313050. Admission free. Guided tours July–Aug. Public gallery open weekdays 11–1.*

7 **Oslo Domkirke** (cathedral), consecrated in 1697, is modest by the standards of those in some other European capital cities, but the interior is rich with treasures, such as the baroque carved wooden altarpiece and pulpit. The ceiling frescoes by Hugo Lous Mohr were done after World War II. Behind the cathedral is an area of arcades, small restaurants, and street musicians. *Stortorvet 1. Admission free. Open weekdays 10–4.*

8 **Akershus Slott,** a castle on the harbor, was built during the Middle Ages but restored in 1527 by Christian IV of Denmark—Denmark then ruled Norway—after it was damaged by fire. He then laid out the present city of Oslo (naming it Christiania, after himself) around his new resi-

dence; Oslo's street plan still follows his design. Some rooms are open for guided tours, and the grounds form a park around the castle. *Entrance from Festningspl, tel. 22412521. Guided tours of the castle, May–Sept., Mon.–Sat. 11, 1, and 3, Sun. 1 and 3.*

9 On the grounds of Akershus Slott are the **Forsvarsmuseet** and **Hjemmefrontmuseum** (the Norwegian Defense and Resistance museums). Both give you a feel for the Norwegian fighting spirit throughout history and especially during the German occupation, when the Nazis set up headquarters on this site and had a number of patriots executed here. *Entrance from Festningspl., tel. 22412521. Admission: NKr 15. Open June–Aug., weekdays 10–6; Sept.–May, weekdays 10–4.*

10 The large redbrick **Rådhuset** (city hall) is on the waterfront. Note the friezes in the courtyard, depicting scenes from Norwegian folklore, then go inside and see murals depicting daily life in Norway, historical events, and Resistance activities. You can set your watch by the astronomical clock in the inner courtyard. *Rådhuspl., tel. 22410090. Admission free. Open May–Aug., Mon.–Sat. 9–5, Sun. noon–4; Sept.–Apr., Mon.–Sat. 9–3:30. Tours weekdays 10, noon, 2.*

From Pipervika Bay, you can board a ferry in the summertime for the seven-minute crossing of the fjord to the **Bygdøy** peninsula, where there is a complex of seafaring museums. *Ferries run May–Sept., daily every ½ hr 8:15–5:45.*

11 **Norsk Folkemuseum** (Norwegian Folk Museum) is a large park where centuries-old historic farmhouses have been collected from all over the country and reassembled. A whole section of 19th-century Oslo was moved here, as was a 12th-century wooden stave church. Look for the guides in period costume throughout the park, and on Sundays, there are displays of weaving and sheepshearing. *First ferry stop, Dronningen. Museumsvn. 10, tel. 22437020. Admission: NKr 50. Open summer, daily 9–6.*

12 **Vikingskipshuset** (Viking Ship Museum) contains 9th-century ships used by Vikings as royal burial chambers, which have been excavated

from the shores of the Oslofjord. Also on display are the treasures and jewelry that accompanied the royal bodies on their last voyage. The ornate craftsmanship evident in the ships and jewelry dispels any notion that the Vikings were skilled only in looting and pillaging. *Huk aveny 35, tel. 22/43–83–79. Admission: NKr 30. Open Apr. and Oct., daily 11–4; May–Aug., daily 9–6; Sept., daily 11–5.*

13 **Munch-museet** (Munch Museum). In 1940, four years before his death, Munch bequeathed much of his work to the city of Oslo; the museum opened in 1963, the centennial of his birth. Although only a fraction of its 22,000 items—books, paintings, drawings, prints, sculptures, and letters—are on display, you can still get a sense of the tortured expressionism that was to have such an effect on European painting. *Tøyengt. 53 (from Rådhuset take Bus 29 or take the T-bane from the Nationaltheatret to Tøyen, an area in northeast Oslo), tel. 22673774. Admission: NKr 40. Open June–Sept. 15, Tues.–Sat. 10–6, Sun. noon–6; Sept. 16–May, Tues., Wed., Fri, Sat. 10–4, Thurs. 10–6, Sun. noon–6.*

Shopping

Oslo has a wide selection of pewter, silver, glass, sheepskin, leather, and knitwear. Prices on handmade articles are government-controlled.

Many of the larger stores are between Stortinget and the cathedral; much of this area is for pedestrians only. The **Basarhallene,** at the back of the cathedral, is an art and handicrafts boutique center. Oslo's newest shopping area, **Aker Brygge,** was once a shipbuilding wharf. Right on the waterfront, it is a complex of booths, offices, and sidewalk cafés. Also check out **Bogstadveien/Hegdehaugsveien,** which runs from Majorstua to Parkveien. This street offers a good selection of stores and has plenty of places to rest your tired feet and quench your thirst. Shops stay open until 5 (Thurs. until 7).

Paris/Le Havre, France

Le Havre is the port city for Paris, one of Europe's most treasured and beautiful cities. Most cruise passengers will find a day far too short to truly explore the city. However, Paris is a compact city, and with the possible exception of the Bois de Boulogne and Montmartre, you can easily walk from one sight to the next. The city is divided in two by the River Seine, with two islands (Ile de la Cité and Ile St-Louis) in the middle. The south, or Left, Bank has a more intimate, bohemian flavor than the haughtier Right Bank. The east–west axis from Châtelet to the Arc de Triomphe, via the rue de Rivoli and the Champs-Elysées, is the principal thoroughfare for sightseeing and shopping on the Right Bank.

Currency The unit of French currency is the franc (fr), subdivided into 100 centimes. At press time, the U.S. dollar bought 5.5 francs.

Telephones The country code for France is 33. In 1996, two digits were added to all phone numbers. The digits are determined by zone: for Paris and the Ile-de-France, the code is 01. (Drop the zero if you are calling France from a foreign country.) Phone booths are plentiful; they are nearly always available at post offices and cafés. Some French pay phones take 1-, 2-, and 5-franc coins (1-fr minimum), but most phones are now operated by *télécartes* (phone cards), which can be used for both local and international calls. The cards are sold in post offices, métro stations, and cafés sporting a red TABAC (tobacco) sign outside (cost: 40 frs for 50 units; 96 frs for 120 units). To call abroad, dial 19 and wait for the tone, then dial the country code, area code, and number. To reach an **AT&T** long-distance operator, dial 0800–990011; **MCI,** 0800–990019; **Sprint,** 0800–990087. Dial 12 for local operators.

Shore Excursions The following is a good choice from Le Havre. It may not be offered by all cruise lines. Time and price are approximate.

Paris. Journey by coach to Paris, where you will tour the Cathedral of Notre Dame, the Eiffel Tower, and Place de la Concorde, and have time to shop. Glimpse the tree-lined Champs-Elysées and Arc de Triomphe, Place de l'Opera, and Pont Neuf. Includes lunch. *10–12 hrs. Cost: $150–$175.*

Coming Ashore Ships dock at Le Havre. The trip to Paris is approximately three hours each way. Cruise lines will typically sell transfers for around $100 to Paris for those who want to explore on their own.

Getting Around Once you're in the city, you'll find that Paris's monuments and museums are within walking distance of one another. A river cruise is a pleasant way to get an overview. The most convenient form of public transportation is the *métro*; buses are a slower alternative, though they do allow you to see more of the city. Taxis are not terribly expensive but are not always easy to hail, either.

There are 13 métro lines crisscrossing Paris and the nearby suburbs, and you are seldom more than a five-minute walk from the nearest station. It is essential to know the name of the last station on the line you take, since this name appears on all signs within the system. A connection (you can make as many as you please on one ticket) is called a *correspondance*. At junction stations, illuminated orange signs bearing the names of each line terminus appear over the corridors that lead to the various correspondances. Métro tickets cost 8 francs each, though a *carnet* (10 tickets for 46 frs) is a far better value.

There is no standard vehicle or color for Paris taxis, but all offer good value. Daytime rates (7 to 7) within Paris are about 2.80 francs per kilometer, and nighttime rates are around 4.50 francs, plus a basic charge of 13 francs. Cruising cabs can be hard to find. There are numerous taxi stands, but these are not well marked. Cruise passengers should be aware that taxis seldom take more than three people at a time.

Exploring Paris *Numbers in the margin correspond to points of interest on the Paris map.*

The most enduring symbol of Paris, and its historic and geographic heart, is the cathedral
1 **Notre-Dame**, around the corner from Cité métro station. Notre Dame has been a place of worship for more than 2,000 years; the present building is the fourth on this site. It was begun in 1163, making it one of the earliest Gothic cathedrals, although it was not finished until 1345. The 387-step climb up the towers is worth the effort for a perfect view of the famous gargoyles and the heart of

Paris. *Pl. du Parvis. Cathedral admission free. Towers admission: 28 frs. Open daily 10–5. Treasury (religious and vestmental relics) admission: 15 frs. Open Mon.–Sat. 10–6, Sun. 2–6.*

2 The Hôtel de Cluny houses the **Musée National du Moyen-Age,** a museum devoted to the late Middle Ages and Renaissance. Look for the *Lady with the Unicorn* tapestries and the beautifully displayed medieval statues. *6 pl. Paul-Painlevé, tel. 01–43–25–62–00. Admission: 27 frs, 18 frs on Sun. Open Wed.–Mon. 9:30–5:15.*

3 **La Sorbonne,** Paris's ancient university, is where students used to listen to lectures in Latin, which explains why the surrounding area is known as the Quartier Latin (Latin Quarter). The Sorbonne is the oldest university in Paris—indeed, one of the oldest in Europe—and has for centuries been one of France's principal institutions of higher learning. *Rue de la Sorbonne.*

4 The **Panthéon,** with its huge dome and elegant colonnade, is reminiscent of St. Paul's in London but dates from a century later (1758–89). The Panthéon was intended to be a church, but during the French Revolution it was earmarked as a secular hall of fame. Its crypt contains the remains of such national heroes as Voltaire, Rousseau, and Zola. The interior is empty and austere, with principal interest centering on Puvis de Chavannes's late-19th-century frescoes, relating the life of Geneviève, patron saint of Paris. *Pl. du Panthéon, tel. 01–43–54–34–51. Admission: 32 frs. Open daily 10–5:30.*

Rue de Navarre and rue Lacépède lead to the
5 **Jardin des Plantes** (Botanical Gardens), which have been on this site since the 17th century. The gardens have what is reputedly the oldest tree in Paris, an acacia Robinia (allée Becquerel) planted in 1636. Natural science enthusiasts will be in their element at the various museums, devoted to insects (Musée Entomologique), fossils and prehistoric animals (Musée Paléontologique), and minerals (Musée Minéralogique). The Grande Galerie de l'Evolution, with its collection of stuffed and mounted animals (some now extinct), is mind-blowing. *36 rue Geoffroy-St-Hilaire. Admission: 12–25 frs. Museums open Wed.–Mon. 9–11:45, 1–4:45; Grande Galerie de l'Evolution: Wed.–Mon., 10–5; Thurs. 10–10.*

Paris

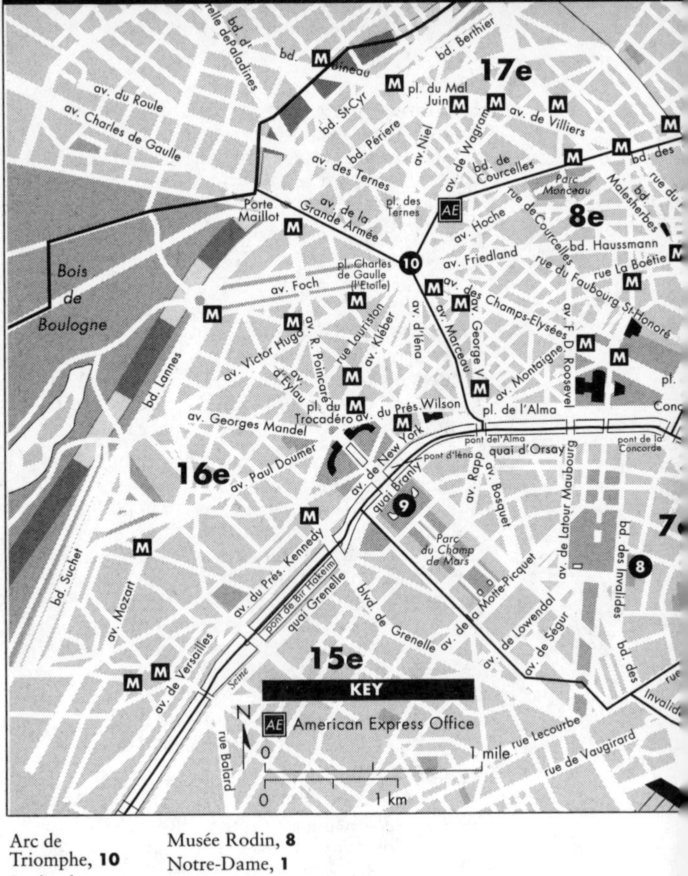

Arc de Triomphe, **10**

Jardin des Plantes, **5**

La Sorbonne, **3**

Louvre, **11**

Musée d'Orsay, **7**

Musée National du Moyen-Age, **2**

Musée Rodin, **8**

Notre-Dame, **1**

Panthéon, **4**

St-Germain-des-Prés, **6**

Tour Eiffel, **9**

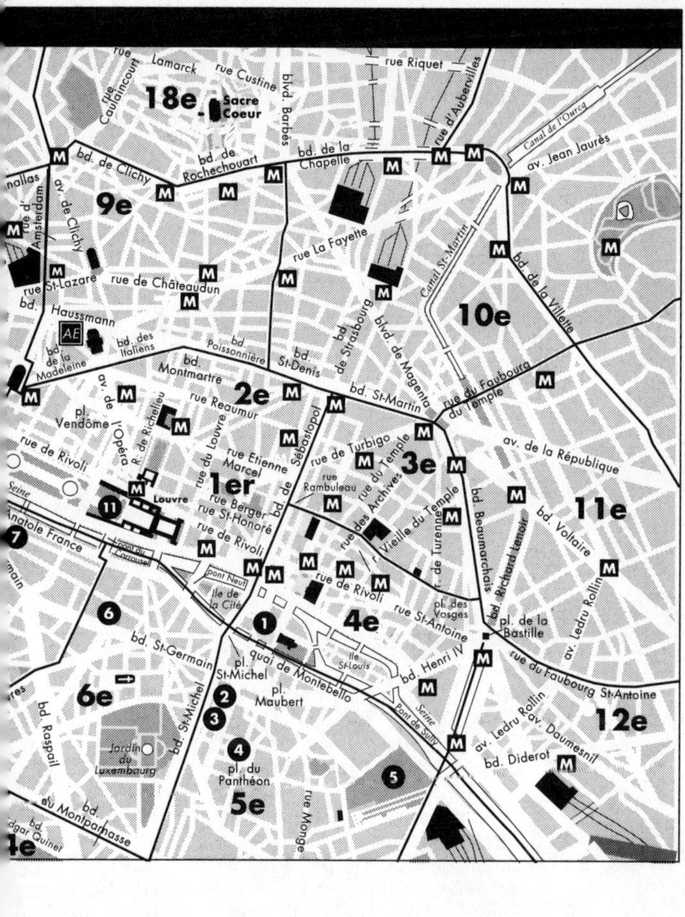

rue Lamarck
rue Custine
rue Caulaincourt
18e
Sacre Coeur
blvd. Barbès
rue Riquet
rue d'Aubervilles
Canal de l'Ourcq
av. Jean Jaurès
bd. de Clichy
bd. de Rochechouart
bd. de la Chapelle
9e
rue d'Amsterdam
av. de Clichy
rue La Fayette
Canal St-Martin
bd. de la Villette
rue St-Lazare
rue de Châteaudun
bd. Haussmann
AE
10e
bd. des Italiens
bd. Poissonnière
bd. St-Denis
bd. de Strasbourg
blvd. de Magenta
bd. de la Madeleine
bd. Montmartre
2e
bd. St-Martin
rue du Faubourg du Temple
pl. Vendôme
av. de l'Opéra
rue Reaumur
R. de Richelieu
rue de Turbigo
3e
av. de la République
rue de Rivoli
rue du Louvre
rue Etienne Marcel
bd. de Sébastopol
rue du Temple
rue Rambuleau
rue des Archives
1er
Louvre
rue Berger
rue St-Honoré
rue Vieille du Temple
r. de Turenne
bd. Beaumarchais
bd. Richard Lenoir
bd. Voltaire
11e
Seine
Anatole France
Pont du Carrousel
Pont Neuf
Ile de la Cité
pl. des Vosges
rue St-Antoine
pl. de la Bastille
av. Ledru Rollin
4e
bd. St-Germain
pl. St-Michel
quai de Montebello
Ile St-Louis
bd. Henri IV
rue du Faubourg St-Antoine
pl. Maubert
Pont de Sully
12e
6e
bd. Raspail
bd. St-Michel
Jardin du Luxembourg
pl. du Panthéon
5e
rue Monge
av. Daumesnil
bd. Diderot
bd. du Montparnasse
bd. Edgar Quinet
1
2
3
4
5
6
7
11

You can hardly miss the sturdy pointed tower of
6 **St-Germain-des-Prés,** the oldest church in Paris (begun around 1160, though the towers date from the 11th century). Note the colorful nave frescoes by the 19th-century artist Hippolyte Flandrin, a pupil of Ingres. *Pl. St-Germain-des-Prés. Weekdays 8–7:30; weekends 8–9.*

7 The **Musée d'Orsay** has become one of Paris's star tourist attractions. Its imaginatively housed collections of the arts (mainly French) span the period 1848–1914 and take up three floors, but the visitor's immediate impression is one of a single, vast hall. This is not surprising: The museum was originally built in 1900 as a train station. *1 rue Bellechasse, tel. 01–40–49–48–14. Admission: 35 frs., 24 frs. on Sun. Open Tues., Wed., Fri., Sat. 10–5:30; Thurs. 10–9:30; Sun. 9–5:30.*

8 The **Musée Rodin** is among the most charming of Paris's individual museums. An old house (built in 1728) and a pretty garden are filled with the vigorous sculptures of Auguste Rodin (1840–1917). The garden also has hundreds of rosebushes, with dozens of different varieties. *77 rue de Varenne, tel. 01–44–18–61–10. Admission: 27 frs, 18 frs Sun. Open Tues.–Sun. 10–5.*

No one will want to miss Paris's most famous
9 landmark, the **Tour Eiffel** (Eiffel Tower). It was built by Gustave Eiffel for the World Exhibition of 1889. Recent restorations haven't made the elevators any faster—long lines are inevitable—but decent shops and two good restaurants have been added. Such was Eiffel's engineering precision that even in the fiercest winds the tower never sways more than a few centimeters. Standing beneath it, you may have trouble believing that it nearly became 7,000 tons of scrap iron when its concession expired in 1909. Only its potential use as a radio antenna saved the day; it now bristles with a forest of radio and television transmitters. The view from 1,000 ft up will enable you to appreciate the city's layout and proportions. *Quai Branly, tel. 01–44–11–23–23. Admission: on foot, 12 frs; by elevator, 20–56 frs, depending on the level. Open July–Aug., daily 9 AM–midnight; Sept.–June, Sun.–Thurs. 9 AM–11 PM, Fri., Sat. 9 AM–midnight.*

Looming over place Charles-de-Gaulle, known
10 to Parisians as “L’Étoile” (the Star), is the **Arc de Triomphe.** This 164-ft arch was planned by Napoléon to celebrate his military successes—but Napoléon had been dead for 15 years when the Arc de Triomphe was finally finished in 1836. From the top of the Arc you can see the “star” effect of Étoile’s 12 radiating avenues and admire two special vistas: one down the Champs-Élysées toward place de la Concorde and the Louvre, and the other down avenue de la Grande Armée toward La Tête Défense, a severe modern arch surrounded by imposing glass and concrete towers. France’s Unknown Soldier is buried beneath the archway. Halfway up the Arc is a small museum devoted to its history. *Pl. Charles-de-Gaulle, tel. 01–43–80–31–31. Admission: 32 frs. Open daily 10–5:30.*

The **Champs-Elysées** is the site of colorful national ceremonies on July 14 and November 11; its trees are often decked with French tricolors and foreign flags to mark visits from heads of state. It is also where the cosmopolitan pulse of Paris beats strongest. The gracefully sloping 2-km (1¼-mi) boulevard was originally laid out in the 1660s by André Le Nôtre as a garden sweeping away from the Tuileries. There is not much sign of that as you stroll past the cafés, restaurants, airline offices, car showrooms, movie theaters, and chic arcades that occupy its upper half, although the avenue was spruced up in the early 1990s with wider sidewalks and an extra row of trees.

Once a royal palace, now the the world’s largest
11 and most famous museum, the **Louvre** has been given fresh purpose by a decade of expansion, renovation, and reorganization, symbolized by I. M. Pei’s daring glass pyramid that now serves as the entrance to both the museum and an underground shopping arcade, the Carrousel du Louvre. The Louvre was begun as a fortress in 1200 (the earliest parts still standing date from the 1540s) and completed under Napoléon III in the 1860s. The museum’s sheer variety can seem intimidating. The main tourist attraction is Leonardo da Vinci’s *Mona Lisa* (known in French as *La Joconde*), painted in 1503. The latest research, based on Leonardo’s supposed homosex-

uality, would have us believe that the subject was actually a man! The *Mona Lisa* may disappoint you: It's smaller than most imagine, it's kept behind glass, and it's invariably encircled by a mob of tourists. Turn your attention instead to some of the less-crowded rooms and galleries nearby, where Leonardo's fellow Italians are strongly represented: Fra Angelico, Giotto, Mantegna, Raphael, Titian, and Veronese. El Greco, Murillo, and Velázquez lead the Spanish; Van Eyck, Rembrandt, Frans Hals, Brueghel, Holbein, and Rubens underline the achievements of northern European art. English paintings are highlighted by works of Lawrence, Reynolds, Gainsborough, and Turner. Highlights of French painting include works by Poussin, Fragonard, Chardin, Boucher, and Watteau—together with David's *Coronation of Napoléon*, Géricault's *Raft of the Medusa*, and Delacroix's *Liberty Guiding the People*. Famous statues include the soaring *Victory of Samothrace* and the eternally fascinating *Venus de Milo*. *Palais du Louvre, tel. 01–40–20–53–17 for information. Admission: 45 frs, 26 frs after 3 PM and Sun. Open Mon. and Wed. 9 AM–9:45 PM, Thurs.–Sun. 9–6.*

Shopping Paris is the home of fashion and perfume. Old prints are sold by *bouquinistes* (secondhand booksellers) in stalls along the Left Bank of the Seine. For state-of-the-art home decorations, the shop in the **Musée des Arts Décoratifs** in the Louvre (107 rue de Rivoli) is well worth visiting.

The top shops are along avenue Montaigne, rue du Faubourg-St-Honoré, and the place des Victoires. The area surrounding St-Germain-des-Prés on the Left Bank is a mecca for specialty shops and boutiques and has recently seen an influx of the elite names in haute couture. If you're on a tight budget, search for bargains along the streets around the foot of Montmartre or in the designer discount shops (Cacharel, Rykiel, Dorotennis) along rue d'Alésia in Montparnasse. The streets to the north of the Marais, close to Arts-et-Métiers métro, are historically linked to the cloth trade, and some shops offer garments at wholesale prices.

The most famous department stores in Paris are **Galeries Lafayette** and **Printemps,** on boulevard Haussmann. Others include **Au Bon Marché** on the Left Bank (métro: Sèvres-Babylone) and the **Samaritaine,** overlooking the Seine east of the Louvre (métro: Pont-Neuf).

Reykjavík, Iceland

Iceland is anything but icy. Though glaciers cover about 10% of the country, summers are relatively warm, and winters are milder than those in New York. Coastal farms lie in green, pastoral lowlands, where cows, sheep, and horses graze alongside raging streams. Distant waterfalls plunge from heather-covered mountains with great spiked ridges and snowcapped peaks. Iceland's name can be blamed on Hrafna-Flóki, a 9th-century Norse settler who failed to plant enough crops to see his livestock through their first winter. Leaving in a huff, he passed a northern fjord filled with pack ice and cursed the country with a name that's kept tourism in cold storage for 1,100 years.

The second-largest island in Europe, Iceland is in the middle of the North Atlantic, where the warm Gulf Stream from the south meets cold currents from the north—just the right conditions for fish, which provide the nation with 80% of its export revenue. Beneath some of the country's glaciers are burning fires that become visible during volcanic eruptions—fires that heat the country's hot springs and geysers. The springs, in turn, provide warmth for the country's homes, hospitals, and public swimming pools, keeping the nation's air smokeless and smogless.

Currency The Icelandic monetary unit is the króna (plural, krónur), which is equal to 100 aurar and is abbreviated kr. locally and IKr internationally. At press time, the rate of exchange was IKr67 to the U.S. dollar.

Telephones The country code for Iceland is 354. All phone numbers in Iceland have seven digits; there are no city codes. Pay phones take IKr 10 and IKr 50 coins and are found in hotels, shops, bus stations, and post offices. Phone cards cost IKr 500 and are sold at post offices, hotels, and so on. For operator assistance with local calls dial 119; for information dial 118. For assistance with overseas calls, dial 115; for direct international calls dial 00. To reach a long-distance operator in the United States from Iceland, use the following international access codes: for **AT&T** dial 800–9001; **MCI,** 999–002; **Sprint,** 800–9003.

Shore Excursions The following are good choices in Iceland. They may not be offered by all cruise lines. Times and prices are approximate.

Golden Circle. Iceland's natural wonders are the focus of this tour, which visits Thingvellir National Park, Gulifoss (the Golden Waterfall), and Strokkur Geyser. You'll also see the second-largest glacier in Iceland and post-glacial lava fields. *5 hrs. Cost: $75.*

City Sights. Reykjavík's naturally heated outdoor swimming pool is a highlight of a half day of sightseeing, which also visits the Arabaer Folk Museum and the National Museum and drives by the University, Old Town, the Parliament, the Cathedral, and residential areas. *3 hrs. Cost: $36.*

Coming Ashore Ships calling in Iceland berth at the dock in Reykjavík. The most interesting sights are in the city center, within easy walking distance of one another.

Getting Around The center of Reykjavík is served by two main bus stops: Brook Square and Hlemmur station. Buses run from 7 AM to midnight. The flat fare for Reykjavík and suburbs is IKr 120. Taxi rates start at about IKr 300; few in-town taxi rides exceed IKr 700. The best taxis to call are Hreyfill (tel. 588–5522), BSR (tel. 561–0000 or 561–1720), and Bæjarleiðir (tel. 553–3500).

Exploring Reykjavík The heart of Reykjavík is **Austurvöllur Square** (East Field), a small square in the center of the city. The 19th-century Albingi (Parliament building), one of the oldest stone buildings in Iceland, faces the square. In the center of the square is a statue of Jón Sigurðsson (1811–79), the national hero who led Iceland's fight for independence, which it achieved fully in 1944.

Next to Albingi is the **Dómkirkjan** (Lutheran cathedral), a small, charming stone church. Behind it is Tjörnin, a natural pond next to Reykjavík City Hall. One corner of the pond does not freeze; here thermal springs feed warm water, making it an attraction for birds year-round. *Austurvöllur Square (East Field), tel. 551–2113. Open Mon. and Tues.–Fri. 9–5, Wed. 10–5, unless in use for services.*

Overlooking Tjörnin stands the **Listasfn Íslands** (National Gallery), which houses a collection of Icelandic art. *Fríkirkjuvegur 7, tel. 562–1000. Admission: IKr 200. Open Tues.–Sun. noon–6.*

At Lækjartorg square, on the right, is the **Bernhöftstorfa** district, a small hill with colorful two-story wooden houses from the mid-19th century, where no modernizing efforts have been made. For a century and a half, the largest building has housed the oldest educational institution in the country, Menntaskólinn í Reykjavík, a college whose graduates have from the early days dominated political and social life in Iceland. *Corner of Amtmannsstígur and Lækjargata.*

Leading west out of Lækjartorg square is Austurstræti, a semipedestrian shopping street with the main post office on the right. From here you can take bus 10 from the bus station for a 20-minute ride to the **Arbæjarsafn** (Open-Air Museum), a "village" of 18th- and 19th-century houses. *Árbær (bus 10 at Hlemmur station), tel. 577–1111. Open June–Aug., Tues.–Sun. 10–6, and by appointment.*

At the **Ásmundur Sveinsson Sculpture Museum,** a few originals of this social realist sculptor are in the surrounding garden, which is accessible at all times free of charge. *v/Sigtún, tel. 553–2155. Admission: IKr 200. Open June–Sept., daily 10–4; Oct.–May, daily 1–4.*

The **Náttúrufræð´istofnun** (Museum of Natural History) has one of the last great auks on display plus several exhibits on Icelandic natural history. *Hlemmtorg, Hverfisgata 116, tel. 562–9822. Admission free. Open Tues., Thurs., and weekends. 1:30–4.*

The **Hallgrímskirkja** (Hallgrim's Church) features a 210-ft gray-stone tower that dominates the city's skyline. The church, which took more than 40 years to build and was completed in the '80s, is open to the public. The church tower offers a panoramic view of the city and its spacious suburbs. *Top of Skólavörðustígur, tel. 551–0745. Admission to tower: IKr 200. Open May–Sept., daily 9–6; Oct.–Apr., daily 10–6.*

The **National Gallery of Einar Jónsson** is devoted to the works of Iceland's leading early-20th-century sculptor. His monumental sculptures have a strong symbolic and mystical content. *Njarðargata, tel. 551–3797. Admission: IKr 200. Open June–mid-Sept., Tues.–Sun 1:30–4; weekends only mid-Sept.–Nov. and Feb.–May; closed Dec.–Jan. Sculpture garden always open.*

At the campus of the **University of Iceland** (founded 1911) is the outstanding phjópminjasafn (National Museum). On display are Viking artifacts, national costumes, weaving, wood carving, and silver works. *Suðurgata 41, tel. 552–8888. Small admission fee. Open mid-May–mid-Sept., Tues.–Sun. 11–5; late Sept.–early May, Tues., Thurs., and weekends noon–5.*

Shopping Many of the shops that sell the most attractive Icelandic woolen goods and arts and crafts are on Apalstræti, Hafnarstræti, and Vesturgata streets. The **Icelandic Handcrafts Center** (Falcon House, Hafnarstræti 3, tel. 551–1785) stocks Icelandic woolens, knitting and tapestry materials, and handmade pottery, glassware, and jewelry. At the **Handknitting Association of Iceland** (Skólavörpustígur 9, tel. 552–1890), you can buy high-quality hand-knitted items through a knitters' cooperative. **Rammagerp´in** (Hafnarstræti 19, tel. 551–7910) stocks a wide range of Icelandic-made clothes, souvenirs, and books. On weekends, try the **flea market** (Harborside Kolaportið in the rear of the Customs House on Geirsgata) between 11 and 5.

Rome/Civitavecchia, Italy

Civitavecchia is the port city for Rome, where antiquity is taken for granted. Successive ages have piled the present on top of the past—building, layering, and overlapping their own particular segments of Rome's 2,500 years of history to form a remarkably varied urban complex. Most of the city's major sights are in a fairly small area known as the *centro*. At its heart lies ancient Rome, where the Forum and Colosseum stand. It was around this core that the other sections of the city grew up through the ages: medieval Rome, which covered the horn of land that pushes the Tiber toward the Vatican and extended across the river into Trastevere; and Renaissance Rome, which was erected upon medieval foundations and extended as far as the Vatican, creating beautiful villas on what was then the outskirts of the city.

Currency The unit of currency in Italy is the lira (plural, lire). At press time, the exchange rate was about 1,595 lire to the U.S. dollar. When your purchases run into hundreds of thousands of lire, beware of being shortchanged, a dodge that is practiced at ticket windows and cashiers' desks, as well as in shops and even banks. Always count your change before you leave the counter.

Telephones The country code for Italy is 39. Most local calls cost 200 lire for two minutes. Pay phones take either 100-, 200-, or 500-lire coins or *schede telefoniche* (phone cards), purchased in bars, tobacconists, post offices, and TELECOM offices in either 5,000-, 10,000-, or 15,000-lire denominations. To place international calls, many travelers go to the Telefoni telephone exchange, where the operator assigns you a booth, can help place your call, and will collect payment when you have finished. Telefoni exchanges (usually marked TELECOM) are found in both cities. To dial an international call, insert a phone card, dial 00, then the country code, area code, and phone number. For **AT&T**, dial access number 172–1011; **MCI,** 172–1022; **Sprint,** 172–1877. You will be connected directly with an operator in the United States.

Shore Excursions Due to the limited amount of time you will have in the city and its wealth of sights, it is a good idea to select a tour in Rome. The following is a good choice. It may not be offered by all cruise lines. Time and price are approximate.

Highlights and History. An excellent choice for first-time visitors who want to span Rome's 2,500 years of history. Highlights include the

Colosseum, the Vatican Museum, St. Peter's Basilica, and the Forum. Travel is by motor coach. *11 hrs. Cost: $160.*

Coming Ashore Ships dock at Civitavecchia, about one hour and 45 minutes from Rome by bus. Cruise lines usually will sell bus transfers to Rome for those who want to explore independently.

Getting Around The layout of the centro is highly irregular, but several landmarks serve as orientation points to identify the areas that most visitors come to see: the Colosseo (Colosseum), the Pantheon and Piazza Navona, the Basilica di San Pietro (St. Peter's Church), the Scalinata di Piazza di Spagna (Spanish Steps), and Villa Borghese. You'll need a good map to find your way around; newsstands offer a wide choice. The important thing is to relax and enjoy Rome. Don't try to see everything, but do take time to savor its pleasures. If you are in Rome during a hot spell, do as the Romans do: Sightsee a little, take a break during the hottest hours, then resume sightseeing.

The best way to see Rome once you arrive is to choose an area or a sight that you particularly want to see, reach it by bus or metro, then explore the area on foot. Wear comfortable, sturdy shoes, preferably with thick rubber soles to cushion you against the cobblestones. You can buy transportation-route maps at newsstands and at ATAC (bus company) information and ticket booths. The metro provides the easiest and fastest way to get around. A BIG tourist ticket, valid for one day on all public transport, costs 6,000 lire. Taxis wait at stands and, for a small extra charge, can also be called by telephone. The meter starts at 4,500 lire. Use the yellow or the newer white cabs only, and be very sure to check the meter. To call a cab, phone 06/3570, 06/3875, 06/4994, or 06/88177.

Exploring Rome *Numbers in the margin correspond to points of interest on the Rome map.*

❶ In the valley below the Campidoglio is the **Foro Romano** (Roman Forum). Once only a marshy hollow, the forum became the political, commercial, and social center of Rome, studded with public meeting halls, shops, and temples. As

Rome declined, these monuments lost their importance and eventually were destroyed by fire or the invasions of barbarians. Rubble accumulated (though much of it was carted off later by medieval home builders as construction material), and the site reverted to marshy pastureland; sporadic excavations began at the end of the 19th century. You don't really have to try to make sense of the mass of marble fragments scattered over the area of the Roman Forum. Just consider that 2,000 years ago this was the center of the Mediterranean world. Wander down the Via Sacra and climb the Palatine Hill, where the emperors had their palaces and where 16th-century cardinals strolled in elaborate Italian gardens. From the belvedere you have a good view of the Circus Maximus. *Entrances on Via dei Fori Imperiali, Piazza Santa Maria Nova, and Via di San Gregorio, tel. 06/699–0110. Admission: 12,000 lire. Open Apr.–Sept., Mon.–Sat. 9–6, Sun. 9–1; Oct.–Mar., Mon.–Sat. 9–3, Sun. 9–1.*

2 Rome's most famous ancient ruin, the **Colosseo** (Colosseum), was inaugurated in AD 80 with a program of games and shows that lasted 100 days. On opening day alone 5,000 wild animals perished in the arena. The Colosseum could hold more than 50,000 spectators; it was faced with marble, decorated with stuccos, and had an ingenious system of awnings to provide shade. Try to see it both in daytime and at night, when yellow floodlights make it a magical sight. The Colosseum, by the way, takes its name from a colossal, 118-ft statue of Nero that stood nearby. You must pay a fee to explore the upper levels. *Piazza del Colosseo, tel. 06/700–4261. Admission: free; 8,000 lire for upper levels. Open Apr.–Sept., Mon.–Tues. and Thurs.–Sat. 9–7, Sun. and Wed. 9–1; Oct.–Mar., Mon.–Tues. and Thurs.–Sat. 9–3, Sun. and Wed. 9–1.*

3 The **Terme di Caracalla** (Baths of Caracalla), numbered among ancient Rome's most beautiful and luxurious, were inaugurated by Caracalla in AD 217 and used until the 6th century. An ancient version of a swanky athletic club, the baths were open to the public; citizens could bathe, socialize, and exercise in huge pools and richly decorated halls and libraries, now towering

Rome

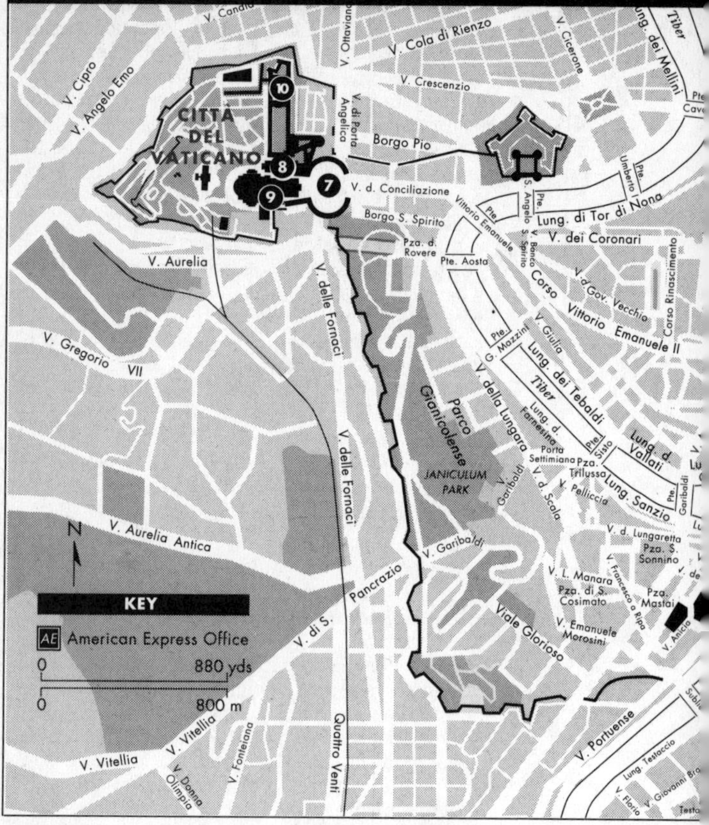

Basilica di San Pietro, **9**

Colosseo, **2**

Fontana di Trevi, **5**

Foro Romano, **1**

Musei Vaticani, **10**

Pantheon, **11**

Piazza San Pietro, **7**

Santa Maria della Concezione, **6**

Scalinata di Piazza di Spagna, **4**

Termi di Caracalla, **3**

Vatican Palace, **8**

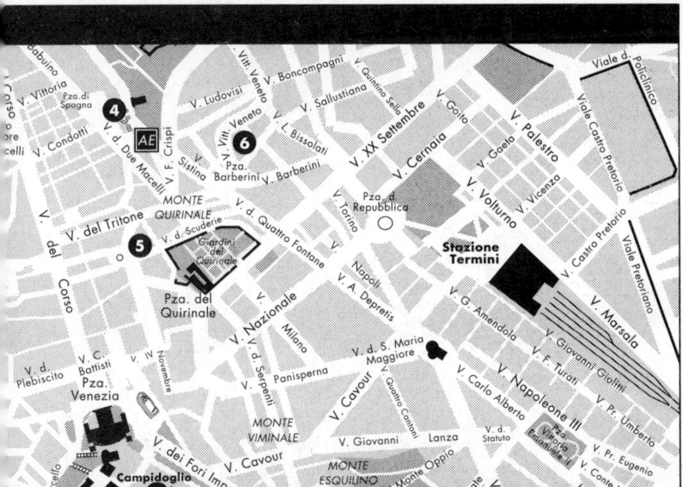

V. Vittoria
Pza. di Spagna
V. Condotti
V. d. Due Macelli
V. F. Crispi
V. Sistina
V. Ludovisi
Vitt. Veneto
V. Boncompagni
V. Quintino Sella
V. Sallustiana
V. L. Bissolati
Pza. Barberini
V. Barberini
V. XX Settembre
V. Goito
V. Cernaia
V. Palestro
V. Gaeta
V. Volturno
V. Vicenza
Viale d. Policlinico
Viale Castro Pretorio
V. Castro Pretorio
Viale Pretoriano
V. Marsala
Stazione Termini
Pza. d. Repubblica
V. Torino
V. d. Quattro Fontane
V. Napoli
V. A. Depretis
V. G. Amendola
V. Giovanni Giolitti
V. F. Turati
V. Napoleone III
V. Pr. Umberto
V. Pr. Eugenio
V. Conte Verde
Pza. Vittorio Emanuele II
V. Carlo Alberto
V. d. Statuto
V. d. S. Maria Maggiore
V. Quattro Cantoni
V. Giovanni Lanza
V. Cavour
V. Panisperna
V. d. Serpenti
V. Milano
V. Nazionale
MONTE QUIRINALE
V. d. Scuderie
Giardini del Quirinale
Pza. del Quirinale
V. del Tritone
V. del Corso
V. d. Plebiscito
V. C. Battisti
V. IV Novembre
Pza. Venezia
MONTE VIMINALE
V. dei Fori Imperiali
Campidoglio
MONTE ESQUILINO
Viale del Monte Oppio
V. Mecenate
V. Merulana
V. Rugg. Bonghi
V. d. Domus Aurea
V. Labicana
V. S. Giovanni in Laterano
Viale Manzoni
V. Emanuele Filiberto
Pza. Giovanni XXIII
V. di S. Stefano Rotondo
V. Claudia
Pza. SS. Giovanni e Paolo
MONTE CELIO
V. di S. Gregorio
MONTE PALATINO
V. di S. Teodoro
V. dei Cerchi
V. del Circo Massimo
V. d. Teatro di Marcello
Lung. d. Pierleoni
Pte. Palatino
Tiber
V. Aventino
COLLE AVENTINO
Pte. Romolo e Remo
V. d. S. Sabina
MONTE AVENTINO
V. S. Prisca
Viale Aventino
V. delle Terme Caracalla
Pza. di Porta Metronia
V. Gallia
V. Pannonia
V. d. Porta Latina
Parco di Porta Capena
V. Guido Bacelli
Terme di Caracalla
Pza. Albania
V. M. Gelsomini
AE
1
2
3
4
5
6

ruins. *Via delle Terme di Caracalla. Admission: 8,000 lire. Open Apr.–Sept., Tues.–Sat. 9–6, Sun.–Mon. 9–1; Oct.–Mar., Tues.–Sat. 9–3, Sun.–Mon. 9–1.*

4 The 200-year-old **Scalinata di Piazza di Spagna** (Spanish Steps), named for the Spanish Embassy to the Holy See, opposite the American Express office, are a popular rendezvous, especially for the young people who throng this area. The steps are banked with blooming azaleas from mid-April to mid-May. *Piazza di Spagna and Piazza Trinità dei Monti.*

5 **Fontana di Trevi** (Trevi Fountain) is a spectacular fantasy of mythical sea creatures and cascades of splashing water. Legend has it that visitors must toss a coin into the fountain to ensure their return to Rome, but you'll have to force your way past crowds of tourists and aggressive souvenir vendors to do so. The fountain as you see it was completed in the mid-1700s, but there had been a drinking fountain on the site for centuries. Pope Urban VIII almost sparked a revolt when he slapped a tax on wine to cover the expenses of having the fountain repaired. *Piazza di Trevi.*

One of Rome's oddest sights is the crypt of the
6 church of **Santa Maria della Concezione.** In four chapels under the main church, the skeletons and scattered bones of some 4,000 dead Capuchin monks are arranged in decorative motifs, a macabre practice peculiar to the baroque age. *Via Veneto 27, tel. 06/462850. Admission free, but donations encouraged. Open daily 9–noon and 3–6.*

Via della Conciliazione, the broad avenue leading to St. Peter's Basilica, was created by Mussolini's architects by razing blocks of old houses. This opened up a vista of the basilica, giving the eye time to adjust to its mammoth dimensions and thereby spoiling the effect Bernini sought when he enclosed his vast square (which is really oval) in the embrace of huge quadruple colon-
7 nades. In **Piazza San Pietro** (St. Peter's Square), which has held up to 400,000 people at one time, look for the stone disks in the pavement halfway between the fountains and the obelisk. From these points the colonnades seem to be formed of a single row of columns all the way around.

When you enter St. Peter's Square (completed in 1667), you are entering Vatican territory. Since the Lateran Treaty of 1929, **Vatican City** has been an independent and sovereign state, which covers about 108 acres and is surrounded by thick, high walls. Its gates are watched over by the Swiss Guards, who still wear the colorful dress uniforms designed by Michelangelo. Sovereign of this little state is John Paul II, 264th pope of the Roman Catholic Church.

8 At noon on Sunday, the pope appears at his third-floor study window in the **Vatican Palace,** to the right of the basilica, to bless the crowd in the square. (Note: Entry to St. Peter's, the Vatican Museums, and all other sites within Vatican City, e.g., the Gardens, is barred to those wearing shorts, miniskirts, sleeveless T-shirts, and otherwise revealing clothing. Women should carry scarves to cover bare shoulders and upper arms or wear blouses that come to the elbow. Men should dress modestly, in slacks and shirts.)

9 **Basilica di San Pietro** (St. Peter's Basilica) is one of Rome's most impressive sights. It takes a while to absorb the sheer magnificence of it, however, and its rich decoration may not be to everyone's taste. Its size alone is overwhelming, and the basilica is best appreciated when providing the lustrous background for ecclesiastical ceremonies thronged with the faithful. The original basilica was built in the early 4th century AD by the emperor Constantine, over an earlier shrine that supposedly marked the burial place of St. Peter. After more than a thousand years, the old basilica was so decrepit it had to be torn down. The task of building a new, much larger one took almost 200 years and employed the architectural genius of Alberti, Bramante, Raphael, Peruzzi, Antonio Sangallo the Younger, and Michelangelo, who died before the dome he had planned could be completed. Finally, in 1626, St. Peter's Basilica was finished. The basilica is full of extraordinary works of art. Among the most famous is Michelangelo's *Pietà* (1498), seen in the first chapel on the right just as you enter the basilica. Michelangelo has four *Pietàs* to his credit. The earliest and best known

can be seen here. Two others are in Florence, and the fourth, the *Rondanini Pietà*, is in Milan.

At the end of the central aisle is the bronze statue of **St. Peter,** its foot worn by centuries of reverent kisses. The bronze throne above the altar in the apse was created by Bernini to contain a simple wood and ivory chair once believed to have belonged to St. Peter. Bernini's bronze *baldacchino* (canopy) over the papal altar was made with metal stripped from the portico of the Pantheon at the order of Pope Urban VIII, one of the powerful Roman Barberini family. His practice of plundering ancient monuments for material to implement his grandiose schemes inspired the famous quip, "*Quod non fecerunt barbari, fecerunt Barberini*" ("What the barbarians didn't do, the Barberini did").

As you stroll up and down the aisles and transepts, observe the fine mosaic copies of famous paintings above the altars, the monumental tombs and statues, and the fine stuccowork. Stop at the **Museo Storico** (Historical Museum), which contains some priceless liturgical objects.

The entrance to the so-called **Vatican Grottoes,** or crypt, is in one of the huge piers at the crossing. It's best to leave this visit for last, as the crypt's only exit takes you outside the church. The crypt contains chapels and the tombs of many popes. It occupies the area of the original basilica, over the necropolis, the ancient burial ground where evidence of what may be St. Peter's burial place has been found. To see the roof and dome of the basilica, take the elevator or climb the stairs in the courtyard near the exit of the Vatican Grottoes. From the roof you can climb a short interior staircase to the base of the dome for an overhead view of the interior of the basilica. Only if you are in good shape should you attempt the very long, strenuous, and claustrophobic climb up the narrow stairs to the balcony of the lantern atop the dome, where the view embraces the Vatican Gardens as well as all of Rome.

Free 90-minute tours of St. Peter's Basilica are offered in English daily (usually starting about

10 AM and 3 PM) by volunteer guides. They start at the information desk under the basilica portico. *St. Peter's Basilica, tel. 06/6988–4466. Open Apr.–Sept., daily 7–7; Oct.–Mar., daily 7–6. Treasury: entrance in Sacristy. Admission: 8,000 lire. Open Apr.–Sept., daily 9–6; Oct.–Mar., daily 9–5. Roof and dome: entrance in courtyard to the left as you leave basilica. Admission: 6,000 lire for elevator, 5,000 lire for stairs. Open Apr.–Sept., daily 8–6; Oct.–Mar., daily 8–5. Vatican Grottoes (Tombs of the Popes): entrance alternates among piers at crossing. Admission free. Open Apr.–Sept., daily 7–6; Oct.–Mar., daily 7–5.*

10 The collections in the **Musei Vaticani** (Vatican Museums) cover nearly 8 km (5 mi) of displays. If you have time, allow at least half a day for Castel Sant'Angelo and St. Peter's and another half day for the museums. Posters at the museum entrance plot out a choice of four color-coded itineraries; the shortest takes about 90 minutes, the longest more than four hours, depending on your rate of progress.

No matter which tour you take, it will include the famed **Capella Sistina** (Sistine Chapel). In 1508, Pope Julius II commissioned Michelangelo to fresco the more than 10,000 square ft of the chapel's ceiling. For four years Michelangelo dedicated himself to painting over fresh plaster, and the result was his masterpiece. Completed cleaning operations have removed centuries of soot and revealed its original and surprisingly brilliant colors. On the wall over the altar is Michelangelo's *Last Judgement*, painted about 30 years after the ceiling was completed.

You can try to avoid the tour groups by going early or late, allowing yourself enough time before the closing hour. In peak season, the crowds definitely detract from your appreciation of this outstanding artistic achievement. To make sense of the figures on the ceiling, buy an illustrated guide or rent a taped commentary. A pair of binoculars also helps.

The Vatican collections are so rich that unless you are an expert in art history, you will probably want only to skim the surface, concentrating on pieces that strike your fancy. Some of the highlights that might be of interest include the Egyptian collection and the *Laocoön*, the *Belvedere Torso*, and the *Apollo Belvedere*, which inspired Michelangelo. The Raphael Rooms are decorated with masterful frescoes, and there are more Raphaels in the *Pinacoteca* (Picture Gallery). At the Quattro Cancelli, near the entrance to the Picture Gallery, a rather spartan cafeteria provides basic nonalcoholic refreshments. *Viale Vaticano, tel. 06/6988–3860. Admission: 15,000 lire; free last Sun. of month. Open Easter wk and mid-Mar.–mid-June and Sept.–Oct., weekdays 8:45–4:45, Sat. 8:45–1:45; Oct.–mid-Mar. and mid-June–Aug., Mon.–Sat. 8:45–1:45. Last Sun. of month 9–1. Ticket office closes 45 mins before museums close. Closed Sun., except last Sun. of month.*

11 Originally built in 27 BC by Augustus's general Agrippa and rebuilt by Hadrian in the 2nd century AD, the **Pantheon** is one of Rome's finest, best-preserved, and perhaps least appreciated ancient monuments. Romans and tourists alike pay little attention to it, and on summer evenings it serves mainly as a backdrop for all the action in the square in front. It represents a fantastic feat of construction, however. The huge columns of the portico and the original bronze doors form the entrance to a majestic hall covered by the largest dome of its kind ever built, wider even than that of St. Peter's. In ancient times the entire interior was encrusted with rich decorations of gilt bronze and marble. *Piazza della Rotonda, tel. 06/6830–0230. Admission free. Open Mon.–Sat. 9–4:30, Sun. 9–1.*

Shopping

Shopping is part of the fun of being in Rome. The best buys are leather goods of all kinds, from gloves to handbags and wallets to jackets; silk goods; and high-quality knitwear. Shops are closed on Sunday and on Monday morning; in July and August, they close on Saturday afternoon as well. **Via Condotti,** directly across from the Spanish Steps, and the streets running parallel to Via Condotti, as well as its cross streets, form the most elegant and expensive shopping area in the city. Romans themselves do much of their shopping along **Via Cola di Rienzo** and **Via Nazionale.**

Seville, Spain

Seville—Spain's fourth-largest city and capital of Andalucía—is one of the most beautiful and romantic cities in Europe. Here in this city of the sensuous Carmen and the amorous Don Juan, famed for the spectacle of its Holy Week processions and April Fair, you'll come close to the spiritual heart of Moorish Andalucía. The downside to a visit to Seville is that petty crime, much of it directed against tourists, is rife. Take only the minimum amount of cash with you when going ashore. If you're unlucky, it's an equally depressing fact that the police have adopted a distinctly casual attitude to such thefts.

Currency The unit of currency in Spain is the peseta (pta.). There are bills of 1,000, 2,000, 5,000, and 10,000 ptas. Coins are 1, 5, 25, 50, 100, 200, and 500 ptas. Note that the 2- and 10-pta. coins and the old 100-pta. bills are no longer legal tender. At press time, the exchange rate was about 145 ptas. to the U.S. dollar.

Telephones The country code for Spain is 34. Pay phones generally take the new, smaller 5- and 25-pta. coins; the minimum charge for short local calls is 25 ptas. Area codes always begin with a 9 and are different for each province. In Madrid province, the code is 91; in Cantabria, it's 942. If you're dialing from outside the country, drop the 9. Calling abroad can be done from any pay phone marked *teléfono internacional*. Use 50-pta. (or 100-pta. if the phone takes them) coins initially, then coins of any denomination to prolong your call. Dial 07 for international calls, wait for the tone to change, then 1 for the United States or 0101 for Canada. For lengthy international calls, go to the telefónica, a telephone office, where an operator assigns you a private booth and collects payment at the end of the call; this is the least expensive and by far the easiest way of phoning abroad. **AT&T** (tel. 900/99–00–11); **MCI** (tel. 900/99–00–14); **Sprint** (tel. 900/99–00–13).

Shore Excursions The following is a good choice in Seville. It may not be offered by all cruise lines. Time and price are approximate.

Survey of Seville. Travel through Seville's past and present on this comprehensive excursion that explores the city's religious, ethnic, and historical diversity. *8½ hrs. Cost: $124.*

Coming Ashore Ships dock at Cádiz for Seville. The drive to and from Seville is around two hours each way.

Getting Around Once in the city, you can walk from some sights to others; hop a cab or even take a horse-drawn carriage to reach other areas.

Exploring Seville *Numbers in the margin correspond to points of interest on the Seville map.*

1 A must is a visit to the **cathedral,** begun in 1402, a century and a half after St. Ferdinand delivered Seville from the Moors. This great Gothic edifice, which took just over a century to build, is traditionally described in superlatives. It's the biggest and highest cathedral in Spain, the largest Gothic building in the world, and the world's third-largest church after St. Peter's in Rome and St. Paul's in London. And it boasts the world's largest carved wooden altarpiece. Despite such impressive statistics, the inside can be dark and gloomy, with too many overly ornate baroque trappings. You'll want to pay your respects to Christopher Columbus, whose mortal vestiges are enshrined in a flamboyant mausoleum in the south aisle. Borne aloft by statues representing the four medieval kingdoms of Spain, it's to be hoped that the great voyager has found peace at last, after the transatlantic quarrels that carried his body from Valladolid to Santo Domingo and from Havana to Seville. *Plaza Virgen de los Reyes, tel. 95/421–4971. Admission to cathedral and Giralda (see below): 550 ptas. Open weekdays 11–5, Sat. 11–4, Sun. 2–4.*

Every day the bell that summons the faithful to prayer rings out from a Moorish minaret, a relic of the Arab mosque whose admirable tower of Abu Yakoub the Sevillians could not bring themselves to destroy. Topped in 1565–68 by a bell
2 tower and weather vane and called the **Giralda,** this splendid example of Moorish art is one of the marvels of Seville. In place of steps, 35 gently sloping ramps climb to the viewing platform 230 ft high. St. Ferdinand is said to have ridden his horse to the top to admire the view of the city he had conquered. Seven centuries later your view of the Golden Tower and shimmering Gua-

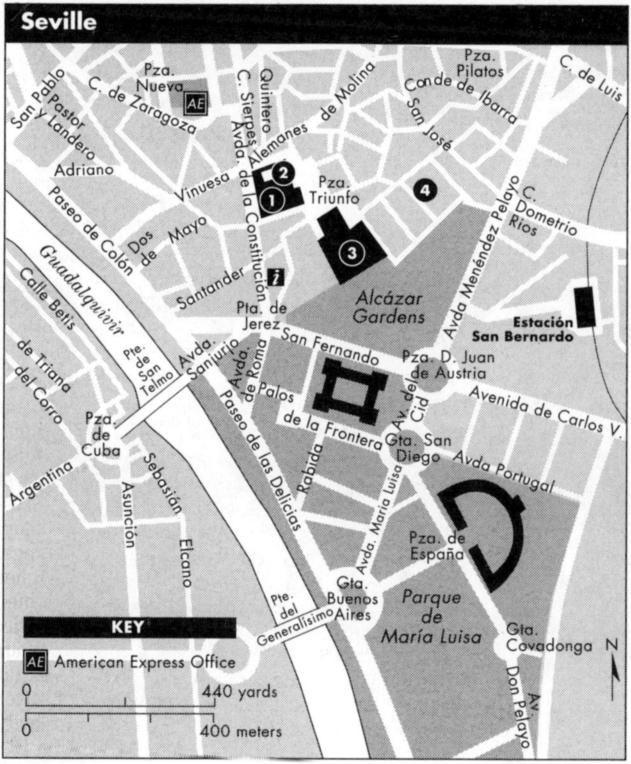

Alcázar, **3**
Barrio de Santa Cruz, **4**
Cathedral, **1**
Giralda, **2**

dalquivir will be equally breathtaking. *Plaza Virgen de los Reyes, tel. 95/456–3321. Open Mon.–Sat. 11–5, Sun. 10–4.*

3 The high, fortified walls of the **Alcázar** belie the exquisite delicacy of the palace's interior. It was built by Pedro the Cruel—so known because he murdered his stepmother and four of his half-brothers—who lived here with his mistress María de Padilla from 1350 to 1369. Don't mistake this for a genuine Moorish palace, as it was built more than 100 years after the reconquest of Seville; rather, its style is Mudéjar—built by Moorish craftsmen working under orders of a Christian king. *Plaza del Triunfo, tel. 95/422–7163. Palace and gardens admission: 600 ptas. Open Tues.–Sat. 10:30–5, Sun. 10:30–1.*

4 The **Barrio de Santa Cruz,** with its twisting alleyways, cobbled squares, and whitewashed houses, is a perfect setting for an operetta. Once the home of Seville's Jewish population, it was much favored by 17th-century noblemen, and today boasts some of the most expensive properties in Seville. All the romantic images you've ever had of Spain will come to life here: Every house gleams white or deep ocher yellow, wrought-iron grilles adorn the windows, and every balcony and patio is bedecked with geraniums and petunias. Ancient bars nestle side by side with antiques shops.

Stockholm, Sweden

The city of Stockholm, built on 14 small islands among open bays and narrow channels, is a handsome, civilized place, full of parks, squares, and airy boulevards; yet it is also a bustling, modern metropolis. Glass-and-steel skyscrapers abound, but in the center you are never more than five minutes' walk from twisting, medieval streets and water views.

Currency The unit of currency in Sweden is the krona (plural, kronor), which is divided into 100 öre and is written as SKr, SEK, or kr. At press time, the exchange rate was 6.8 SKr to the U.S. dollar.

Telephones The country code for Sweden is 46. Sweden has plenty of pay phones; to use them you'll need either SKr 1, SKr 5, or SKr 10 coins, since a local call costs SKr 2. You can also purchase a *telefonkort* (telephone card) from a Telebutik, hospital, or *Pressbyrån* store for SKr 35, SKr 60, or SKr 100. International calls can also be made from any pay phone. For calls to the United States and Canada, dial 009, then 1 (the country code), then wait for a second dial tone before dialing the area code and number. You can make calls from Telebutik offices. To reach an **AT&T** long-distance operator, dial 020/795611; **MCI,** 020/795922; **Sprint,** 020/799011.

Shore Excursions The following are good choices in Stockholm. They may not be offered by all lines. Times and prices are approximate.

City and Vasa Museum. Visit City Hall and Golden Hall, the site of the Nobel Prize banquet. Pass the Senate Building and Royal Opera House on the way to the Vasa Ship Museum. *3½ hrs. Cost: $44.*

Royal Palace and Millesgarden. A complete tour of the royal residence precedes a visit to Millesgarden, the home, studio, and gardens of Sweden's famous modern sculptor, Carl Milles. In between, you'll stroll the streets of Old Town and drive through Stockholm Center past the Royal Opera House. *3 hrs. Cost: $44.*

Coming Ashore Ships berth at Stockholm's pier within view of the Royal Palace in Old Town.

Getting Around The most cost-effective way of getting around Stockholm is to buy a Stockholmskortet (the Key to Stockholm card). Besides unlimited transportation on city subway, bus, and rail services, it offers free admission to 60 museums and several sightseeing trips. The card costs SKr 185 for 24 hours. It is available from the tourist information centers at Sweden House and the Kaknäs TV tower, and at the Hotellcentralen accommodations bureau at the central train station.

Maps and timetables for all city transportation networks are available from the Stockholm Transit Authority (SL) information desks at Sergels Torg, the central train station, and at Slussen in Gamla Stan. You can also obtain information by phone (tel. 08/600–1000).

The subway system, known as T-banan (the *T* stands for tunnel), is the easiest and fastest way of getting around the city. Station entrances are marked with a blue T on a white background. Trains run frequently between 5 AM and 2 AM. Bus and subway tickets are interchangeable. Fares are based on zones, starting at SKr 14, good for travel within one zone, such as downtown, for one hour. You pay more if you travel in more than one zone. Single tickets are available at station ticket counters, but it is cheaper to buy the SL Tourist Card, which is valid on buses and the subway and also gives free admission to a number of sights and museums. It can be purchased at Pressbyrån newsstands and SL information desks and costs SKr 60 for 24 hours.

A 10-km (6-mi) taxi ride will cost SKr 97 between 9 AM and 4 PM on weekdays, SKr 107 on weekday nights, and SKr 114 on weekends. Major taxi companies are Taxi Stockholm (tel. 08/150000), Taxikurir (tel. 08/300000), and Taxi 020 (tel. 020/850400).

Exploring Stockholm

Numbers in the margin correspond to points of interest on the Stockholm map.

Anyone in Stockholm with limited time should give priority to a tour of **Gamla Stan** (the Old Town), a labyrinth of narrow, medieval streets, alleys, and quiet squares on the island just south of the city center. Ideally, you should devote an entire day to this district.

1 **Stadshuset** (city hall) was constructed in 1923; architect Ragnar Östberg's ornate facade has become a Stockholm landmark. Lavish mosaics adorn the walls of the Golden Hall, and the Prince's Gallery features a collection of large murals by Prince Eugen, brother of King Gustav V. Take the elevator halfway up, then climb the rest of the way to the top of the 348-ft tower for a magnificent view of the city. *Hantverkargatan 1, tel. 08/508–29000. Admission: SKr 30. Tours daily at 10 and noon; also at 11 and 2 in summer. Tower admission: SKr 15. Tower open May–Sept., daily 10–4:30.*

2 You should get to **Kungliga Slott** (Royal Palace), preferably by noon, when you can see the colorful changing-of-the-guard ceremony. The smartly dressed guards seem superfluous, as

tourists wander at will into the palace courtyard and around the grounds. Several separate attractions are open to the public. Be sure to visit the Royal Armory, with its outstanding collection of weaponry and royal regalia. The Treasury houses the Swedish crown jewels, including the regalia used for the coronation of King Erik XIV in 1561. You can also visit the State Apartments, where the king swears in each successive government. *Gamla Stan, tel. 08/666–4466. Admission: SKr 45 for Armory; SKr 40 for Treasury; SKr 45 for State Apartments. Call ahead for opening hrs, as they are subject to change.*

A short walk from the city center is the large island of **Djurgården,** where attractions include Waldemarsudde (tel. 08/662–2800), an art museum in the former summer residence of Swedish prince Eugen, on a peninsula in Djurgården. *Tel. 08/662–2800. Call ahead for prices and times; they're subject to change.*

The *Vasa,* a restored 17th-century warship, is one of the oldest preserved war vessels in the world and has become Sweden's most popular tourist sight. It sank ignominiously in Stockholm Harbor on its maiden voyage in 1628, reportedly because it was not carrying sufficient ballast. Recovered in 1961, the ship has been restored to its original appearance and is housed in a spectacular museum, **Vasamuseet.** It has guided tours, films, and displays. *Gälarvarvet, tel. 08/666–4800. Admission: SKr 45. Open Thurs.–Tues. 10–5, Wed. 10–8.*

3

4 **Gröna Lund,** Stockholm's only amusement park, is a family favorite, with traditional rides and new attractions on the waterfront each season. *Djurgårdsvägen, tel. 08/670–7600. Open late Apr.–early Sept. Call ahead for prices and hrs, as they are subject to change.*

5 **Nordiska Museet** (the Nordic Museum) provides insight into the way Swedish people have lived over the past 500 years. The collection includes displays of peasant costumes, folk art, and Sami culture. Families with children should visit the delightful "village life" play area on the ground floor. *Djurgårdsvägen 6–16, tel. 08/666–4600. Admission: SKr 50. Open Tues.–Sun. 11–5.*

Stockholm

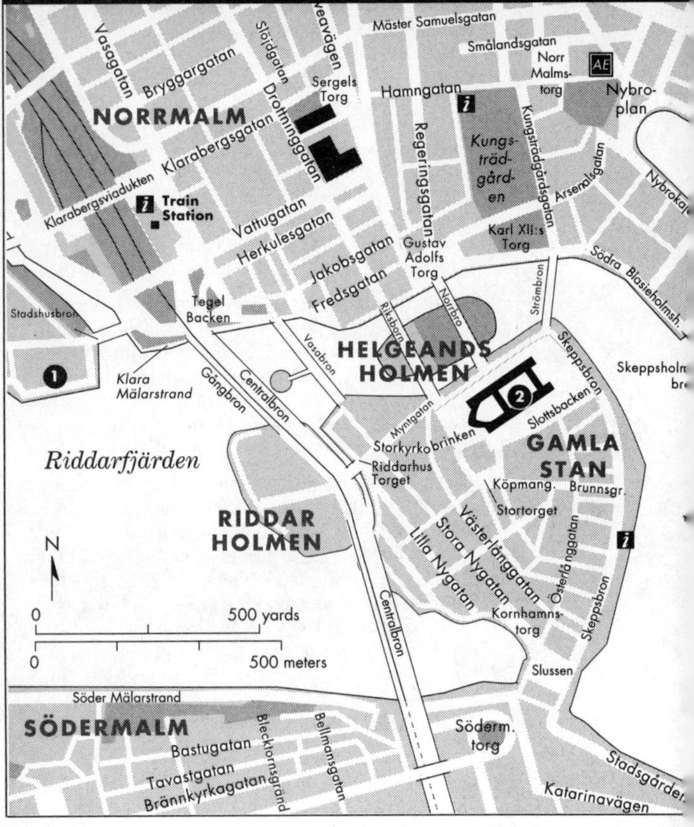

Gröna Lund, **4**
Kungliga Slott, **2**
Nordiska Museet, **5**
Stadshuset, **1**
Vasa Museet, **3**

Linnégatan
Storgatan
ddargatan
Styrmangatan
Strandvägen
Strandvägen
Djurgårdsbron
Djurgårdsbrunnsviken
5
Rosendalsvägen
3
DJURGÅRDEN
EPPSHOLMEN
Svensksundsvägen
Alkärret
Djurgårdsvägen
Falkenbergsg.
Djurgårds Slätten
Sollidsbacken
Allmänna Gränd
4
KASTELL-
HOLMEN
Saltsjön
BECKHOLMEN
KEY
Tourist Information
Rail Lines
AE American Express Office

Shopping **Västerlånggatan,** one of the main streets in the Old Town, is a popular shopping area brimming with boutiques and antiques shops. Walk down to the Skeppsbron waterfront, then head back toward the center over the Ström bridge, where anglers cast for salmon.

Turkish Coast

Some of the finest reconstructed Greek and Roman cities, including the fabled Pergamum, Ephesus, Aphrodisias, and Troy, are found along the Aegean. Bright yellow road signs pointing to historical sites or to those currently undergoing excavation are everywhere here. There are so many Greek and Roman ruins, in fact, that some haven't yet been excavated and others are going to seed. Grand or small, all the sites are steeped in atmosphere and are best explored early in the morning or late in the afternoon, when there are fewer crowds. You can escape the heat of the day on one of the sandy beaches that line the coast.

Currency The monetary unit is the Turkish lira (TL). At press time, the exchange rate was 116,060 TL to the U.S. dollar. These rates are subject to wide fluctuation, so check close to your departure. Be certain to retain your original exchange slips when you convert money into Turkish lira—you will need them to reconvert the money. Because the Turkish lira is worth a lot less than most currencies, it's best to convert only what you plan to spend.

Telephones The country code for Turkey is 90. All telephone numbers in Turkey now have seven local digits plus three-digit city codes. Intercity calls are preceded by 0. (If calling from outside the country, drop this zero when dialing.) Pay phones are yellow, push-button models. Most take *jetons* (tokens) although an increasing number, particularly in large cities, take phone cards. Multilingual directions are posted in phone booths. For all international calls dial 00, then dial the country code, area or city code, and the number. You can reach an international operator by dialing 132. To reach an **AT&T** long-distance operator, dial 00800–12277; **MCI,** 00800–11177; **Sprint,** 00800–14477.

Shore Excursions

The following are good choices along the Turkish coast. They may not be offered by all cruise lines. Times and prices are approximate.

In İzmir

City Tour. Visit the fairly well-preserved Velvet Fortress and Archaeological Museum followed by a belly-dancing performance and a folkloric show. *3¾ hrs. Cost: $30.*

Ephesus. Drive 1 hour and 15 minutes to reach Ephesus, once the Roman Capital of Asia Minor, where you'll tour the spellbinding ruins of Ephesus. Major sights include the Great Theater, the Library of Celsus, the Temple of Hadrian, and Curetes Street. *4½ hrs. Cost: $45.*

In Kuşadası

Ancient Ephesus. This is the tour to take—it explores one of the best-preserved ancient cities of the world. Be prepared to do a lot of walking. *4 hrs. Cost: $39.*

In Bodrum

The Castle of Bodrum is easily explored on your own and is within walking distance of the tender drop-off point.

Wooden Boat Ride. Sail one of the wooden boats that line Bodrum's harbor to small coves and bays for swimming and snorkeling. *3½ hrs. Cost: $59.*

Coming Ashore

Whether your ship docks or drops anchor along the Turkish Coast, landing sites are conveniently located for independent exploration.

In İzmir

Ships calling at İzmir's harbor dock along the waterfront boulevard called Kordon. Depending on what you want to see, you can walk, take a bus, or hire a taxi to explore the sights.

In Kuşadası

Ships either dock or tender passengers ashore at Kuşadası. Shops and restaurants are within walking distance of the port.

In Bodrum

Ships calling at Bodrum tender passengers ashore in the main harbor. Walking Bodrum's streets is truly the best and most pleasurable way to explore local sights.

Exploring the Turkish Coast

İzmir

The center of the city is **Kültürpark,** which is a large green park that is the site of İzmir's industrial fair from late August until late September.

On top of İzmir's highest hill is the **Kadifekale** (Velvet Fortress), built in the 3rd century BC by

Lysimachos. It is easily reached by dolmuş and is one of the few ancient ruins that was not destroyed in the fire after the war for Turkish independence.

At the foot of the hill is the restored **Agora,** the market of ancient Smyrna. The modern-day marketplace is in Konak Square, a maze of tiny streets filled with shops and covered stalls. *Open Mon.–Sat. 8–8.*

Kuşadası The major attraction near Kuşadası is **Ephesus,** a city created by the Ionians in the 11th century BC and now one of the grandest reconstructed ancient sites in the world. It is the showpiece of Aegean archaeology. Ephesus was a powerful trading port and the sacred center for the cult of Artemis, Greek goddess of chastity, the moon, and hunting. The Ionians built a temple in her honor, one of the Seven Wonders of the Ancient World. During the Roman period, it became a shrine for the Roman goddess Diana. Today, waterlogged foundations are all that remain of the temple. Allow yourself the full day for Ephesus. *4 km/2½ mi west of Selçuk on Selçuk–Ephesus Rd., tel. 232/892–6402. Open daily 8:30–6 (summer), 8:30–5 (winter).*

Bodrum Sitting between two crescent-shape bays, Bodrum has for years been the favorite haunt of the Turkish upper classes. One of the outstanding sights in Bodrum is **Bodrum Kalesi** (Bodrum Castle), known as the Castle of St. Peter. Between the two bays, the castle was built by crusaders in the 11th century. It has beautiful gardens and the Museum of Underwater Archaeology. *Kale Cad., tel. 252/316–2516. Castle and museum admission: $3. Open Tues.–Sun. 8:30–noon and 1–5.*

The peninsula is downright littered with ancient Greek and Roman ruins, although getting to some of them involves driving over rough dirt roads. Five km (3 mi) from Bodrum is **Halikarnas,** a well-preserved 10,000-seat Greek amphitheater built in the 1st century BC and still used for town festivals. *Admission free. Open daily 8:30–sunset.*

Varna, Bulgaria

Bulgaria, a land of mountains and seascapes, of austerity and rustic beauty, lies in the eastern half of the Balkan peninsula. From the end of World War II until recently, it was the closest ally of the former Soviet Union and presented a rather mysterious image to the Western world. This era ended in 1989 with the overthrow of Communist party head Todor Zhivkov. Since then, Bulgaria has gradually opened itself to the West as it struggles along the path toward democracy and a free-market economy.

Founded in 681 by the Bulgars, a Turkic tribe from central Asia, Bulgaria was a crossroads of civilization even before that date. Archaeological finds in Varna, on the Black Sea coast, give proof of civilization from as early as 4600 BC. Bulgaria was part of the Byzantine Empire from AD 1018 to 1185 and was occupied by the Turks from 1396 until 1878. The combined influences are reflected in Bulgarian architecture, which has a truly Eastern feel. Five hundred years of Muslim occupation and nearly half a century of Communist rule did not wipe out Christianity, and there are many lovely, icon-filled churches to see.

Currency The unit of currency in Bulgaria is the lev (plural, leva), divided into 100 stotinki. At press time, the exchange rate was 350 leva to the U.S. dollar. All unspent leva must be exchanged before you depart the country, and you will need to present your official exchange slips to prove that the currency was legally purchased—so exchange only as much as you plan to spend.

Telephones The country code for Bulgaria is 359. Local calls cost 2 leva and can be made from your hotel, from pay phones, or with the two types of phone cards, *Betkom* and *Bulfon*, both of which can also be used for calls throughout Bulgaria and Europe. Phone cards can be purchased at post offices and major hotels. Calls to the United States must be made from your hotel, for a surcharge, or placed from a post office. To place a call using an **AT&T USADirect** international operator, dial 00–800–0010.

Shore Excursions

The following is a good choice in Varna. It may not be offered by all cruise lines. Time and price are approximate.

Varna Tour. You'll see the city's major sites before visiting one of the area's renowned Black Sea spas. *Half day. Cost: $42.*

Coming Ashore

Ships calling at Varna dock at the city harbor. Varna's main sights can be reached on foot. Buses are inexpensive; make sure to buy your ticket in advance from the kiosks near the bus stops.

Exploring Varna

Begin with the **Archeologicheski Musei** (Museum of Art and History), one of the great—if lesser-known—museums of Europe. The splendid collection includes the world's oldest gold treasures from the Varna necropolis of the 4th millennium BC, as well as Thracian, Greek, and Roman treasures, and richly painted icons. *41 bul. Osmi Primorski Polk, tel. 052/23–70–57. Open Tues.–Sat. 10–5.*

In Mitropolit Simeon Square, the monumental **Tsurkva Yspenie Bogorodichno** (Cathedral of the Assumption), 1880–86, is worth a look for its lavish murals. Opposite the cathedral, in the city gardens, is the Old **Clock Tower,** built in 1880 by the Varna Guild Association. *Nezavisimost Sq.*

On the corner of Knyaz Boris I Boulevard and Shipka Street are the remains of the **Roman fortress wall.**

The **Holy Virgin Church** of 1602 also features the substantial remains of the **Rimski Termi** (Roman baths) dating from the 2nd to the 3rd century AD. Buy the excellent English guidebook here to get the most out of your visit. *Ul. Han Krum.*

The **Morski Muzei** (Marine Museum) displays the early days of navigation on the Black Sea and the Danube. *No. 2 Primorski Blvd., tel. 052/22–26–55. Open weekdays 8–4.*

In the extensive and luxuriant **Primorski Park** (Seaside Park) are restaurants, an open-air theater, and the fascinating Copernicus Astronomy Complex, near the main entrance. *Southern end of Primorski Blvd. Astronomy Complex: tel. 052/22–28–90. Open weekdays 8–noon and 2–5.*

Eight kilometers (5 miles) north along the coast from Varna is **Sveti Konstantin,** Bulgaria's oldest Black Sea resort. Small and intimate, it spreads through a wooded park near a series of sandy coves. Warm mineral springs were discovered here in 1947, and the five-star Grand Hotel Varna (tel. 052/86–14–91), the most luxurious on the coast, offers all kinds of hydrotherapy under medical supervision.

The lively **Zlatni Pyasutsi,** better known as **Golden Sands,** lies 16 km (10 mi) nort of Varna. It's known for its extensive leisure amenities, mineral-spring medical centers, and sports and entertainment facilities.

Just over 4 km (2 mi) inland from Golden Sands is **Aladja Rock Monastery,** one of Bulgaria's oldest, cut out of the cliff face and made accessible to visitors by sturdy iron stairways. *Southwest of Golden Sands (Bus No. 33 from Varna or Golden Sands). Open Tues.–Sun. 9–5.*

Venice, Italy

For hundreds of years Venice—La Serenissima, the Most Serene—was the unrivaled mistress of trade between Europe and the Orient, and the staunch bulwark of Christendom against the tide of Turkish expansion. Though the power and glory of its days as a wealthy city-republic are gone, the art and exotic aura remain. The majority of its magnificent palazzi are slowly crumbling, but somehow in Venice the shabby, derelict effect is magically transformed into one of supreme beauty and charm. Hot and sultry in the summer, Venice is much more welcoming in early spring and late fall.

Currency The unit of currency in Italy is the lira (plural, lire). At press time, the exchange rate was about 1,595 lire to the U.S. dollar. When your purchases run into hundreds of thousands of lire, beware of being shortchanged, a dodge that is practiced at ticket windows and cashiers' desks, as well as in shops and even banks. Always count your change before you leave the counter.

Telephones The country code for Italy is 39. Most local calls cost 200 lire for two minutes. Pay phones take either 100-, 200-, or 500-lire coins or *schede telefoniche* (phone cards), purchased in bars, tobacconists, post offices, and TELECOM offices in either 5,000-, 10,000-, or 15,000-lire denominations. To place international calls, many travelers go to the Telefoni telephone exchange (usually marked TELECOM), where the operator assigns you a booth, can help place your call, and will collect payment when you have finished. To dial an international call, insert a phone card, dial 00, then the country code, area code, and phone number. For **AT&T,** dial access number 172–1011; **MCI,** 172–1022; **Sprint,** 172–1877. You will be connected directly with an operator in the United States.

Shore Excursions The following are good choices in Venice. They may not be offered by all cruise lines. Times and prices are approximate.

Canals of Venice. See Venice from the water on this boat tour that glides down the bustling Grand Canal as well as some of the city's more intimate, narrow canals. Take time out for a visit to a glass factory. *3½ hrs. Cost: $52.*

Venice Tour. Visit St. Mark's Square and Cathedral, Doge's Palace, and the Bridge of Sighs. *2½ hrs. Cost: $42.*

Coming Ashore Ships typically dock in Venice at the main port terminal, an unappealing building whose saving grace is its relative nearness to St. Mark's Square.

Getting Around Cruise passengers may find that getting around Venice presents some unusual problems: the complexity of its layout (the city is made up of more than 100 islands, all linked by bridges); the bewildering unfamiliarity of waterborne transportation; the apparently illogical house numbering system and duplication of street names in its six districts; and the necessity of walking whether you enjoy it or not. It's essential to have a good map showing all street names and water-bus routes; buy one at any newsstand, and count on getting lost more than once.

Walking is the only way to reach many parts of Venice, so wear comfortable shoes. ACTV water buses run the length of the Grand Canal and circle the city. There are several lines, some of which connect Venice with the major and minor islands in the lagoon. Line 1 is the Grand Canal local, calling at every stop, and continuing via San Marco to the Lido. (It takes about 45 minutes from the station to San Marco.) As the result of (extremely confusing and unpopular) rerouting, there are now two Line 52 routes: one running from the railway station to San Zaccaria, skirting the north of the city, via Fondamente Nove (where boats leave for the islands of the northern lagoon) and Murano, and continuing via the Arsenal; the other acting as a fast service via Zattere on the Giudecca Canal, south of the city, to San Marco and the Lido. There are also two Line 82 routes from the Tronchetto: One goes via Piazzale Roma, the railway station, and Rialto, and continues during the day down the Grand Canal, with fewer stops than the Line 1, to San Marco and, in the summer, on to the Lido. The other takes the southern route through the Giudecca Canal, via Zattere and also stopping on Giudecca, to San Marco and, in the summer, continues to the Lido. The fare is 3,500 lire on most lines. A 24-hour tourist ticket costs 15,000 lire. Timetables are posted at every landing stage, but there is not always a ticket booth operating. You may get on a boat without a ticket, but you will have to pay a higher fare on the boat. For this reason, it may be useful to buy a *blochetto* (book of tickets) in advance. Landing stages are clearly marked with name and line number, but check before boarding, particularly with the 52 and 82, to make sure the boat is going in your direction.

Motoscafis, or water "taxis," are excessively expensive, and the fare system is as complex as Venice's layout. A minimum fare of about 50,000 lire gets you nowhere, and you'll pay three times as much to get from one end of the Grand Canal to the other. Always agree on the fare before starting out.

Few tourists know about the two-man gondolas that ferry people across the Grand Canal at various fixed points. It's the cheapest and shortest gondola ride in Venice, and it can save a lot of walking. The fare is 600 lire, which you hand to one of the gondoliers when you get on. Look for TRAGHETTO signs.

Exploring Venice

Numbers in the margin correspond to points of interest on the Venice map.

1 Even the pigeons have to fight for space on **Piazza San Marco,** the most famous piazza in Venice, and pedestrian traffic jams clog the surrounding byways. Despite the crowds, San Marco is the logical starting place for exploring Venice. Napoléon called this "the most beautiful drawing room in all of Europe."

2 The **Basilica di San Marco** (St. Mark's Basilica) was begun in the 11th century to hold the relics of St. Mark the Evangelist, the city's patron saint, and its richly decorated facade is surmounted by copies of the four famous gilded bronze horses (the originals are in the basilica's upstairs museum). Inside, golden mosaics sheathe walls and domes, lending an extraordinarily exotic aura: half Christian church, half Middle Eastern mosque. Be sure to see the Pala d'Oro, an eye-filling 10th-century altarpiece in gold and silver, studded with precious gems and enamels. From the atrium, climb the steep stairway to the museum: The bronze horses alone are worth the effort. *Piazza San Marco. Basilica open Mon.–Sat. 9:30–5, Sun. 2–5; free admission. Pala d'Oro and Treasury, tel. 041/522–5205; open Apr.–Sept., Mon.–Sat. 9:30–5, Sun. 1–4:30; Oct.–Mar., Mon.–Sat. 10–4, Sun. 1–4:30 (may vary slightly). Gallery and Museum open Apr.–Sept., daily 10–5; Oct.–Mar., daily 10–4:30.*

3 During Venice's heyday, the **Palazzo Ducale** (Doge's Palace) was the epicenter of the Serene Republic's great empire. More than just a palace, it was a combination White House, Senate, Supreme Court, torture chamber, and prison. The building's exterior is striking; the lower stories consist of two rows of fragile-seeming arches, while above rests a massive pink-and-white marble wall, whose solidity is barely interrupted by its six great Gothic windows. The interior is a maze of vast halls, monumental staircases, secret corridors, and the sinister prison cells and torture chamber. The palace is filled with frescoes, paintings, and a few examples of statuary by some of the Renaissance's greatest artists. Don't miss the famous view from the balcony, overlooking the piazza and St.

Mark's Basin and the church of San Giorgio Maggiore across the lagoon. *Piazzetta San Marco, tel. 041/522–4951. Admission: 10,000 lire. Open Apr.–Oct., daily 8:30–5; Nov.–Mar., daily 9–4. Last entry 1 hr before closing time.*

4 For a pigeon's-eye view of Venice, take the elevator up to the top of the **Campanile di San Marco** (St. Mark's bell tower) in Piazza San Marco, a reconstruction of the 1,000-year-old tower that collapsed one morning in 1912, practically without warning. Fifteenth-century clerics found guilty of immoral acts were suspended in wooden cages from the tower, sometimes to live on bread and water for as long as a year, sometimes to die of starvation and exposure. Look for them in Carpaccio's paintings of the square, which hang in the Accademia (*see below*). *Piazza San Marco, tel. 041/522–4064. Admission: 5,000 lire. Open daily 9:30–5:30; closed Dec.–Jan.*

5 The **Galleria dell'Accademia** (Accademia Gallery) is Venice's most important picture gallery and a must for art lovers. Try to spend at least an hour viewing this remarkable collection of Venetian art, which is attractively displayed and well lighted. Works range from 14th-century Gothic to the Golden Age of the 15th and 16th centuries, including oils by Giovanni Bellini, Giorgione, Titian, and Tintoretto, and superb later works by Veronese and Tiepolo. *Campo della Carità, tel. 041/522–2247. Admission: 12,000 lire. Open Tues.–Thurs. 9–7, Fri.–Sat. 9–2, Sun. 9–1.*

6 The church of Santa Maria Gloriosa dei Frari—known simply as the **Frari**—is one of Venice's most important churches, a vast, soaring Gothic building of brick. Since it is the principal church of the Franciscans, its design is suitably austere to reflect that order's vows of poverty, though paradoxically it contains a number of the most sumptuous pictures in any Venetian church. Chief among them are the magnificent Titian altarpiece, the immense *Assumption of the Virgin*, over the main altar. Titian was buried here at the ripe old age of 88, the only one of 70,000 plague victims to be given a personal church burial. *Campo dei Frari, tel. 041/522–2637. Admission: 1,000 lire. Open Mon.–Sat. 9–noon and 2–6, Sun. 3–6.*

Venice

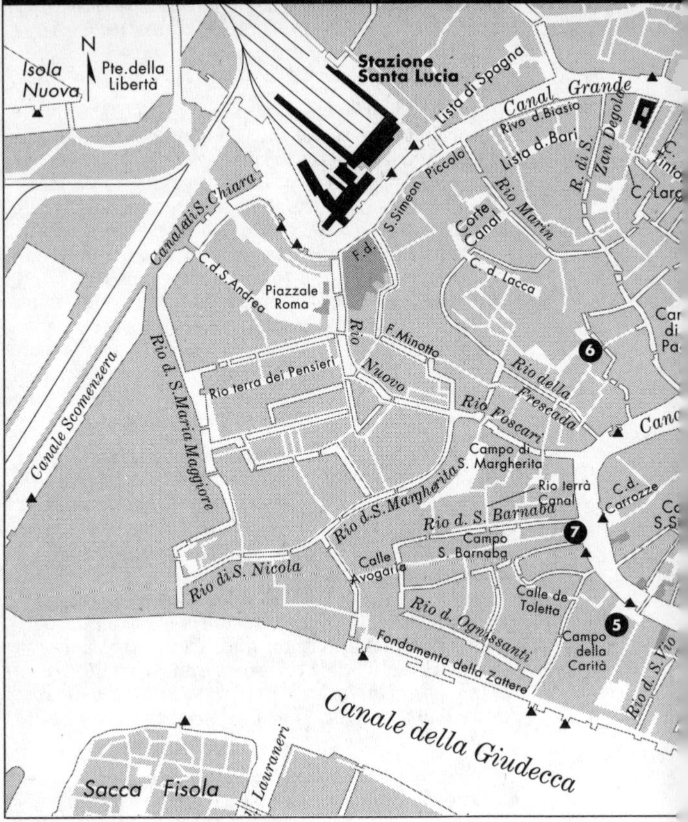

Basilica di San Marco, **2**

Ca' Rezzonico, **7**

Campanile di San Marco, **4**

Frari, **6**

Galleria dell' Accademia, **5**

Palazzo Ducale, **3**

Piazza San Marco, **1**

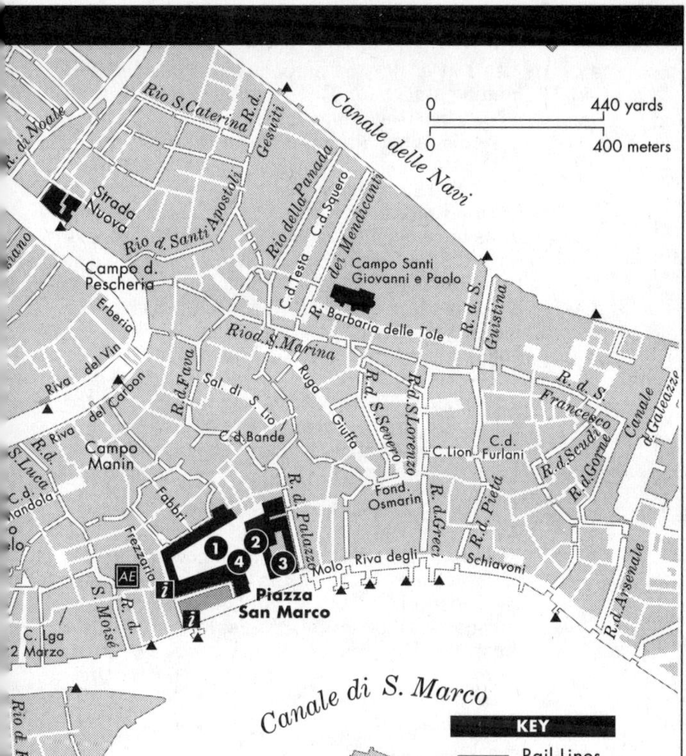

Rio S.Caterina
R.d. Gesuiti
Canale delle Navi
0 440 yards
0 400 meters
R. di Noale
Strada Nuova
Rio d. Santi Apostoli
Rio della Panada
C.d.Squero
dei Mendicanti
Campo Santi Giovanni e Paolo
Campo d. Pescheria
C.d.Testa
R. Barbaria delle Tole
R. d. S. Guistina
Erberia
Riod.S.Marina
Riva del Vin
Ruga Giuffa
R.d. S.Severo
R.d.S.Lorenzo
R. d. S. Francesco
Canale d.Galeazzo
Riva del Carbon
R.d.Fava
Sal. di S. Lio
C.d.Bande
C.Lion
C.d. Furlani
R.d.Scudi
R.d.Gorne
R.d. S.Luca
Campo Manin
C.d. Mandola
Fabbri
R. d. Palazzo
Fond. Osmarin
R. d.Greci
R.d. Pietà
Frezzaria
AE
Molo
Riva degli
Schiavoni
R.d.Arsenale
Piazza San Marco
S. Moisè
R. d.
C. Lga 22 Marzo
Canale di S. Marco
Rio d. Fornace
KEY
Rail Lines
Boat stop
Tourist Information
American Express Office
Isola di S. Giorgio Maggiore

Just off Piazzetta di San Marco (the square in front of the Doge's Palace) you can catch Vaporetto 1 at either the San Marco or San Zaccaria landing stages (on Riva degli Schiavoni), to set off on a boat tour along the **Grand Canal.** Serving as Venice's main thoroughfare, the canal winds in the shape of an S for more than 3½ km (2 mi) through the heart of the city, past some 200 Gothic-Renaissance palaces. Although restrictions have been introduced to diminish the erosive effect of wash on buildings, this is still the route taken by vaporetti, gondolas, water taxis, mail boats, police boats, fire boats, ambulance boats, barges carrying provisions and building materials, bridal boats, and funeral boats. Your vaporetto tour will give you an idea of the opulent beauty of the palaces and a peek into the side streets and tiny canals where the Venetians go about their daily business. *Vaporetto 1. Cost: 3,500 lire.*

7 The **Ca' Rezzonico**—the most spectacular palace in all of Venice—was built between the mid-17th and 18th centuries and is now a museum of sumptuous 18th-century Venetian paintings and furniture. The Ca' Rezzonico is the best chance to glimpse Venetian splendor and is a must-see. *Fondamenta Rezzonico, S. Barnaba, tel. 041/522–4543. Admission: 8,000 lire. Open Apr.–Oct., Sat.–Thurs. 10–5; Nov.–Mar., Sat.–Thurs. 10–4.*

Shopping

Venetian glass is as famous as the city's gondolas, and almost every shop window displays it. There's a lot of cheap glass for sale; if you want something better, among the top showrooms are **Venini** (Piazzetta dei Leoncini 314), **Pauly** (Piazza San Marco 73–77), and **Salviati** (Piazza San Marco 79B). Carlo Moretti's chic, contemporary designs are on show at **L'Isola** (Campo San Moisè 1468, near Piazza San Marco). On the island of Murano, where prices are generally no lower than those in Venice, **Domus** (Fondamenta dei Vetrai) has a good selection.

For Venetian fabrics, **Norelene** (Calle della Chiesa 727, in Dorsoduro, near the Guggenheim) has stunning hand-painted material that makes wonderful wall hangings or elegantly styled jackets and chic scarves. **Venetia Studuim** (Calle Larga XXII Marzo 2430) is famous for Fortunyinspired lamps, furnishings, clothes, and accessories.

Try to visit the famous **Rialto market** when it's in full swing (start from the Salizzada S. Giovanni side of the bridge on Tues.–Sat. mornings; Mon. is quiet because the fish market is closed), with fruit and vegetable vendors hawking their wares in a colorful and noisy jumble of sights and sounds.

Ports of Embarkation and Disembarkation

Athens/ Piraeus Athens is the gateway for cruises to the Greek Islands and to the eastern Mediterranean, including cruises of the Black Sea.

From the Airport Piraeus lies 10 km (6 mi) from Athens. You can take a taxi for about 1,100 dr. or buy a transfer from the cruise line in advance.

Istanbul Istanbul is a major jumping-off point for cruises of the eastern Mediterranean.

From the Airport Atatürk Airport lies very close to the pier, but traffic in Istanbul is notoriously bad, so plan on half an hour for the transfer. You can take a cab from the airport to the ship, but buying a cruise-line transfer in advance is a good idea.

Rome/ Civitavecchia For reasons as much geographical as historical, Rome is a very popular port to begin or end a cruise of the eastern Mediterranean or the western Mediterranean.

From the Airport Civitavecchia, the port city for Rome, is an hour and 15 minutes from the city. Cruise-line transfers are your best bet for getting to the ship.

Southampton Southampton is where the *Queen Elizabeth 2* arrives and departs on transatlantic crossings. There's not much in the immediate vicinity except a coffee shop and berths for ferries going to the Isle of Wight. The train station is about a quarter mile from the pier.

From the Airport Southampton is 90 km (56 mi) southwest of London. The trip by BritRail takes an hour and 40 minutes from central London's Waterloo Station. Driving from London to Southampton takes less than two hours.

3 Itineraries

Sailing Schedules

Itineraries are for the 1998 Europe season. Ports of call are described in Chapter 2. Ship deployments and itineraries are subject to change; ports of call may also vary with departure date. Check with your cruise line or travel agent.

Clipper Cruise Line

Clipper Adventurer Ten-night **Mediterranean** loop from Lisbon. Fourteen-night **northern Europe** cruise between Lisbon and Amsterdam. Eleven-night **northern Europe** cruise from Amsterdam to Stockholm or from Stockholm to Dover (England). Twelve-night British Isles cruises between Dover and Edinburgh. Eight-, 10-, or 12-night **northern Europe** cruises from Edinburgh to Copenhagen, Copenhagen to Bergen, and between Bergen and Spitsbergen. Ten-, 12-, and 14-night **transatlantic/Canada crossings** from Bergen to Narsarssuaq (Greenland) or Narsarssuaq and Churchill (Canada) or Narsarssuaq to Halifax.

Club Med

Club Med 2 Seven-night **Mediterranean** cruises with ports to be announced.

Costa Cruise Lines

CostaAllegra Ten-night **northern Europe/Baltic Sea** loops from Amsterdam call at Stockholm, Copenhagen, Helsinki, and other ports. Eleven-, 12-, and 13-night **Norwegian Fjords** loops from Amsterdam.

CostaClassica Seven-night **Mediterranean** loops from Venice call at the Greek Islands.

CostaMarina Seven-night **northern Europe/Baltic Sea** and **Norwegian Fjords** loops from Copenhagen call at Stockholm, Helsinki, Bergen, Oslo, and St. Petersburg.

CostaRiviera Ten- and 11-night **Canary Island** loops from Savona (Italy) call at Barcelona, the Canary Islands, and other ports. Ten- and 11-night **Mediterranean** loops from Savona call at the Greek Islands, the Napoli Coast, and other ports. Ten-

and 11-night **Mediterranean** loops from Genoa (Italy) call at the Napoli Coast, Greek Islands, Turkish Coast, and other ports. Ten-night **Canary Islands** loops from Genoa call at Barcelona, the Canary Islands, and other ports.

CostaVictoria Seven-night **Mediterranean** loops from Venice call at the Turkish Coast, Athens/Piraeus, and other ports.

Crystal Cruises

Crystal Symphony Fifteen-night **Arabian Sea/Red Sea/Mediterranean** segment from Bombay to Athens/Piraeus; and a 16-night **Mediterranean/northern Europe** segment from Athens/Piraeus to London, calling at Barcelona, Lisbon, and other ports. Ten-night **northern Europe/Mediterranean** cruise from London to Rome/Civitavecchia calls at Lisbon, the French Riviera, and other ports. Twelve-night **Mediterranean** cruises between Rome/Civitavecchia and Athens/Piraeus call at the Greek Islands, Turkish Coast, Venice, and other ports. Twelve-night **Mediterranean** cruise from Athens/Piraeus to Barcelona calls at the Turkish Coast, Greek Islands, Florence/Livorno, and other ports. Eleven- and 12-night **northern Europe** cruises between Barcelona and London call at Cannes, Lisbon, Dublin, and other ports. Twelve- and 14-night **northern Europe** cruises between London and Copenhagen call at Oslo, Stockholm, Helsinki, Edinburgh, and other ports. Twelve-night **Mediterranean** cruise from Barcelona to Venice calls at Florence/Livorno and other ports. Twelve-night **Mediterranean** cruise from Venice to Athens/Piraeus calls at the Turkish Coast, Greek Islands, and other ports.

Cunard Line Limited

Queen Elizabeth 2 Eight- or 16-night **Mediterranean** loops from Southampton call at Istanbul and Florence/Livorno. Ten-night **Canary Islands** loop from Southampton calls at Lisbon and Cadiz/Seville. Six-night **northern Europe** loop from Southampton calls at Amsterdam and other ports. Fifteen-night **northern Europe** loop from Southampton calls along the Norwegian fjords. Six-night **northern Europe** loop from Southampton calls along the Irish and Scottish coasts.

Royal Viking Sun Fourteen-night **northern Europe** cruises from Paris/Rouen to Copenhagen, between Copenhagen and London/Dover, and loops from London/Dover call at the Norwegian coast, Dublin, and Edinburgh. Six-, 8-, and 14-night **northern Europe** cruises between London/Dover and Venice call at the Napoli Coast. Seven- and 14-night **Mediterranean/Red Sea** cruises between Venice and Athens/Piraeus call at the Greek Islands and the Turkish Coast.

Sea Goddess I Five-night **Canary Islands** cruise between Tenerife and Malaga (Spain). Seven-night **Mediterranean** loops from Monte Carlo or Malaga (Spain) or between Monte Carlo and Venice, Malaga and Monte Carlo, Monte Carlo and Nice, or Nice and Venice call at the Napoli Coast and other ports.

Sea Goddess II Ten-night **Mediterranean** cruise from Ashod (Jordan) to Venice calls at the Greek Islands. Seven-night **Mediterranean** cruises from Venice to Athens, Istanbul to Venice, or Athens to Istanbul call at the Greek Islands and the Turkish Coast.

Vistafjord Five- to 14-night **Mediterranean** cruises from Barcelona to Venice or Venice to Athens/Piraeus or Amsterdam to Venice call at the Greek Islands. Six- to 14-night **northern Europe** cruises from Athens/Piraeus to Copenhagen, Copenhagen to Amsterdam, or loops from Amsterdam call at the Norwegian coast and other ports.

Holland America Line

Rotterdam **Mediterranean and northern Europe** cruises to be announced.

Norwegian Cruise Line

Norway Twelve, 14-, and 15-night **Mediterranean** and **northern Europe** cruises from Lisbon, Marseilles (France), London/Southampton, and Barcelona.

Norwegian Dream Twelve- and 13-night **northern Europe** cruises from London/Dover. Twelve-night **Mediterranean** cruises from Rome/Civitavecchia.

Orient Lines

Marco Polo Eleven- to 17-night **Mediterranean** cruise-tours from Rome/Civitavecchia, Istanbul, Athens/Piraeus, or Barcelona call at the Greek Islands and along the Italian and French rivieras and the Black Sea.

Princess Cruises

Grand Princess Twelve-night **Mediterranean** cruises between Barcelona and Istanbul.

Island Princess Twelve- and 14-night **Mediterranean** cruises between Istanbul and Rome/Civitavecchia. Twelve-night **northern Europe** cruises between Rome/Civitavecchia and London/Dover or 12-night **northern Europe** loops from London/Dover.

Pacific Princess Twelve- and 14-night **Mediterranean** cruises between Istanbul and Rome/Civitavecchia. Twelve-night **northern Europe** cruises between Rome/Civitavecchia and London/Dover or 12-night **northern Europe** loops from London/Dover.

Royal Princess Thirteen-night **Mediterranean** cruises from Barcelona to Lisbon, Lisbon to Athens/Piraeus, or Athens/Piraeus to London/Dover. Thirteen-night **northern Europe** loops from London/Dover.

Radisson Seven Seas Cruises

Radisson Diamond Seven- to 11-night **Mediterranean** and **northern Europe** cruises.

Song of Flower Seven- and 10-night **Mediterranean** cruises between Athens/Piraeus and Istanbul. Eight- and 10-night **Mediterranean** cruises between Istanbul and Venice. Eleven- and 12-night **Mediterranean** cruises between Venice and Barcelona. Nine-night **Mediterranean** cruise from Lisbon (Portugal) to Rouen (France). Nine-night **Mediterranean** cruise from Rouen (France) to Lisbon (Portugal). Ten-night **Mediterranean** cruise from Edinburgh to Stockholm. Eleven-night **Mediterranean** cruises between Stockholm and London. Nine-night **Mediterranean** cruise from London to Copenhagen. Seven-night **Mediterranean** cruise from Copenhagen to Stockholm.

Eleven-night **Mediterranean** cruise from London to Barcelona.

Renaissance Cruises

Renaissance V Five-night **Mediterranean** cruises between Barcelona and Rome/Civitavecchia call at the French Riviera, Florence/Livorno, and other ports. Ten-night **Mediterranean** cruises between Athens/Piraeus and Istanbul, the Greek Islands, and other ports.

Renaissance VI Five-night **Mediterranean** cruises between Barcelona and Rome/Civitavecchia call at the French Riviera, Florence/Livorno, and other ports. Ten-night **Mediterranean** cruises between Athens/Piraeus and Istanbul call at the Greek Islands and other ports. Seven-night **northern Europe** cruises between Stockholm and Copenhagen call at Helsinki and other ports.

Renaissance VIII Five-night **Mediterranean** cruises between Athens/Piraeus and Istanbul call at the Greek Islands. Five-night **Mediterranean** cruises between Barcelona and Rome/Civitavecchia call at the French Riviera, Florence/Livorno, and other ports. Ten-night **Mediterranean** cruises between Athens/Piraeus and Istanbul call at the Greek Islands and other ports.

Royal Caribbean International

Enchantment of the Seas *Splendour of the Seas* Twelve-night **Mediterranean** loops from Barcelona call at the French Riviera, Florence/Livorno, the Napoli Coast, Rome/Civitavecchia, and Venice. Twelve-night **northern Europe** cruise from Barcelona to Harwich (England) calls at Lisbon, Paris/Le Havre, and Oslo. Twelve-night **northern Europe** loops from Harwich (England) or from Barcelona to Harwich call at Oslo, Stockholm, Helsinki, Copenhagen, Bergen, and Dublin.

Vision of the Seas Seven-night **northern Europe** cruise from Southampton to Barcelona calls at Lisbon, Gibraltar, and other ports. Seven-night **Mediterranean** loops from Barcelona call at the French Riviera, Livorno/Florence, and Rome/Civitavecchia. Seven-night **northern Europe** cruise from Barcelona to Harwich (England) calls at Lisbon, Gibraltar, and other ports.

Royal Olympic Cruises

Odysseus Twelve-night **Mediterranean** cruises between Lisbon and Athens/Piraeus call at Florence/Livorno, Rome/Civitavecchia, the French Riviera, and other ports. Ten- and 14-night **Mediterranean/Baltic/northern Europe** cruises.

Olympic Three- and four-night **Mediterranean** loops from Athens/Piraeus call at the Greek Islands and the Turkish Coast.

Orpheus Seven-night **Mediterranean** loops from Athens/Piraeus call at the Greek Islands and Crete.

Stella Oceanis Seven-night **Mediterranean** loops from Athens/Piraeus call at the Greek Islands, Turkish Coast, Egypt, and Israel. Twelve-night **Mediterranean** loops from Athens/Piraeus.

Stella Solaris Seven-night **Mediterranean/Black Sea** loops from Athens/Piraeus call at the Greek Islands, the Turkish Coast, and other ports.

Triton Seven-night **Mediterranean** loops from Athens/Piraeus call at the Greek Islands, Istanbul, and the Turkish Coast.

Seabourn Cruise Line

Seabourn Pride Thirteen-night eastbound **transatlantic crossing** from Fort Lauderdale to Lisbon (Portugal) calls at Bermuda. Thirteen-night **Mediterranean/Canary Islands** loop from Lisbon calls at the Canary Islands and Seville. Fourteen-night **western Europe** cruise from Lisbon to London/Southampton. Twelve- and 14-night **northern Europe** cruises from Lisbon to London/Southampton and Copenhagen to London, loops from London, and loops from Copenhagen call at Edinburgh/Leith, Dublin, Stockholm, St. Petersburg, Helsinki, and Bergen.

Seabourn Spirit Eleven- and 12-night **Mediterranean** cruises between Athens/Piraeus and Venice call at the Greek Islands and other ports. Fourteen-night **Mediterranean** cruises between Rome/Civitavecchia and Lisbon call at the French Riviera and other ports. Ten-night **western Europe** cruises between Lisbon and Paris/Rouen.

Fourteen-night **Mediterranean** cruises between Istanbul and Rome/Civitavecchia, from Haifa (Israel) to Athens/Piraeus, and a loop from Istanbul call at the Turkish Coast and the Greek Islands.

Silversea Cruises

Silver Cloud Ten- to 18-night **Mediterranean/northern Europe/Baltic** cruises from Athens, Monte Carlo, Barcelona, Lisbon, London/Southampton, St. Petersburg, or Copenhagen.

Silver Wind Seven-, 11-, 12-, and 14-night **Mediterranean** cruises from Istanbul, Athens/Piraeus, Rome/Civitavecchia, Monte Carlo, Barcelona, Lisbon, or Malta call at the Greek Islands, the Napoli Coast, the Canary Islands, the French Riviera, Florence/Livorno, and the Turkish Coast.

Special Expeditions

Caledonian Star **Northern Europe** and **Mediterranean** cruises call at Amsterdam, Helsinki, Oslo, Stockholm, Copenhagen, the Napoli Coast, the Greek Islands, and the Turkish Coast.

Star Clippers

Star Clipper Six- to 9-night **Mediterranean** cruises from Malaga to Monaco or Cannes, Cannes to Monaco or Athens, Cyprus to Athens, Athens to Cannes, or loops from Cannes. Seven-night **Mediterranean** loops between Cannes and Monaco.

Star Flyer Ten-night **Mediterranean** cruises between Athens/Piraeus and Kuşadası (Turkey) call at the Greek Islands. Seven-night **Mediterranean** loops from Kuşadası (Turkey) call at the Greek Islands and Turkish Coast.

Windstar Cruises

Wind Song Seven- and 14-night **Mediterranean** cruises from Lisbon to Barcelona or from Barcelona to Rome/Civitavecchia or from Lisbon to Rome/Civitavecchia. Seven-day **Mediterranean** loops from Rome/Civitavecchia call at the Napoli Coast.

Wind Spirit Seven-, 13-, and 14-night **Mediterranean** cruises from Lisbon to Barcelona, Barcelona to Rome/

Civitavecchia, and Rome to Athens/Piraeus. Seven-night **Mediterranean** cruises between Athens/Piraeus and Istanbul call at the Greek Islands and the Turkish Coast.

Wind Star Thirteen-night **Mediterranean** cruise from Lisbon to Nice calls at Gibraltar and the French Riviera. Seven- and 14-night **Mediterranean** cruises from Nice to Rome/Civitavecchia, Rome/Civitavecchia to Athens/Piraeus, or Nice to Athens/Piraeus call at the Napoli Coast and the Greek Islands. Seven-night **Mediterranean** cruises between Athens/Piraeus and Istanbul call at the Greek Islands and the Turkish Coast.

Index